The New Universalism

FAITH MEETS FAITH

An Orbis Series in Interreligious Dialogue

Paul F. Knitter, General Editor

In our contemporary world, the many religions and spiritualities stand in need of greater intercommunication and cooperation. More than ever before, they must speak to, learn from, and work with each other, in order to maintain their own identity and vitality and so to contribute to fashioning a better world.

FAITH MEETS FAITH seeks to promote interreligious dialogue by providing an open forum for the exchanges between and among followers of different religious paths. While the series wants to encourage creative and bold responses to the new questions of pluralism confronting religious persons today, it also recognizes the present plurality of perspectives concerning the methods and content of interreligious dialogue.

This series, therefore, does not want to endorse any one school of thought. By making available to both the scholarly community and the general public works that represent a variety of religious and methodological viewpoints, FAITH MEETS FAITH hopes to foster and focus the emerging encounter among the religions of the world.

Already published:

Toward a Universal Theology of Religion, Leonard Swidler, Editor
The Myth of Christian Uniqueness, John Hick and Paul F. Knitter, Editors
An Asian Theology of Liberation, Aloysius Pieris, S.J.
The Dialogical Imperative, David Lochhead
Love Meets Wisdom, Aloysius Pieris, S.J.
Many Paths, Eugene Hillman, C.S.Sp.
The Silence of God, Raimundo Panikkar
The Challenge of the Scriptures, Groupe de Recherches
    Islamo-Chrétien
The Meaning of Christ, John P. Keenan
Hindu-Christian Dialogue, Harold Coward, Editor
The Emptying God, John B. Cobb, Jr. and Christopher Ives, Editors
Christianity through Non-Christian Eyes, Paul J. Griffiths, Editor
Women Speaking, Women Listening, Maura O'Neill
Bursting the Bonds?, Leonard Swidler, Lewis John Eron, Lester Dean, and
    Gerard Sloyan
Christian Uniqueness Reconsidered, Gavin D'Costa, Editor
One Christ—Many Religions, S. J. Samartha

FAITH MEETS FAITH SERIES

The New Universalism

Foundations for a Global Theology

David J. Krieger

ORBIS BOOKS

Maryknoll, New York 10545

The Catholic Foreign Mission Society of America (Maryknoll) recruits and trains people for overseas missionary service. Through Orbis Books, Maryknoll aims to foster the international dialogue that is essential to mission. The books published, however, reflect the opinions of their authors and are not meant to represent the official position of the society.

Copyright © 1991 by Orbis Books
Published by Orbis Books, Maryknoll, New York 10545
Printed in the United States of America

Library of Congress Cataloging-in-Publication Data

Krieger, David J.
    The new universalism: foundations for a global theology / by
David J. Krieger.
        p.   cm. — (Faith meets faith)
    Includes bibliographical references and index.
    ISBN 0-88344-728-2 — ISBN 0-88344-727-4 (pbk.)
    1. Religions — Relations.   2. Christianity and other religions.
3. Religious pluralism.   I. Title.   II. Series.
BL410.K75   1991
291.2 — dc20   90-48833
                                                              CIP

Contents

ACKNOWLEDGMENTS   vii

A NOTE ON ORTHOGRAPHY   ix

INTRODUCTION   1

1. OPENING UP THE HORIZON FOR A GLOBAL THEOLOGY   9
   Theology between Orthodoxy and Secularism   9
   A Genealogy of Pluralism   18
   Presuppositions for a Global Theology   37

2. METHOD   45
   Theology and Intercultural Encounter: Raimundo Panikkar   45
   Diatopical Hermeneutics   47

3. FOUNDATIONS   77
   The Problem of Ideology   80
   Objectivism versus Relativism in Intercultural Understanding   89
   Can There Be a Universal Discourse?   102
   Rationality, Irrationality, and Other-Rationality   120

4. THE NEW UNIVERSALISM   124
   The Universality of Argumentation   132
   The Universality of Hermeneutics   140
   Satyagraha: Towards a Global Form of Life   150

NOTES   163

BIBLIOGRAPHY   203

INDEX   213

Acknowledgments

Parts of the material presented here have appeared in the following publications: *Indische Religionen und das Christentum im Dialog*, ed. by H.-J. Braun and D. J. Krieger (Zürich: Theologischer Verlag Zürich, 1986); and *Das Interreligiöse Gespräch: Methodologische Grundlagen der Theologie der Religionen* (Zürich: Theologischer Verlag Zürich, 1986).

Special thanks are due to Gibson Winter, Langdon Gilkey, David Tracy and Wendy Doniger, who not only carefully read and commented upon earlier versions of this work, but also encouraged me to present it to a broader public; to Raimundo Panikkar who read and commented upon chapter 2; to Prof. Dr. Hans-Jürg Braun, Director of the *Evangelische Studiengemeinschaft an den Zürcher Hochschulen*, who entrusted me with the direction of the institute's research project on interreligious dialogue and provided untiring support and inspiration for over four years; to my associates in the *Religionstheologische Arbeitsgruppe* in Zürich, especially Christian Jäggi. The book is dedicated to my parents Mary E. and Robert J. Krieger, to my wife Verena and to Pierre Riches.

A Note on Orthography

The problem of rendering non-Western systems of writing into Roman letters for English and other modern European languages is notoriously difficult. Joining many publishers who do not insert diacritical marks for words such as the Sanskrit *Śūnyatā*, this book also omits them.

Scholars and others who know languages such as Sanskrit, Pali, Arabic, or Japanese do not need the diacritical marks to identify words in their original written form. And persons who do not know these languages gain little from having the marks reproduced. We recognize that languages employing different orthographic systems have a richness and distinctiveness that *are* partially conveyed by the orthographics of diacritical marks. And while we do not wish to be part of flattening out the contours of our linguistically plural globe, the high cost of ensuring accuracy in using the diacritical marks does not justify reproducing them here.

The New Universalism

Introduction

Truly, it is not by believing people
that you turn them into liars!
—Tao Te King XVII

The age of the "flight of the gods" seems to be coming to an end. Everywhere there are signs of a reawakened awareness of the sacred. The many "languages" of Babel (worldviews, ideologies, cultures), when seen from the perspective of an approaching global Pentecost, appear to be true *religions*. The task is no longer to search for and somehow make contact with the sacred, but rather to mediate and synthesize its many conflicting manifestations. It is the purpose of an intercultural hermeneutics understood as a *theology of religions* to fulfill this task confronting contemporary humanity.

There are, however, many questions which must be answered before a theology of religions can go to work. It will be objected that it is impossible for a single, unified theology to express adequately the apparently very different truths of humanity's religions. Is not every theology grounded in its own particular tradition? Does not every religion define itself through a faith commitment to a unique revelation and a systematic explication of its content to the exclusion of other religions? Must not, therefore, the relations between religions from the outset be of an apologetic and polemical nature? It would appear that the attempt to avoid all apologetics and polemics, so noble as it may be, endangers one's own faith. To open oneself without reservation to other religions would seem inevitably to bring with it a denial of all that is concrete and unique in one's own tradition.

Even if the difficulties these questions express could be overcome and the *possibility* of a theology of religions established, it would still remain questionable if such an enterprise is at all *necessary*. What right have we, after all, to interfere in the "internal affairs" of other religions? And would it not be a more prudent and modest undertaking to first solve the many problems we have at home before busying ourselves with those of others?

Perhaps a familiar story from the Buddhist tradition can help us at this point. The Buddha is said to have told this story when his followers came to him troubled by the many different religions they had heard about from wandering teachers:

1

In former times a Raja sent for all the blind men in his capital and placed an elephant in their midst. One man felt the head of the elephant, another an ear, another a tusk, another the tuft of its tail. Asked to describe the elephant, one said that an elephant was a large pot, others that it was a winnowing fan, a ploughshare, or a besom. Thus each described the elephant as the part which he first touched, and the Raja was consumed with merriment. "Thus," said the Buddha, "are those wanderers who, blind, unseeing, knowing not the truth, yet each maintain that it is thus and thus."[1]

The moral of this well-known story is clear: The many religions are like blind men who, although they only perceive a part of the truth, nonetheless claim to possess it wholly. We can easily imagine the scene before the Raja's throne, how the blind men bump into each other and begin arguing, each declaring the other a heretic and a fool, and how the Raja ridicules them.

We might imagine, however, another ending to this story. What if the blind men were able and willing to listen to one another and to perceive that they all had, indeed, experienced some truth? What if, instead of condemning each other, each took the other by the hand and led him to that point where he had touched the elephant? Each would then see that the description which the other had given was justified. It would turn out that the elephant really was as each had described it. All could now admit this. For each would find not only his own description of the elephant confirmed, but also *completed* through the description of the other.[2] If they trusted each other and followed one another, then they would all know much better what the truth is. The Raja would no longer find them ridiculous; instead, he would consider them wise!

If this version of the story speaks for the possibility and the need for a theology of religions, then it remains to ask *how* such a theology could be carried out. How can we, who have so long seen the world through the "glasses" of our own culture that we are like blind men when it comes to seeing the truths of other cultures and religions, how can we find our way in the present *global situation*, where many different peoples are "bumping" into each other, just as the blind men before the Raja's throne? What method of *theological* thinking is able to respond to the call of all religions? And what sort of *science* of religions—without which such a universal theology would be inconceivable—could accommodate itself to the faith-commitment which characterizes religious thought? The wisdom of those blind men who were able to trust and follow each other lies, it would seem, in the *methodological foundations* for a global theology.

Originally "method" meant "way." The word comes from the Greek "methodos," which means "a going after" or "pursuit" as, for example, of knowledge. Contemporary philosophy understands "method" to be a systematic procedure, technique, or mode of inquiry. The metaphor of the "way" or "path" is helpful because it illustrates a peculiar structure consisting first of a point of departure, second a goal, and third an area, region or horizon through which the path leads. The horizon may be said to consist of the presuppositions which open up the region within which a certain subject matter first becomes visible *as* that which it is and as something *questionable*. A way, therefore, is first opened up when the horizon through which it leads is disclosed. Only when the horizon is opened up does it become possible to see the point of departure and the goal. And only when we know in advance where we must begin and in what direction we must go does a methodical procedure, as opposed to merely wandering aimlessly about, become possible. Disclosing the horizon and determining the point of departure, the procedure and the goal of a course of inquiry is therefore an important task in its own right. *Methodology* is the discipline which accomplishes this task.

Methodology literally means "speaking" about the "way." But the "logos" is not idle talk. It is also "ground" and "foundation." Speaking about the way, therefore, must *demonstrate* the possibility and necessity of the inquiry in question.

Under the conditions of human historicity, however, to demonstrate the necessity of a certain path of inquiry means that we are not allowed to appeal to absolute first principles or ahistorical, eternal truths. The historical conditionedness of all human knowing implies that any attempt at grounding, beyond mere formalism, can at best become clear about the way upon which we are already travelling. Methodology, therefore, is essentially a *hermeneutical* discipline, that is, an explication, a process of coming to know where we already are, where we have come from, and where we are going. Consequently, the methodological foundation for a global theology must begin from our present historical situation and show that the path which leads out beyond the confines of any particular religious tradition into the space of encounter and dialogue between religions is the inevitable task of our historical moment, our "kairos."

Chapter 1, therefore, attempts to open up the *horizon* of the theology of religions. If it is so that Christian theology has traditionally understood its task to be the preservation and systematic articulation of the Gospel in the "world," then it has located itself within a unified, non-pluralistic horizon defined by orthodoxy on one side and secularism on the other. Within the framework of a discussion of Paul Tillich, I will show that this "frame" is no longer tenable and that theology must redefine itself within a horizon which can be characterized as *radical pluralism*.

The task of theology can be seen to be that of a theology of religions only within the horizon of a radical pluralism. It is, therefore, important to see that what is here called radical pluralism is a quite recent phenomenon, or event, in the history of Western thought and that it owes its existence above all to two specific developments. One is the differentiation and successful self-assertion of secularism as a universalist mode of thought modeled after and in opposition to Christian universalism. Here my thesis is that *both* Christian and Secular Humanist thought share the same basic structure, which may be called *apologetic universalism*.

Universalism is the way in which any human community establishes its collective identity, orients itself in the "world" and articulates its basic common convictions about what is real, meaningful and of value. Apologetic universalism is that form of encompassing worldview constituted by the presupposition of its own absolute totality and the denial of the validity and truth of other worldviews. It is based upon a principle of exclusion/inclusion which nurtures the hope that eventually all opposition will be overcome. The fact that neither Christianity nor Secular Humanism, throughout the long history of their conflict within Western culture, could fully neutralize and incorporate the other into its view may be seen to have undermined the credibility of the entire apologetic project and thus to have opened up the question of whether we must give up the idea of the unity of the mind altogether or whether a *non-apologetic* universalism is possible. But the internal tension between universalist claims and particularist reality haunting both Christian theology and Secular Humanism would not have been enough to open a global horizon within which the need for a *new universalism* could appear, were it not for the second factor, namely, the rise and fall of colonialism, which challenged the heretofore unquestioned claims of the West to cultural supremacy from without and thus made men and women sensitive to the fact of cultural relativism.

It is this latter event which offers the key to interpreting the inner fragmentation of the Western mind caused by the Christianity–Secularism split. The more or less explicit conviction lying at the base of both theological and secular apologetics — namely, that there is no "other" truth — becomes untenable once Western culture *as a whole* has been relativized. Just as the walls which had hitherto safely insulated Western convictions of supremacy against the meaning and value of other cultures gave way early in this century to a global horizon within which every culture and religion could appear as an equally valid possibility for human existence, so also did those walls collapse which had hitherto defined the *one* world we live in exclusively from either a Christian or a secular point of view. At the moment when the Western world, in the aftermath of decolonization, suddenly appeared as merely one worldview among others, the boundaries of Western thought expanded to encompass the possibility of other forms of truth. Christian and Secular Humanist traditions suddenly found themselves afloat upon a wide ocean of historical and cultural relativism. It became apparent that no one, neither Christian nor secularist, stands on solid, neutral ground. Everyone has the same access to truth; which can only mean that every worldview is as true as every other. *The* truth, if there still is "one," is that truth is many and not one. Seen from within, "pluralism" is the name for that event in the history of Western thought which Heidegger has called the "end of metaphysics" and which has come to demarcate our time as "postmodern." What this means for the self-understanding and practice of theology is the question I am concerned with in Chapter 1. The answer is that this event is only adequately grasped once it is seen as opening up the horizon for a theology of religions.

Chapter 2 attempts to answer the question of *how* a global theology can actually be carried out. It presents a method, a step-by-step procedure. Here I rely almost exclusively upon the pioneering work of Raimundo Panikkar. Although Panikkar has not yet offered a systematic presentation of his method for doing cross-cultural theology, the reflections on method scattered throughout his works do allow for a systematic *reconstruction*. The result of such a reconstruction is a seven-step method based upon a *diatopical model* of communication in which the idea of an *intra*-religious dialogue and a conception of "methodological conversion" emerge as central for any adequate interreligious and intercultural understanding.

Chapter 3 tackles the thorny philosophical questions which arise as soon as one admits the fact of radical pluralism on the one hand, and on the other hand still wishes to avoid skepticism and relativism and uphold the possibility of universal understanding and communication. How, for example, is it possible for people from different cultures, with different convictions about reality and meaning, to communicate their deepest truths to one another? If ways of thinking, perceiving and feeling are in fact relative to cultural identity, then intercultural and interreligious understanding seem to be condemned to failure at the outset. Chapter 3 attempts to answer these questions by carrying the discussion beyond the borders of traditional theological concerns into the realm of *philosophical foundations*.

If it is so that all traditions tend to see the "world" from their own perspective and thus uncritically blind out their relativity, then this can be said all the more for programs of thought which claim to lay philosophical foundations. The suspicion with which foundational thinking today must be approached requires that I begin with a discussion of the problem of ideology. This is not "false consciousness," as ideology has often been understood. It is the problem arising from the inevitable tendency of the human mind to theoretically reinforce and legitimate the taken-for-granted rightness and reasonableness of the lifeworld horizon in which thought is embedded by attempting to ground it in the "way things are." This is no less the case for views which have traditionally been labeled "ideological" as for those which have considered themselves able to expose and criticize ideology. This "objectivist" tendency is not overcome simply by abandoning any claim to universality and admitting the relativity of all thought, for "relativism" merely subjectivizes what was previously held to be objective and thus ends in nihilistic skepticism. Consequently, the task of grounding intercultural understanding, as well as the critique of ideology, can only be fulfilled by *overcoming both objectivism and relativism*.

If the critique of ideology and a universal language which does not suppress otherness is to be possible, then what is required is a theory of meaning which sets itself the task of discovering the *conditions for coherence and consensus beyond shared lifeworld horizons.* This is the way the problem of the universality and relativity of thought has been posed in the methodology of those social sciences whose task it is to understand other cultures. The problem of going beyond objectivism and relativism must, therefore, be taken up in terms of the *locus classicus* for the discussion of rationality and relativism, the famous article by Peter Winch on understanding a primitive society. I show that intercultural understanding only becomes problematic the moment we admit that talk about "another culture" supposes radically different criteria of intelligibility. This leads to the question of whether or not a *universal discourse* in which different traditions, with incompatible criteria of truth, meaning and reality, can communicate and mutually appropriate each other is at all possible.

The question of the foundations for a theology of religions thus becomes the philosophical and epistemological question of a possible *global thinking.* The inquiry into this problem takes us back to the thought of that man who, more than any other, is held to be the father of contemporary relativism, Ludwig Wittgenstein. Is Wittgenstein really a relativist? Does his philosophy of language-games lead directly into skepticism, as much post-Wittgensteinian and postmodern thought has claimed? Contrary to contemporary fashion in Wittgenstein interpretation, I will argue that Wittgenstein's philosophy shows the way beyond both objectivism and relativism by demonstrating that the recognition of a genuine *other-rationality* is a necessary condition of our own reasonableness. Language-games are not windowless monads but are constituted by an opening toward another interpretation of the "rules" which constitute them—that is, an opening toward a horizon of infinite variation, a truly universal horizon.

Still more, the linguistic turn which Wittgenstein brought about is at the same time a "pragmatic turn." Not only does the language-game model of communication open up a universal horizon for philosophy in a non-metaphysical way, but it accomplishes this by rooting thought in modes of action, in pragmatic conditions of intelligibility, in "forms of life." Meaning is use. And to say something is to do something, to enter into *communicative action.* Thus arises an epistemological priority of praxis for any discourse claiming universality. Global thinking must be grounded in a *global form of life.*

In Chapter 4 the discussion of the conditions which make a universal discourse possible focuses upon the pragmatic conditions of communicative action. The question becomes: What must we do in order to communicate with members of other cultural and religious communities, what *pragmatic* conditions must be met before intercultural and interreligious understanding become possible? Upon the basis of the diatopical model of communication which distinguishes three levels of discourse—argumentation, proclamation and disclosure—I try to show that the way out of the alternatives of objectivism and relativism, which a proper understanding of Wittgenstein's thought reveals, does not lead into a new humanism understood as global secularism, but rather into a *new universalism* understood as theology of religions.

In order to make this claim good, however, I must enter into the debate concerning the universality of those modes of discourse and their pragmatic conditions which inspire the programs of orthodox as well as secular apologetic universalism. My question is whether or not the attempt to universalize argumentative discourse undertaken by Karl-Otto Apel and Jürgen Habermas in the name of a *theory of communicative action* and an *ethics of discourse* is successful. If not, it remains to ask if the alternative attempt to universalize hermeneutical discourse which Hans-Georg Gadamer has undertaken in the name of a *philosophical hermeneutics* is any more promising. They both claim to go beyond objectivism and relativism and thus to represent universal forms of rationality and communication. Do they, however, successfully incorporate Wittgenstein's fundamental discovery of "other-rationality" into their programs? I will argue that the universalist intentions of both programs can only be preserved upon a higher level of discourse which may be called a "discourse of disclosure."

Although the ethics of discourse appears to take the plurality and discontinuity of thought seriously, its program of universalizing argumentation conceives of the *other* as merely the *alienated self* which it is the task of reason to recover. The radical *other* which must be acknowledged, if the problem of intercultural understanding is to be adequately addressed, does not come into view. For *philosophical hermeneutics*, the presupposition of the unity and continuity of tradition indeed grounds understanding, but it fails to take account of the radical pluralism of lifeworlds characteristic of the global situation and of the effects which violence arising from the conflict of these lifeworlds has upon language and thought.

My conclusion will be that neither theory sufficiently recognizes the extent to which Wittgenstein's discovery of "other-rationality" determines the task of any thinking claiming universality in today's global situation. Neither theory can find a way between the two equally unacceptable alternatives of an imperialistic objectivism or a skeptical and finally self-contradictory relativism. My thesis is that this can only be found if philosophical hermeneutics, the theory of communicative action and the ethics of discourse are incorporated into a *pragmatics of non-violence*. For the question of the possibility of global thinking can only be answered affirmatively once it is shown that this is really the question of a *global form of life*; that is, that the universality of discourse cannot be affirmed in abstraction from a method for resolving those conflicts which are not merely theoretical, but which arise beyond the normal bounds of discourse and argumentation in the realm of irrational force and radical conflict. A global form of life, however, is only possible as a pragmatics of non-violence which itself is grounded in transcendence, that is, in a *cosmotheandric solidarity*.

Thus is the task which this foundational study sets itself clearly outlined. Chapter 1 begins with an analysis of our present situation and shows how the problem of a theology of religions has emerged as *the* task confronting the human community today. From the peculiar way in which intercultural theology has in fact become a problem for us in our Western Christian and Secular Humanist traditions, Chapter 2 lays out a method which is capable of solving this problem; that is, of actually realizing the possibilities inherent in the present situation. With this, however, the work is not yet done, for there remain serious doubts about the entire project of a theology of religions which cannot go unanswered. Against the objection that a theology of religions is not possible, or when possible, not necessary, the *presuppositions* discovered in Chapter 1 and the *method* derived from them in Chapter 2 must, in Chapter 3, be philosophically *grounded*. Finally, Chapter 4 shows that the theology of religions is no merely theoretical preoccupation of theologians and philosophers, but a unique form of *communicative action* which is rooted in a global form of life.

1

Opening up the Horizon for a Global Theology

THEOLOGY BETWEEN ORTHODOXY AND SECULARISM

Among contemporary theologians who have dealt with the problem of interreligious dialogue,[1] no one has penetrated more deeply into the basic issues than has Paul Tillich. In his last public lecture, "The Significance of the History of Religions for the Systematic Theologian,"[2] Tillich saw that a new orientation in theology had become unavoidable, and he stated the presuppositions necessary to realize it. Christian theology can no longer define itself in terms of the apologetic struggle with Secularism, but rather, has to open itself in a non-apologetic way to the entire spectrum of the religions of humanity. This task, however, can only be adequately perceived and carried out once two major decisions have been made. First, the theologian must decide to overcome an orthodox-exclusivism which regards all religions other than its own as false. Secondly, one must free oneself from the temptation to see all religions from the universal, but indifferent, standpoint of a secular science of religions which denies the claims of revelation altogether.

Both of these basic positions stand in the way of a theological appropriation of the non-Christian religions. On the one side, thought does not get beyond confessional borders, and on the other, it does not attain to what is authentically *religious* in other religions. Therefore, according to Tillich:

A theologian who accepts the subject, "The Significance of the History of Religions for the Systematic Theologian," and takes this subject seriously, has already made, explicitly or implicitly, two basic decisions. On the one hand he has separated himself from a theology which rejects all religions other than that of which he is a theologian. On the other hand if one accepts the subject affirmatively and seriously, he has rejected the paradox of a religion of non-religion, or a theology without theos, also called a theology of the secular.[3]

Therefore, as theologians, we have to break through two barriers against a free approach to the history of religions: the orthodox-exclusive one and the secular-rejective one.[4]

The importance of these two decisions is fully appreciated only when it is recalled that Christian orthodoxy, on the one hand, and Secularism, on the other, are deeply rooted in the history of Western culture. Orthodoxy reaches back into the doctrine of "authority" as the basis of all true knowledge and the conviction in the divine authorship of the scriptures, whereas Secularism traces its heritage to Descartes' foundation of knowledge upon the self-certainty of the autonomous, rational subject.

Ever since the Enlightenment these two traditions have been locked in a life-or-death struggle which does not allow peaceful coexistence between them. For both traditions claim absolute and universal validity. Consequently, there can neither be a just and lasting victory of one over the other, nor can they peacefully coexist, nor even can they be synthesized into a third position, since this would merely posit another contender in the struggle and all the problems would begin again. It would seem that the only way out of this situation would insist on a new orientation for both theological *and* secular thinking away from apologetics towards dialogue. As we shall see, this is in fact the proposal which Tillich makes.

The following discussion will attempt to trace the path which led Tillich to the clear realization that the task of theology is to become a theology of religions. On one level, this path leads through an analysis of Tillich's work. I will begin by briefly recalling the historical roots of the conflict between Christianity and Secularism. I will then argue that Tillich, in his early work on the philosophy of religion, grasped the radical implications of this conflict for the task of theology. And finally, I attempt to show that in his later work, he lost sight of this problematic, and only at the very end of his life, through the encounter with another religion and culture, returned to his earlier, radical conception.

But on another level, the path which leads toward opening up the horizon for a theology of religions goes beyond Tillich and follows the trace of those historical developments which led to the emergence of radical pluralism in our time. Here I will attempt to provide a "genealogy" of pluralism; first from a standpoint within the Western tradition and then from a standpoint which views the emergence of pluralism from outside of Western culture, that is, in the historical interaction of the West with other peoples. *Within* the Western tradition pluralism may be seen to emerge as a consequence of the development of Christian and secular thinking as *apologetic universalism*. Seen from *without*, pluralism is the result of the rise and fall of colonialism. Without these two perspectives the problem motivating Tillich's thought, the problem of theology as *universalism*, a problem which led to the insight that theology must become a "global theology" or a "theology of religions," cannot adequately be grasped. Finally, I will attempt to systematically lay out the decisions and presuppositions, with which Tillich opens up and secures the horizon of the theology of religions.

Let us now begin by recalling the origins of the contemporary struggle between Christianity and Secularism. This will serve to set the stage for the analysis of Tillich's work which frames this chapter.

At the beginning of the medieval period, Augustine laid down the principle of all Christian orthodoxy when he said: "Greater is the authority of the Scriptures than all the powers of the human mind."[5] This precept, which we may call the principle of *authority*, remained the foundation for all knowledge until the modern period. In all important matters one did not rely upon one's own reason or experience so much as upon "authorities," which were handed down by tradition and acknowledged by all. These were first, the sacred Scriptures, then the Fathers of the church followed by Aristotle, and only at the end of the list came "natural reason," or the wisdom of common sense.

The first sentence of Descartes' *Meditations* overthrows the principle of authority and sets up in its place a new principle—the principle of *autonomy*:

It is now some years since I detected how many were the false beliefs that I had from my earliest youth admitted as true, and how doubtful was everything I had since constructed on this basis; and from that time I was convinced that I must once for all seriously undertake to rid myself of all the opinions which I had formerly accepted, and commence to build anew from the foundation, if I wanted to establish any firm and permanent structure in the sciences.[6]

Where, it may be asked, does Descartes take the *authority* to "rid" himself of "all the opinions [he] had formerly accepted" and to "commence to build anew" all which could claim the name of science? And how does he propose to reach the "foundation"? Briefly stated, he places himself upon his own authority, that is, upon the ability of his own reason; upon exactly that, which, according to Augustine, could not ground secure knowledge in those important matters concerning the certainty of being. For Descartes, all knowledge which comes to us from *outside*, perceptions of the external world as well as the opinions which tradition has handed down to us, are subject to distortion and thus the only absolutely certain knowledge we may attain must be found *within*. The unshakable foundation of truth (*fundamentum inconcussum veritatis*) must be sought *before* (*a priori*) all experience which comes to us from without. The only thing which is given before all experience, however, is my own consciousness.[7]

I discover myself not, as it were, outside among the things of the world, but rather, I must already exist as the knower before anything else can be known. Before all experience, the *subject* of experience must exist. The existence of the knowing subject is, therefore, not deducible from anything other than itself. The *ego cogito* is certain of itself because it "gives" itself to itself. It is its own authority in the original sense of "author," or "creator" of itself. It is, therefore, *autonomous* and may "rid" itself of all opinions which it has not sanctioned and "commence anew" with itself as the "foundation" of all true knowledge.

From here it is only a short step to Kant's famous definition of enlightenment:

Enlightenment is man's leaving his self-caused immaturity. Immaturity is the incapacity to use one's own intelligence without the guidance of another. Such immaturity is self-caused if it is not caused by lack of intelligence, but by lack of determination and courage to use one's intelligence without being guided by another. *Sapere Aude!* Have the courage to use you own intelligence! is therefore the motto of the enlightenment.[8]

Since the immaturity characterized by the acceptance of authority is not due to lack of intelligence, but to lack of will and is thus "self-caused," we must be capable of making the decision for maturity and consequently for intellectual and moral independence. We need no longer be subjugated to opinions and ordinances which come down to us from the past. We can and must give the law to ourselves. This is the meaning of "autonomy" — to give oneself the law. Autonomy thus becomes the motto not only of the 18th century, but of the entire modern movement of Secular Humanism. For it expresses, as no other word, the self-definition of modern men and women.[9] Clearly, from now on, religion is possible "within the limits of reason alone."

Thus are roughly staked out *the* two basic positions—we could even say worldviews—between which modern Western thought moves: The authority principle of Christian orthodoxy and Secularism's principle of autonomy. These two positions determine theological thinking even today. On the one side, there is *faith*, the exclusive confession of the truth of Holy Scripture — a position which has recently experienced a revival among neo-confessional, evangelical and fundamentalist movements; and on the other side, we have autonomous reason, critical of all faith commitments and convinced of its ability to secure a human future independent of tradition and religious authority. Depending upon where theology takes its point of departure and whether it proceeds in a conciliatory or defensive and polemical manner, it may be termed "orthodox," "neo-orthodox," "confessional," "evangelical," "liberal" or even "radical."

It is not necessary here to describe all these different attempts to solve the problem of a Christian theology in the 20th century;[10] instead, we may ask if they have adequately understood the problem. For, if it should turn out that neither conciliatory mediation between these two basic positions, nor repudiation of one or the other can do justice to the present situation, then perhaps it is the *question* which theology is trying to answer which is in need of revision. It is precisely in this respect that Tillich, I contend, saw the present predicament of Christian theology most clearly. Although his major work, as we shall presently see, fell behind his deepest insights into the problematic of a Christian theology today, at the end of his life he returned to his earlier, more radical view. It is to this "circular" development in Tillich's thought which we now turn.

In his early work on "The Philosophy of Religion" (1925),[11] Tillich attained to a deeper understanding of the problem facing Christian theology today than any of the above-mentioned theological options, all of which believe that they can take their stand on one side of the conflict between Christian orthodoxy and Secularism or the other, or somewhere in-between. For Tillich repudiates the basic frame, the space or horizon within which all these positions are located, namely, the *presupposition of continuity, unity, sameness and totality* which denies radical otherness, difference, discontinuity and plurality. Only within a presupposed horizon of unity can the conviction that whatever the other says is either error, or a part of one's own truth be sustained. Consequently, he rejects in principle every attempt, either of the one or the other to defeat each other, or, through some third position, to mediate between them.

It is worthwhile quoting Tillich's statement of the problem in full. In order to understand what is being said here one must know that Tillich is concerned with a "philosophy of religion." For it is the very purpose of a philosophy of religion to raise the question of the relationship between faith and reason and to bridge the gap between these two positions. Consequently, it is within the domain of a philosophy of religion that they directly confront each other and their mutual irreconcilability may become clear. Tillich asks what the object and the methods of a free and critical (i.e., secular) investigation into religion can be, and he discovers thereby the fundamental problematic facing Christian theology in the present situation:

The subject matter of philosophy of religion is religion. This elementary definition, however, raises a problem at the outset. It is, generally speaking, the basic problem of the philosophy of religion. In religion, philosophy encounters something that resists becoming an object of philosophy. The stronger, purer, and more original the religion, the more emphatically it makes the claim to be exempt from all generalizing conceptual structures. . . . For that reason it closes its mind to philosophy of religion and opens itself at most to theology, insofar as the latter is nothing other than a "science" of revelation. Thus philosophy of religion is in a peculiar position in face of religion. It must either dissolve away the object it wishes to grasp or declare itself null and void. If it does not recognize religion's claim to revelation, then it misses its object and does not speak of genuine religion. If, on the other hand, it acknowledges the claim to revelation, then it becomes theology.[12]

It is important to notice that Tillich is not interested in the well-known neo-orthodox distinction between "faith" and "religion," but rather in overcoming such distinctions through a deeper understanding of the problem. He insists, on the one hand, that philosophy has a certain right over religion. Indeed, as free and critical inquiry, it has an inalienable right over every possible object of human knowledge, including religion together with religion's claim to possess revealed truth. But as soon as this inquiry attains to its "real" object, it loses its identity *as* philosophy and becomes theology, for theology alone can adequately respond to revelation. Philosophy, therefore, would fulfill itself in its own dissolution, were it not for the fact that it is hindered both by an exclusivistic theology which closes itself to autonomous thought and by its own commitment to autonomous rationality which blocks acknowledgment of revelation. This creates a problem for philosophy which Tillich describes thus:

If there is one object that remains fundamentally closed to philosophy, then philosophy's claim over every object is brought into question. For then it would certainly be in no position to draw for itself the borderline between this reserved subject matter (i.e., religion) and other fields of research.[13]

Were philosophical thought not capable from out of itself, that is, *autonomously*, to set its limits and itself determine what lies beyond its reach, then neither could it determine what lies within its powers of knowledge.[14] It would thereby lose its right over all objects of knowledge, even those within areas it could claim for its own competence. For if philosophy could not determine the limits of knowledge *as such*, it could not know how and whether any object at all could be known with certainty. It would lose its claim to be an autonomous judge of truth and error and thus give up its independence over against other sources of knowledge, for example, tradition. Secular thought, therefore, *must* claim universality and absoluteness.

On the other hand, Tillich points out that religion and revelation *also* must claim universality:

As a matter of fact, revelation does make this claim. If revelation is the breakthrough of the Unconditional into the world of the conditioned, it cannot let itself be made into something conditioned, becoming one sphere alongside others, religion alongside culture. It must rather consider the truth it proclaims as the foundation of all knowledge of truth. ... It cannot admit that there is a conditioned perspective of equal value alongside its unconditioned perspective. To do that would be to annul its own unconditionality.[15]

Revelation cannot allow itself to be "defined" and "delimited" by secular reason as one area of inquiry among others. It knows itself as unconditioned and must, therefore, on the basis of this absolute claim, assume the right and the competence to determine not only reason itself, but all other areas of culture; that is, if it is to exist *as* revelation at all.[16]

Christianity and Secularism, therefore, cannot peacefully coexist side by side, nor can one or the other hope to establish uncontested supremacy except by violent means. For between two absolute claims there can be neither common ground nor peaceful accommodation. And it is equally impossible to take up some third position somewhere between the two, as liberalism attempts to do. As Tillich puts it:

> ... no marking off of boundaries can bring about a solution. It denies the philosophical conviction of truth as much as it denies the unconditionality of revelation to allow either of them to be forced into one sphere alongside others. Every attempt of this kind must miscarry. As a way of answering the question who should determine the limits of the two disciplines, the method of demarcating boundaries fails by necessity, because both sides claim this right. And yet the opposition cannot be allowed to remain, for it leads to the shattering of the unity of consciousness and to the dissolution of religion or culture. As long as a naive faith holds one position or the other as obviously authoritative—whether it be the doctrine of revelation or philosophy—and derogates the other position as subsidiary, the conflict is disguised.[17]

Once the naive optimism of Secularism and the equally naive fundamentalism of Christian orthodoxy have been shattered, then the conflict is not laid to rest; instead, it openly breaks out in full vigor. The "common ground" which each side covertly claimed as its own disappears. The *one* world breaks up into *many*, and a situation of *radical pluralism* arises.

"Pluralism" has itself a plurality of meanings. It is, therefore, necessary to state at the outset in what sense the word is here being used. Radical pluralism is not the "methodological" pluralism of different scientific disciplines, nor is it a "social" pluralism of different "finite provinces of meaning" (A. Schutz) within the same "paramount reality," for example, the "aesthetic" realm of the arts, the "technical" realm of science and industry, the "theoretical" realm of the pure sciences, the "ethical" realm of personal value decisions, or the "world" of play, or of religious faith, and so on. The pluralism we are here concerned with is a *radical* pluralism in the sense that it is a matter of different worldviews, that is, different ways of thinking and forms of life which are constituted by their own criteria of *meaning, truth* and *reality,* and which, therefore, claim absolute validity.[18] Radical pluralism refers to the unique historical situation of the late 20th century wherein humanity finds itself on the threshold of a *global* culture.

It must be emphasized that this is not the pluralism of the sort long known to sociology (Durkheim, Weber). That is to say, it is not a matter of a religious worldview being broken apart and fragmented under the pressure of technological innovations, the division of labor and rational critique of traditional institutions into distinct and autonomous (= secular) spheres such as "law," "art," "science," "economics" and also "religion." This well-known scenario of "rationalization" is itself a thesis of secular universalism which traces all cultural achievements back to the self-creative activity of the autonomous rational subject.[19] The "sociological" conception of pluralism is not an adequate description of the problem, but merely another version of the secular worldview; and thus, itself part of the problem. Contrary to its own self-understanding, it does not represent an impartial and objective viewpoint from which religious experience may be seen as "relative," but stands over against that which it calls "religion" in general and Christianity specifically as *another* universalist position. In a *radically pluralistic* situation "reason" is not a neutral instrument, or a universal common ground through which, and upon which, all competing ideologies can meet and be mediated.[20] Radical pluralism does not mean that religious beliefs have become *relativized*; it means that religious conviction has become *pluralized*. In such a situation thinking has always already *decided* for one worldview or the other. It is from this point of view, I suggest, that Tillich's formulation of the problem facing Christian theology, as well as secular philosophy, must be understood. The outcome is that not only Christian theology, but Secularism as well, must first legitimate its right to speak for "all" men and women, before it can go to work.[21]

At that time, 1925, Tillich saw the solution in a method of "synthesis," which would seek out "a point in the doctrine of revelation and philosophy at which the two are one." From there the attempt to "construct a synthetic solution could be undertaken."[22] But we may ask, *upon what common ground could such a point of union be found? What would guide our search for such a point? According to what criteria (theological or philosophical?) could we know that we have found it?* And finally, *from where could such an inquiry take its point of departure; from revelation, or from reason, or from something other than both?* Since, as Tillich himself says, "a calculated return to naivete is a delusive step," and because "only the way forward remains, namely, the way toward the inner overcoming of the antithesis,"[23] the project of a Christian theology stands or falls with the answers to these *methodological* questions.[24]

That Tillich, at the very moment when he conceived the problematic of Christian theology in all its radicalness, nevertheless, lost sight of the fundamental issues, may be seen in reference to the "method of correlation" upon which he bases his major work, the *Systematic Theology* (1951–1963).[25] Here, he no longer speaks of synthesis but of "correlation." He claims that it is the task of Christian theology to correlate revelation with the "situation," that is, with secular reason, whereby the mode of correlation is determined by the way an answer relates to a question:

> The following system is an attempt to use the "method of correlation" as a way of uniting message and situation. It tries to correlate the questions implied in the situation with the answers implied in the message.[26]

From out of the situation, that is, from out of secular reason, or the self-interpretation of a period, the questions are to be taken, and then these questions are to be correlated with answers taken from revelation. In order, however, to bring Christianity and Secularism into such a relation to begin with, it is necessary to presuppose continuity between the two and consequently to suppress the essential characteristic of Secularism, namely, its claim to autonomy, to self-sufficiency and independence. Secularism defines itself not as a mere "question" awaiting an answer from without to fulfill it, but as having its own answers which in no way stand in need of completion from an alleged revelation.

Even if we acknowledge the pluralistic structure of Tillich's systematic theology, it is difficult to see how he can succeed in realizing a truly dialogical theology so long as he remains committed to the method of correlation. From a certain point of view, therefore, it may be said that he has fallen behind the clarity and depth with which he had grasped the problem in his earlier work. There, at least in the formulation of the problem, when not in the attempted "synthetic" solution, he did not admit the possibility for the theologian to retreat into a bastion called the "theological circle"[27] protected by the bulwark of a "decision" (*Entscheidung*).[28] Despite his earlier insights, theology, for Tillich, remained as it had always been, an *apologetic* enterprise.[29]

This brings us face to face with a problem with which we shall be concerned, in various ways, throughout this study, namely, the fact that it seems impossible to conceive of a universalist thinking which is not at the same time apologetic. This is no accident, but the result of specific historical developments, both within and without Western culture. It is essential for an adequate understanding of the situation of radical pluralism confronting us today to understand that this situation is the outcome of what may be called the rise and fall of *apologetic universalism*. We must at this point, therefore, leave the discussion of Paul Tillich and attempt what might be called a *genealogy of pluralism*. I will show first how pluralism resulted from an *internal split*, a break in the continuity of Western cultural identity. This entails showing how Christian theology arose from an apologetic impulse and how, to this day, the *pragmatics*[30] of theological thinking, indeed all

Western thinking, remain determined by what may be called the *apologetic method*. Only after it has become clear that *both* Christian theology and Secular Humanism represent forms of *apologetic universalism* and that this form of universalism, after the failure of colonial imperialism and the emergence of a global horizon, is no longer tenable, will we be in a position to return to Tillich's final work and appreciate the extent to which he was able to foresee the basis upon which any future theology would be possible.

A GENEALOGY OF PLURALISM

The Internal Split: Western Thought as Apologetic Universalism

The Christ-event came into the world as "an obstacle to the Jews and to the pagans madness" (1 Cor 1:23). That the carpenter's son from Nazareth, who died as a common criminal on the cross, was the Messiah, could only be blasphemy for the Jews. And that the eternal, immutable *logos* could be a mere man, indeed, a Jew, was for the Greeks unthinkable. One might ask what difference this could make to the Christians, who had found their salvation in faith in Jesus. But in fact, the Christians could not remain indifferent towards their Jewish and Hellenic environment. They could not withdraw into an elitist sectarianism and ignore the questions, attacks and accusations from without. For quite apart from the need to justify themselves in the face of persecution, out of the life and suffering of Jesus of Nazareth there had gone forth a *universal* claim. Christ had come "for all men." He is the light, the truth and the way. The proclamation of the salvation he brings comes from a *universal* mission to "make disciples of all nations" (Mt 28:19).

Jesus' proclamation of the Kingdom of God became, after the Easter-event and the coming of the Holy Spirit, the proclamation of Christ, which was directed through the Spirit and the church to all men and women, indeed, to the entire "world." The baptism of Cornelius (Acts 10:23–47), and the conflict concerning the mission to the gentiles (Acts 15:1–29), give witness to the growing universalistic consciousness of the church. As Jaroslav Pelikan puts it:

> The early church as a community and its theologians were obliged to clarify, for friend and foe alike, how the gospel was related to its preparations and anticipations in the nation where it arose as well as in the nations to which it was being borne.[31]

Just as universalism belongs to the nature of Christianity, so the transition from the *regula fidei* of the early church to systematically worked-out dogmas followed naturally and automatically.[32] The various teachings of the Apostles and the different liturgical practices of the churches pressed for unification and synthesis, not only with each other, but also with the Jewish and Hellenic environment. This unification, however, could only be achieved through generally valid formulations of what was to count as "correct" teaching, i.e., orthodoxy. Dogma as a means of unification arose immediately out of the universal claim of the proclamation itself and realized itself as *theology. Christian universalism expresses itself as theology.* It was the task of theology to demonstrate that the Christ-event was also valid for Jews and Hellenes, that is, it had to show the universal significance and validity of Christian truth.[33]

It was in the struggle with Judaism that the early Christians first developed their most effective instrument and weapon — *apologetics.* The question of the continuity of the new faith with Jewish tradition and also of the differences had to be answered. To begin with, the apologetic consisted in the fact that the Christians claimed the Jewish Scriptures for themselves. The Scriptures, therefore, belonged not to the Jews, who did not understand their true meaning, but to the Christians, who possessed in Christ the key to understanding what the prophecies really meant. Typical of this attitude is a remark of Justin Martyr in his *Dialogue with Trypho,* where, during the course of the argument with his Jewish interlocutor, he says that the prophecies about Christ "are contained in your Scriptures, or rather not yours, but ours."[34] The Jews, he argued, had received the Scriptures as a preparation for, and education to faith in Christ, but they had not understood this *praeparatio evangelica.* The Christians, however, possess in Christ the full revelation of God and the fulfillment of the Law. Pelikan notes:

> Against Judaism the apologists consistently maintained that the Jews did not understand their own Bible properly because they had not accepted Jesus as the Christ.[35]

Therefore, the Scriptures and "all of the saints and believers back to Abraham and even to Adam"[36] were claimed by Christianity as its own.

In *A History of Christian Thought,* Tillich maintains that "The apologetic movement can rightly be called the birthplace of a developed Christian theology" and he describes three things that characterize every apologetic method:[37]

> First of all, if you want to speak meaningfully with someone, there must be a common basis of some mutually accepted ideas. The truth that is common to both Christians and pagans must first be elaborated. If they have nothing in common, no conversation is possible and no meaningful address to the pagans is possible. ... Thus the Apologist had to show that here is something in common. Secondly, the Apologists had to point out defects in the ideas of paganism. There are things which contradict the pagan ideas. It can be shown that for centuries pagan philosophers have brought forth criticism of these ideas. This is the second step of apologetics, namely, showing the

negativity in the other. Thirdly, it must be shown that one's own position is not to be accepted as something from outside, but rather that Christianity is the fulfillment of a longing and desire in paganism.[38]

The apologetic method, therefore, has three steps: First, a common ground, a continuity, a unitary horizon within which the two opposing views may meet is projected; for example, the horizon of a "salvation history" within which the Scriptures of the Jews may appear as Christian. In a second step, the weaknesses of the opponent are discovered, for example, the alleged misunderstanding of the prophecies on the part of the Jews. And finally, in a third step the apologist must show opponents that the solution to their problems and the answer to their questions lies in Christian revelation; that is, the apologist must *correlate* the *question* of the opponent with the *answer* offered in Christ.

It is important for what comes later to note that this method has a pragmatic structure which articulates the relation of *self* and *other* in such a way that the opponents' very right to existence is disputed, first by *neutralizing* the right of the other to independent truth, secondly by *expropriating* what truths the other does have and third, by *incorporating* the other's position into one's own. This pragmatic structure of apologetics leads directly to the claim that "Judaism, with its laws, had had its day."[39] Pelikan remarks that the Christians "no longer looked upon the Jewish community as a continuing participant in the holy history that had produced the Church."[40]

At the same time that the Christians were developing this method in their dealings with the Jews, they began to apply it in that area where, as the above citation from Tillich indicates, it was to experience its complete development, namely in the struggle with Hellenism. Indeed, after the destruction of Jerusalem in 70 A.D., the apologetic against the Jews became much less important than the controversies with Hellenic culture. Here again the three-step method described above was employed. Since it was impossible to deny that the Greek philosophers had had true insights, and equally impossible for Christian universalism to admit the existence of a source of truth outside its own symbols, Greek philosophy must somehow have come from Christian sources. With the great example of Paul before them — "the God whom I proclaim is in fact the one whom you already worship without knowing it" (Act 17:23) — many Christians, as we shall see, claimed that all that was of positive value in Greek culture was either taken from Moses, or immediately revealed to the philosophers and poets by Christ himself as the pre-existent *logos*. In both cases it came to the same: What the Greeks had of truth, actually belonged to the Christians; for it was in Christ, the *logos* himself, that all truth is revealed.

For Justin, the philosophers, poets and historians all "spoke well in proportion to the share [they] had of the seminal Logos (*logos spermati-*

kos)."[41] He therefore concluded: "Whatever things were rightly said among men are the property of us Christians."[42] Origen claimed that the "Logos who came to dwell in Jesus . . . inspired men before that."[43] Theophilus of Antioch supposed that the poets and philosophers had "plagiarized from the Scriptures to make their doctrines plausible,"[44] and Clement of Alexandria asserted that certain teachings of Plato had come "from the Hebrews,"[45] but he also explains the element of truth in philosophy on the basis of a "universal revelation."[46] In any case, these truths were given to men to prepare them for faith in Christ. Clement writes:

> Accordingly, before the advent of the Lord, philosophy was necessary to the Greeks for righteousness. . . . For this was a schoolmaster to bring the Hellenic mind, as the law, the Hebrews, to Christ. Philosophy, therefore, was a preparation, paving the way for him who is perfected in Christ.[47]

Pelikan summarizes the central aim and achievement of the apologists so:

> In various ways they joined to assert the thesis that Christ had come as the revealer of true philosophy, ancient and yet new, as the correction and also the fulfillment of what the philosophical mind had already grasped.[48]

In the event that educated pagans did not wish to acknowledge that the *logos*, which they supposedly only dimly glimpsed, is now fully revealed in Christ, then it could be asserted that they no longer understood their own philosophers and poets correctly, and consequently, could not claim to be their rightful heirs. In this way, the Christians "inherited" antique culture.

If, however, Jews or Greeks attempted to make use of the same method and apologetically appropriate the Christian Scriptures for themselves, that is, to interpret Christ apocalyptic-prophetically (Montanism), or Hellenistic-Gnostically (Marcion, Valentinian, etc.), then they were attacked and accused of being heretics. Just as theology defended itself against external enemies by means of apologetics, so it defended itself internally by means of *dogma*. Here again the universalistic motive was decisive. For heresy was understood by the early church to be a separation from the one universal church, and heretical theology was always seen as a one-sided emphasis of a certain aspect of the complete revelation.[49] The divinity of Jesus, for example, was emphasized while his humanity was neglected. Or the unity of God was emphasized at the expense of the Trinity to which the Scriptures also gave witness.

Christianity could not have survived the first three centuries if the Christian symbols had not been capable of taking up into themselves and uniting the most diverse tendencies in the ancient world. In reference to the two major heretical views — pagan polytheism and Jewish monotheism — against which the apologists had victoriously fought, Gregory of Nyssa offers a concise summary of the synthetic movement of apologetic thought:

Truth passes in the mean between these two conceptions, destroy-ing each heresy, and yet accepting what is useful to it from each. The Jewish dogma is destroyed by the acceptance of the Logos and by the belief in the Spirit, while the polytheistic error of the Greek school is made to vanish by the unity of the [divine] nature abrogating this notion of plurality. Yet again, of the Jewish conception, let the unity of the nature stand; and of the Greek only the distinction as to per-sons. . . . It is as if the number of the Trinity were a remedy in the case of those who are in error as to the One, and the assertion of the unity for those whose beliefs are dispersed among a number of divin-ities.[50]

In summary, it may be said that Christian theology realized its univer-salist program by means of a parallel development of apologetics and dog-matics, whereby the *pragmatic* structure of this *apologetic universalism* was based upon the projection of a unified and continuous horizon allowing for a threefold procedure of "neutralization" of the other's truth, of "expro-priation" of whatever truths the opponent had which could not be denied, and of "incorporation" of the other within one's own universal horizon.

The central dogmas developed at this time in service of this program were the Christological and the Trinitarian dogmas, which received their definitive formulation at the Councils of Nicea (325) and Chalcedon (451). The doctrine of God as three divine persons in the one divine nature, and of Christ as two natures, divine and human in one person managed to gather up and weld together the deepest and most powerful currents in the ancient world and form a new vision of reality in which all the others could be incorporated. The jealous, paternalistic and monotheistic Yahweh of the Jewish Scripture and the immutable, eternal and immanent Logos of Greek philosophy were united with the popular yearning for salvation in Jewish apocalyptic and the Hellenistic mystery cults. God was at once unspeakably transcendent and yet so near and approachable. Christian universalism proved itself capable of incorporating the various peoples and cultures of the ancient world by taking up these conflicting currents of thought and welding them together in its symbols.

The significance of this dogmatic synthesis cannot be overestimated, for it was over these symbols that a millennium and a half later modern Sec-ularism had to fight its most decisive battle with Christianity. It was Hegel's *Aufhebung* of the Trinitarian and Christological symbols into the pure, log-ical categories of reason and into a new and more powerful synthesis that carried the struggle of the Enlightenment to victory and shattered the hegemony of Christian universalism. Secular Humanism succeeded in establishing an entirely independent *secular universalism* in the form of a *philosophy of religion.*[51] We cannot here enter into the history of modern rationalism; nonetheless, it is important to see that secular universalism exhibits the same pragmatic structure and uses the same methods to establish and propagate itself which its opponent used before it. This is the major thesis of Panajotis Kondylis' monumental study of the Enlightenment.[52] Kondylis shows how modern Secularism arises from a "polemical" motive to which he also ascribes its universalistic claims. The search for truth is never independent from the personal and social struggle for a particular interpretation of reality as a whole. Meaning does not lie around ready made, but is constituted as a "polemical" universalism:

> The search for truth takes place within the bounds of a struggle against an opponent, and since the opponent stands in the way of "truth", the search for truth necessarily becomes polemical. And for this very reason it must present itself in the form of a systematic theoretical alternative, which widely transgresses the limits of indubitable and certain knowledge. If it did not do this, then it could not make use of that most precious of all weapons, universality.[53]

Applying this insight to modern rationalism, Kondylis concludes:

> The rationalistic plea to let an issue be decided in common from all sides through experiment and observation is neither impartial nor unselfish: it presupposes that the opponent *a limine* must accept the worldview within which experiment and observation are meaningful; but this would necessitate that he gives up not only his own rationalism, but also his entire worldview even before he could begin to fight for them.[54]

In fact the surest sign that modern secular rationalism is a universalistic thought-form is the *apologetic method*, which now, in the name of autonomous reason, is turned against Christianity. Already in Lessing's concept of the "education of mankind," it is clear that the Christian symbols themselves have become *praeparatio evangelica* and that the apologetic method has been appropriated by secular thought. Revelation is now seen to be a preparation for, and education to autonomous reason. Let us recall that for the early Christian apologists, philosophy and reason were given to men and women in order to prepare them for the truth which, in the fullness of time, was revealed in Christ. In words reminiscent of Clement, Origen or Justin, Lessing writes in *The Education of the Human Race*:

> You have seen in the childhood of the human race, in the doctrine of the unity of God, that God makes immediate revelations of mere truths of reason, or has permitted and caused pure truths of reason to be taught, for a time, as truths of immediate revelation, in order

to promulgate them the more rapidly, and ground them the more firmly. As we by this time can dispense with the Old Testament for the doctrine of the unity of God, and as we are gradually beginning also to be less dependent on the New Testament for the doctrine of the immortality of the soul: might there not be mirrored in this book also other truths of the same kind, which we are to gaze at in awe as revelations, just until reason learns to deduce them from its other demonstrated truths, and to connect them with them? For instance, the doctrine of the Trinity. Let it not be objected that speculations of this nature upon the mysteries of religion are forbidden. ... the development of revealed truths into truths of reason is absolutely necessary, if the human race is to be assisted by them. When they were revealed they were certainly not truths of reason, but they were revealed in order to become such.[55]

Here it is biblical revelation which makes up the *praeparatio* for the "good news" of philosophy. This program was carried to completion by Hegel. For it was Hegel who succeeded in fully transforming the revealed mysteries, the *Vorstellung*, into rational concepts, the *Begriff*. Theology became a *philosophy of religion*. It is altogether possible to place Hegel's entire philosophy under this title. He saw religion as the second highest manifestation of the Absolute Spirit, whose fulfillment lay in the realization of philosophy. Out of its last and most extreme alienation in religion, reason returns to itself in philosophy.

Hegel defines the Idea or Spirit so:

Spirit is essentially the result of its own activity: Its activity is the transcending of immediate, simple, unreflected existence – the negation of that existence, and the returning into itself.[56]

Spirit *can* return into itself because it finds itself in its *other*:

Spirit becomes an object to itself and contemplates itself as an objective existence.[57]

Therefore, in knowing its object, its other, Spirit does not remain outside itself, lost, as it were in an "other," but it rebounds (*resultare*) back into itself.

As the result of its own activity Spirit is self-produced, or *causa sui*, which corresponds to the classical definition of God. Thus arises the possibility of assimilating the traditional doctrine of God to this philosophical concept. As dynamic self-emptying and self-uniting, Hegel's "Spirit" can account for the classical inner Trinitarian "mystery" of the generation of the Son from the Father and of the procession of the Holy Spirit, in whom Father and Son are united, from both Father and Son (*filioque*), in purely logical categories. Insofar as the claim can now be made that the meaning of these symbols lies with philosophy, they can be declared the rightful possession of secular universalism and taken away from the church, which has failed to understand them.

Autonomous rationality, grounded in itself, becomes the new center of a purely secular universalism, which operates with exactly the same apologetic method as Christian universalism before it. The inherent truth and value of Christianity is "neutralized," what it has of lasting value is "expropriated" and finally the Christian worldview as a whole is "incorporated" into the allegedly wider and more encompassing truth of secular universalism. This creates an entirely new situation for Christian theology, which we can only clearly grasp once we have seen how Schleiermacher attempted to revive Christian apologetics within this new situation.

Schleiermacher accepts the apologetic method, but places it upon an entirely new basis, namely, upon the concept of "religion." He thereby becomes the founder of all modern Christian apologetics, which, after him, consist in the attempt to claim autonomous rationality *for* Christianity, in that it is asserted that "reason" is essentially *religious*. A new concept is thus introduced and firmly established between Christianity and Secularism. It will henceforth be the purpose of the concept of "religion" to serve as the *common ground*, the horizon of *continuity* upon which the apologetic may operate. The destiny of modern Christian theology will from now on be decided by who controls and defines the concept of "religion" — Christianity or Secularism.

Schleiermacher took over from Kant the newly opened up horizon of transcendental subjectivity for religion. This required, however, that he dissociate it from the rationalism of the speculative philosophies of Fichte, Schelling and Hegel. What for idealism was a matter either of *reason*, or a matter of the *will*, became for Schleiermacher a matter of "intuition" and "*feeling*."[58] The romantic climate in which he lived encouraged him to believe he had thus found a standpoint from which he could speak to the "cultured despisers" of religion.[59] To have religion, Schleiermacher declares, means to have an "intuition" or "immediate consciousness of all finite things, in and through the Infinite, and of all temporal things in and through the Eternal."[60] This intuition awakens in us a "feeling of absolute dependence."[61] This is the essence of "religion." And it is precisely this, argues Schleiermacher, which is mediated by all the achievements of secular culture, such as science, art, and so on — that is, if they only understood themselves properly! Those who criticize religion upon the basis of the accomplishments of secular culture and despise it do not know what they are doing, and above all they do not know upon what ground they themselves are standing. Repeating the well-known apologetic formula that "what you possess, but don't understand properly belongs to us," Schleiermacher cries out to the cultured despisers of religion:

See then, whether you wish it or not, the goal of your highest endeavors is just the resurrection of religion. By your endeavors this event must be brought to pass, and I celebrate you as, however unintentionally, the rescuers and cherishers of religion.[62]

That the cultured despisers of religion do not admit their secular achievements to be essentially religious is their weakness (the second step of the apologetic method!), and at the same time it is the strength of the theologian, who knows that the intuition of the "infinite in the finite," which Secularism, whether admittedly or not, strives for, is not only the essence of religion, but also the essence of Christianity. Schleiermacher thus carries out the third step of the apologetic method when he triumphantly proclaims:

From all finite things we should see the Infinite. We should be in a position to associate religious feelings and views with all sentiments, however they may have arisen, and with all actions, whatever be their object. That is the true and highest aim of mastery in Christianity.[63]

Following the classical apologetic method, Schleiermacher uses the concept of religion first, as the common ground upon which he can neutralize Secularism; secondly, he expropriates secular truth by claiming science and the arts for religion; and thirdly, he incorporates the entire realm of religion into Christianity. Thus would the apologetic have reached its goal, if only the concept of "religion" had anything to do with orthodox Christianity. Tillich, for example, considers it to be a "philosophical concept," and he says:

[Schleiermacher] subjects Christianity to a concept of religion which at least by intent was not derived from Christianity but from the whole panorama of the world's religions.[64]

The transition from religion to Christianity, from secular philosophy of religion to dogmatics, remained for Schleiermacher, and remains still today, broken and unmediated. As soon as Christianity is subordinated to the concept of "religion," there is a *continuity* established between it and all other religious phenomena, which is a threat to its self-understanding as unique and superior. Christ may indeed be the highest and most perfect mediator,[65] but the problem is not thereby solved, for the superiority of Christianity becomes a merely relative one, a matter of more or less.[66] The thesis of continuity inescapably carries with it the danger that the absoluteness and uniqueness of Christian revelation is no longer tenable. And it is precisely against the background of this modern apologetic strategy that "absoluteness" and "uniqueness," concepts which stand at the center of the discussion concerning the relation of Christianity to other religions today, could come to the fore. Despite disclaimers, Christian symbols are subsumed under "higher" categories, that is, categories which are controlled by an opposing universalism. Christianity becomes, for example, one form of "religion" among others; Jesus is seen as one "mediator" among others, and so forth. The door is thus opened for a secular *science of religion*, a history and phenomenology of religion to take possession of these concepts and apologetically expropriate Christianity.

In a remark critical of the entire project of liberal apologetics, Tillich concludes:

> What we need, however, is to be aware of the fact that the method of Schleiermacher, Troeltsch, Harnack, and others, is not sufficient, namely, first defining Christianity as a religion, and then saying it is the highest or absolute religion.[67]

What is insufficient in the liberal project is that modern Christian apologetics continuously falls back into a philosophy of religion from where it opens itself to expropriation by a science of religion. Contrary to the expectations of modern Christian apologetics, the concept of "religion" cannot be wrested from the grip of Secularism.[68] Consequently, after the decisive defeat which Christianity suffered on the metaphysical plane at the hands of Hegel and the subsequent loss of interest in speculation, the apologetic battle shifted to the empirical realm. Religion became the object of an empirical "science of religions" and was subjected to its methods and presuppositions, whereas theology, as a consequence, was forced to defend itself on exegetical and historical critical terrain, which accounts for the tremendous importance of these disciplines in the last century.

This created the following situation with which we are faced today: If the old apologetic projected a unitary horizon and operated with the schema of a divine revelation which came into a more or less neutral "world," to which it was related as an answer to a question, then in the new situation, which is characterized by an independent secular universalism and a horizon of radical pluralism, theology must operate with a schema wherein the "world" is no longer merely an empty receptacle awaiting fulfillment from without, but is itself filled with absolute truth and demands to be considered on the same level as revelation. This implies that the apologetic method, which had served theology so long, is totally obsolete — for its necessary presupposition is that the "other" has no truth of his own.

All the major theologians of the first half of the 20th century have sensed this problem and have reacted to it in different ways. Karl Barth, for example, was well aware that apologetics was no longer possible, and he consequently rejected any mediating theology whatever, without giving up universalist claims, thus *jumping-back* into an *orthodox-exclusivism*.[69] This move is exemplary for all neo-confessionalist, evangelical and fundamentalist programs today. Ernst Troeltsch, on the other hand, also deeply experienced the collapse of Christian theology, but chose the opposite alternative from Barth, namely, the "world." Troeltsch *jumped-over* to a secular position, which historically relativized all absolute truth claims and thus opened the door to liberal programs.[70]

Neither Barth's exclusivist neo-orthodoxy, nor Troeltsch's mediating liberalism, however, represent a genuine solution to *the* problem facing Christian theology. This problem might be formulated thus: How can the absolute truth and universalism of Christian symbols be understood and expressed in a situation characterized by radical pluralism? Clearly, the exclusivist and fundamentalist denial of pluralism represents only the futile attempt to solve the problem by ignoring it. But it would be equally useless to attempt to solve the problem by somehow renewing the apologetic enterprise. Instead, we must ask if the very question which Christian theology has been attempting to answer by means of apologetics is at all the right one, and if the question could not—and perhaps, should not—be placed differently. As we shall see when we return to the discussion of Tillich, this means asking whether the problematic and task of theology should not from the outset be conceived as *theology of religions*.

At the same time that Secular Humanism and a renewed Christian theology were squaring off in a battle of mutually exclusive apologetic universalisms, a desperate struggle which led to the disintegration of Western cultural unity *from within*, there was taking place beyond the borders of Europe a momentous historical event, namely, the global expansion of Western power and influence. The history of colonialism documents the emergence of a global culture and an equally significant fragmentation of universalist presumptions. It is to this drama of the unfolding global imperialism of the West, its collapse after the Second World War and the consequences this has for Western thought that we now must turn in order to understand the full implications of the pluralist horizon and the new question facing theology within this horizon. Again we will orient our discussion of these events around the work of Paul Tillich.

The External Split: Colonialism and the Global Community

In 1960 Tillich visited Japan. The result of this encounter with a completely foreign culture and religion found its first expression in the small book, *Christianity and the Encounter of the World Religions*, which Tillich published in 1963.[71] Although in this book he is primarily interested in what he calls "quasi-religions" (forms of what we have called secular universalism), that is, liberalism, humanism, communism, and so on, it was clear that Tillich's thinking had taken a new orientation towards dialogue with non-Christian religions.

This new interest can only be fully appreciated against the background of the knowledge that there is hardly any significant problem today, whether it be political, social or economic, which is not at the same time a *global* problem. This situation, in turn, is only understandable as a consequence of the colonial expansion of Europe during the last five centuries. Let us briefly recall the major phases of this development before turning to a more detailed analysis of its effects.

European colonial expansion began in the 15th century and went through three phases before it ended in the decolonization process in this century. The historical factors which led to the overseas expansion of Europe were complex. The obstacles which Turkish power created for trade with the East, the political weakness of Asia, Africa and the Americas, together with the advances in weaponry and naval technology in Europe encouraged and enabled Europeans to seek their own routes to the riches of the East. European explorers and traders set out in three directions: east to India, Indonesia, China and Japan; west to America and Canada; and south to Africa.

Thanks to its lead in national consolidation and its favorable geographical position for navigation, it was Portugal which first succeeded in establishing a worldwide trade imperium. Vasco da Gama reached India in 1497 by going around Africa. Shortly thereafter there arose Portuguese trading stations along the coast of the Malaysian Archipelago and commercial relations with China and Japan. Portuguese dominion in eastern trade, however, did not go unchallenged. With the discovery of the West Indian Islands by Columbus, Spain began its successful conquest of the Americas. California, Middle and South America were quickly brought under Spanish control and exploitation. It came to conflicts between the two "world powers" and in the Contract of Tordesillas (1494) the Pope ceremoniously divided the world between Portugal and Spain.

This agreement, of course, did not go uncontested. The next century saw a second wave of European expansion led by the Netherlands, England and France. Decisive for this phase was the establishment of permanent colonies. It was no longer merely a question of trading with the East or the newly discovered peoples of Africa and America, but of taking possession of the land and producing what one needed.

The third phase may be termed the phase of colonial imperialism in the proper sense. During the 19th century, European domination of the world reached its climax. The distinguishing characteristic of this third wave of overseas expansion was determined by the new political and economic situation in Europe. The industrial revolution, the ideology of free trade and the new political constellation with the independent colonies of America and the never-completely conquered nations of Asia and Africa all led to an imperialism based upon indirect domination and control of trade. The major events of this period were no longer the dazzling discoveries of heretofore unknown lands and peoples or the heroic founding of new colonies, but political and diplomatic struggles among the European powers themselves, such as the dividing up of Africa from about 1884/5 through 1900, the rise of Germany as a colonial power, the consolidation of British Empire around control of India, the suppression of the Boxer Revolt in China and the division of China into commercial and political spheres of influence between England, Germany and Russia.

With the two world wars in the early decades of the 20th century, this worldwide system of domination and exploitation collapsed. One after the other, the ex-colonies and protectorates attained national independence, each in its own way: the Philippines in 1946, India in 1947, Burma and Sri Lanka in 1948, Malaya in 1957, Ghana in 1957, Kenya in 1963, Nigeria in 1966. The world primacy which Europe had built up since the 15th century was principally shaken. The West was no longer the most important "actor" upon the stage of history. Other peoples and cultures now asserted their right to "make" history. It has become clear that a serious and honest dialogue with these peoples and cultures is no longer avoidable, if all forms of imperialism are finally to be overcome.

An analysis of the *typical forms of cultural encounter* which have arisen during the history of colonialism show us not only that the need for dialogue with other cultures is of central importance today, but also that the real possibilities for intercultural encounter are conditioned in a specific way. Ethnological investigations as well as the historical study of colonialism show that our history has given us four typical forms of intercultural encounter. Following the terminology of Urs Bitterli, we may categorize them as follows: 1) meeting of cultures, 2) contact of cultures, 3) conflict of cultures and 4) interaction of cultures, or mutual acculturation. We will briefly discuss each of these forms with the intention of showing how they determine the possibilities of the concrete existential situation in which we are today living.

In his thorough and careful study of the history of colonialism, *Die "Wilden" und die "Zivilisierten,"*[72] Urs Bitterli defines "cultural meeting" as "the meeting of a small group of travelers with representatives of a closed archaic society, which is of short duration or following upon long interruptions."[73] According to Bitterli, this form of cultural encounter was characteristic of the early voyages of discovery and amounts to little more than becoming aware of the fact that other peoples exist. We know from reports how the first meetings of Portuguese or Spanish sailors, adventurers and tradesmen with the indigenous peoples of Africa and America transpired, and how on both sides feelings of curiosity, threat, embarrassment and mistrust dominated the encounter. It is, therefore, not surprising that this unstable and precarious situation quickly took on other forms.

"Cultural contact," says Bitterli, "arose in those cases where, on the one hand, the connections back to the mother-land could be secured and expanded, and on the other, a permanent condition of mutual relations to the indigenous people developed out of the first meeting."[74] When one recalls that the presuppositions and the motivating forces behind the overseas expansion of Europe were *missionary zeal, military and technical superiority*, and above all *commercial interests*, it is easily understandable why cultural contact limited itself to trade relations and mission.

As conquerors and tradesmen, the first Europeans to encounter other peoples were, on the basis of their education and interests, the least suited to understand a foreign culture. Simple sailors, uneducated adventurers and tradesmen as they were, the first Europeans to encounter other peoples were completely incapable of overcoming the barriers of a strange language, unknown customs and a foreign view of the world. They avoided personal contact and reduced their relations to the minimum necessary to secure effective trade. The situation was still further burdened by the fact that the Europeans were very early on aware of their military superiority and fled from the task of understanding and dialogue. In their position as the stronger, they were allowed to dictate the conditions of the relationship, as well as to legitimate their actions by means of prejudices against the natives.

Bitterli describes how *ethnocentrism*, which became typical of the European attitude towards other peoples, arose from these first contacts:

> The same incapacity to deal intellectually with the phenomenon of archaic culture, which politically led to the application of violent means, led philosophically and psychologically to the tendency to discriminate against representatives of other races. The embarrassment of the European in the face of such a meeting with another culture, did not usually give way to a serious effort to impartially come to know the foreign culture, rather, it turned into an undifferentiated and general condemnation of the native, who was once and for all declassed as a "barbarian" or a "savage." In that the European self-righteously set up his own form of life as an absolute norm above all others, and branded whatever deviated from it as inferior and perverted, he introduced a distinction between culture and nature, which was founded upon no scientific considerations whatever, and assigned the native to the second area, while appointing himself with the greatest self-evidence lord of creation, without even considering the responsibilities which such a presumption implies.[75]

Equally extreme as fleeing from the encounter with the other and springing back into the false security of prejudice bolstered by degrading indigenous peoples to the level of mere "savages," was the opposite reaction; one gave oneself over to the fascinating power of the strange and exotic. For it also came to pass that Europeans "went over" to the "savages." The phenomenon of "jumping over," as we may call it, occurred not only in situations where Europeans came into contact with other high cultures, but also in Africa and America. There were those who turned away from European civilization and were taken up into the tribes. The Portuguese, who among the colonialists tended most to mix with the foreign peoples in the form of mixed marriages, were also the most brutal in condemning to death those who jumped over to another culture. Jesuit missionaries in North

America reported with astonishment that Europeans had joined the Indians. According to Bitterli, these people "by their actions, clearly placed the exemplary quality of Western-Christian culture in question."[76]

When one looks at the problem of the Christian mission, one can see most clearly the futility of both these forms of reacting to the encounter of cultures. On the one hand, the Christian religion was considered to be the only valid way to attain salvation for all men and women. This missionary consciousness legitimated not only the attempts to convert native peoples to Christianity, but also the political and military domination of the "savages" by Europeans. This is clearly expressed in the Laws of Burgos (1512), which were in part conceived as a response to missionary critique of the brutality of Spanish colonialism. Bitterli writes:

> The holy Catholic faith is according to these laws the major legitimation for the right of the mother-land to subjugate these areas of the world. Far from placing colonial expansion into question, the mission showed itself to be intimately connected with the political and military actions of the absolutistic state, and even represented, at least in theory, its juridical legitimation.[77]

On the other hand, however, it was the missionaries above all who most sharply criticized the unethical actions of the European conquerors and colonialists. For it was the missionaries, who, because of their high degree of education and close contact with the indigenous peoples, were the first to recognize the value of these cultures and to see that in comparison with the brutality of the Europeans these peoples were not at all inferior. Missionaries continually found themselves in the embarrassing situation of having to uphold the claims to absoluteness and universality of Christianity, while at the same time having to admit that Christian–Western culture was highly unethical. This led them into the following dilemma: they could neither fully support a total integration of foreign peoples into European culture, nor really acknowledge the independent truth of the foreign cultures and religions.[78]

In such a situation the mission was bound to fail. So long as a serious dialogue between cultures was lacking, as it still is today, the mission is reduced to emphasizing merely external acts like Baptism, Communion, church attendance, etc. The lacking readiness for dialogue inevitably expresses itself in relations of domination of one sort or another, to which the widespread paternalism and the more-or-less explicit cultural imperialism typical of much missionary activity bear witness.

It is clear that, under the conditions of such misunderstanding and outright unwillingness to understand, the relations between Europeans and the peoples of Asia, Africa and America could not always develop without tension and conflict. When a people resisted, the Europeans quickly sought a military solution. The result was often the annihilation, expulsion, or enslavement of entire peoples. This violent form of cultural encounter Bitterli terms "cultural conflict," and he cites as examples the annihilation of the original population of Santo Domingo in 1500, the expulsion of the Amerindians from their home lands and their containment in reservations, and the enslavement of millions of Africans. Other examples, of course, would be easy to find throughout the entire colonial period. The history of these events is well-known, and their consequences are still today so near to us that we do not need to discuss them here at greater length.

The fourth form of cultural encounter, which has arisen in the course of the history of colonialism, is "cultural interaction" or "mutual acculturation." This form presupposes that peoples from different cultures live and work together for a long period of time in the same geographical area. Bitterli defines it in the following way:

> While it is trade or the mission which, in the relation which we have termed cultural contact, stand in the foreground, cultural interaction (*Kulturverflechtung*) occurs against the background of an intense social interpenetration. This interpenetration takes the place of the historically more frequently observable conflict of cultures when between two or more cultures there arises the necessity of cooperation in order to secure their existence and the consciousness of a binding mutual dependence. Acculturation and cultural interaction are processes which extend over several generations and which can actually never be considered as having come to an end; ... they achieve their historical independence only when there arises from the close and constant encounter of cultures a new mixed culture, which contains all areas of economic, social and religious life of the partners and which sublimates more and more the contradictions of the original cultural situation.[79]

Bitterli finds it difficult to give already existing examples of acculturation. We may, therefore, take his description of this form of cultural encounter as the description of *the task* for the present historical situation. The decolonization process of the last fifty years, therefore, in no way means a return to cultural isolationism. On the contrary, the global interrelations and dependencies on the economic and political level require social and religious acculturation if we are to survive. For it is an undeniable result of the history of colonialism that all peoples now find themselves within the "same geographical area" and are thus forced to "work together in order to secure their existence." The outcome of the last five centuries of colonialism is the fact that only through mutual acculturation can we avoid the alternative of a destructive conflict of cultures and find stable solutions to the problems of development, freedom, and peace which threaten the world today.

The four typical forms of cultural encounter which have developed in the course of the history of colonialism have not, then, been overcome and left behind in the present phase of decolonization. On the contrary, they are all still with us, *determining the structure of the existential situation* facing all of us.[80] The process of intercultural encounter is not something which takes place, as it were, on distant shores, but is an important and even a decisive factor determining how we think and feel here at "home" and what existential options are available to us. The "intercultural field" is no longer defined by national boundaries, but extends into groups, confessions and parties to include each of us personally in one way or another. Indeed, a phenomenological analysis of the existential situation in which we live reveals three structural moments determined by the event of an emerging global culture.

First, it is an undeniable fact that each of us is rooted and "at home" in some particular culture and religion. This fact may be explicitly known or not. We may be aware of ourselves, for example, *as* Westerners, i.e., as men or women *of* a certain culture among other cultures, which we may regard as either equally humane and valid as our own, or as inferior, holding our own worldview and way of life to be obviously the only right one. Nevertheless, the fact remains that we are equipped with entire systems of thinking, habits, and forms of life which make up what we call our "culture" and which we simply take for granted, whether we know this or not, whether we relate to these things critically or if we uncritically accept them as valid and true.

Secondly, our situation today is such that we are not only rooted in a specific culture and worldview, but we also live in a relatively "open" world. The history of colonialism has created a global horizon within which we are always being confronted with influences from other cultures. We have always already to some extent, through education and the media, come into contact with other religions and worldviews. We have, as it were, automatically acquired a certain "understanding" of one or more of these other worldviews. This knowledge can, of course, be consciously appropriated and augmented or we can repress it and reject it. The fact of the encounter, however, remains decisive for our attitude toward reality, for we are compelled to take a stand and make a decision, even if only unconsciously and in the mode of a defensive repression.

The third structural moment of our existential situation follows upon the second. Acquaintance with another religion or worldview tends to become real knowledge, and at a certain point this knowledge becomes an *insight* into the *truth* of the other view. We become — whether all of a sudden or only over a long period of time is unimportant — *convinced* of the truth of what we have before only been indifferently acquainted with; what was previously foreign becomes familiar and tends to take on the same obviousness as our own worldview. This is not merely an intellectual process, for there is a tendency toward praxis in all understanding, such that the understanding of a new worldview automatically brings with it new possibilities for life. These new ways of life, in turn, confirm and legitimate the new views of reality.[81]

In order to grasp the significance of these three structural moments of our "pluralistic situation," it is important to note that it belongs to the very nature of worldviews and religions that they exercise a great fascination and power of attraction over us; for they offer, after all, complete solutions to the problems of life and undeniably contain deep truths and even authentic revelations and experiences of being and of the holy.[82] This means that in our present situation, determined as it is by the presence and accessibility of a plurality of worldviews, we are, as it were, exposed and surrendered over to the power of these many "realities." The psychological and social tensions created by this unprecedented "conflict of worlds" have given rise to three specific options or stances which we may, for the sake of convenience, term *jumping-back, jumping-over* and *jumping-in-between*.

If we acknowledge the fact of intercultural encounter and furthermore admit that acquaintance leads to knowledge and finally to conviction, we may suppose that it is not unusual today for persons to carry within themselves two convictions and move in two systems of taken-for-granted truths—that into which they were born and the one that has been taken over through the encounter of cultures. It is to be expected that these two worldviews do not harmoniously coincide. Indeed, in most cases they radically contradict each other in basic principles and therefore mutually exclude each other. For the person who finds himself or herself with two such views of reality, this creates a psychologically precarious situation bordering on schizophrenia.[83] One is, as it were, torn in two. One feels oneself being claimed by both worlds. This condition can become pathological if some sort of *mediation* or other "solution" is not found.[84]

We have seen that it was in order to flee from the psychological stress of intercultural encounter that European explorers and colonialists *jumped-back* into ethnocentrism. Since then the basic situation has not changed. When we cannot bear the psychological burden created by the claims of other worldviews, we react out of fear and *jump-back* into the worldview, religion or culture in which we were originally rooted, whether that be Christianity or some form of Secularism. The current upsurge of neo-confessional, evangelical and fundamentalist movements of all sorts shows that by jumping-back in this way we build a wall around our own beliefs and habits of thought and take up a polemical attitude towards other religions and worldviews. It is this reaction to the emerging global culture which, whether explicitly acknowledged or not, lies at the basis of the conservative radicalism and isolationism typical of our present religious and political climate. This may indeed be a way to avoid psychological disorientation and "schizophrenia," but one pays a high price for one's peace of mind. For jumping-back can neither practically, nor theoretically deal with the actual situation. In the long run, such defensive reactions can neither psychologically/socially, nor scientifically/theologically lead to real and lasting solutions.

Jumping-back is typical of all forms of ethnocentrism, cultural imperialism and exclusivism. Despite its untenableness, it still remains *the* standard solution to the problems caused by encounters with the foreign, the anomalous, the unknown, of which the encounter with other cultures and worldviews is today the major example. Historically, as we have seen, it received its legitimation from the military and technological superiority of European culture, as well as from the missionary consciousness of Christianity. Although today, under the conditions of changing power relations in the East–West and North–South conflicts, jumping-back has become politically obsolete, it has, nonetheless, lost none of its *psychological* power. It continues, therefore, to affect almost all dimensions of life: personal, social, religious, economic and political, as the tremendous upsurge of neo-confessional and fundamentalist movements shows.

The present situation, however, contains another option which appears in the great popularity of the "new religious movements" and the success of Indian and Asian missions in the West: namely, the possibility of *jumping-over* into the other culture or religion. Never before has it been so easy to solve the problem of the encounter of cultures simply by giving up one's own culture and accepting the other in toto. The difficulties that come with this solution are, however, apparent. For one is forced to cut off all connections to one's original beliefs, values and way of life. As a consequence of the "jump," one takes up the same sort of exclusive, polemical attitude toward one's former convictions, as the one who has jumped-back into a conservative affirmation of the original worldview. Here too, a high price is paid for one's peace of mind. A person who jumps over into another culture without any mediation or reconciliation with his or her mother culture runs the risk of becoming uprooted and never again being able to strike roots. Even if new roots do grow, the danger remains that they will have little life so long as the problem of a pluralistic reality has not been acknowledged and adequately dealt with.

Jumping-over is structurally similar to jumping-back in that both are forms of exclusivism. Both are essentially defensive reactions. In this structural identity we may see at least one of the reasons why jumping-over is today no longer considered criminal—for one cannot prohibit others from doing that which one does oneself! The fragmentation of the human spirit into a plurality of ideologies, all of which are committed to polemicizing against each other, and among which there can be no common ground, but only the *decision* for or against, is a major characteristic of the existential situation of contemporary humanity.

The third option available in the present situation arises out of the inadequacies of the other two. For, if it is not a real solution to jump-back or to jump-over, then there remains only the possibility of *jumping-in-between*. One attempts to bring the different worldviews into *dialogue* with each other. The only possibility of enduring the psychological stress of two conflicting systems of beliefs is somehow to relate them to each other by placing them into a *horizon of encounter* so that they can come into a fruitful and transforming contact with each other. This alternative coincides with that form of cultural encounter which Bitterli termed "acculturation." It is, therefore, this alternative which becomes the task of all practical and theoretical efforts to adequately face the existential situation in which we find ourselves. For theology, this can only mean that its task lies in the direction which Tillich pointed out for it; namely, in the direction of a theology of religions.[85]

PRESUPPOSITIONS FOR A GLOBAL THEOLOGY

We are now in a position to return to Paul Tillich and consider his last work. Only at the end of his life did Tillich succeed in breaking through to a real solution to the problem of Christian theology. He did so, however, not by means of an apologetic synthesis of Christianity and Secularism, but instead, by means of a *new question*. Tillich proposed to reformulate the question of Christian theology as the question of a *theology of religions*. It was Tillich's insight that the question of the relation between orthodoxy and Secularism cannot be adequately placed, either within the framework of a merely *Christian* theology—be it ever so liberal—nor within the framework of a *philosophy* of religion, which remains committed to the tradition of Western metaphysics. The question can only be appropriately asked within a truly *global horizon*, wherein the different cultures, religions and worldviews, each in its validity, may come forward.[86]

This new insight was further deepened during two years of seminars held together with the historian of religions, Mircea Eliade, at the University of Chicago. Tillich's last public lecture, "The Significance of the History of Religions for the Systematic Theologian,"[87] was a result of this cooperative endeavor.

In this lecture Tillich broke through to the insight that the decisive task for theology did not lie in the apologetic against Secularism—the problematic which had guided his theological work for decades and informed his great *Systematic Theology*—but rather in an "interpenetration of systematic theological study and religious historical studies."[88] Later, Eliade described his impressions of this lecture:

In the course of that superb and moving lecture, Professor Tillich declared that, had he time, he would write a new *Systematic Theology* oriented toward, and in dialogue with, the whole history of religions. In his *Systematic Theology* Tillich had addressed himself to modern Western man, at grips with history and totally involved in the secular world of science and technology. He felt now that a new systematic theology was needed—a theology taking into consideration not only the existential crisis and the religious vacuum of contemporary Western societies, but also the religious traditions of Asia and the primitive world, together with their recent crises and traumatic transformations.[89]

Upon what methodological foundation, we may ask, could such a systematic theology of religions be realized? Tillich could not work out a complete methodology for this new systematic theology, but he did clearly state the *presuppositions* which open up the horizon within which such a theology first becomes possible:

> A theologian who accepts the subject, "The Significance of the History of Religions for the Systematic Theologian," and takes this subject seriously, has already made, explicitly or implicitly, two basic decisions. On the one hand he has separated himself from a theology which rejects all religions other than that of which he is a theologian. On the other hand if one accepts the subject affirmatively and seriously, he has rejected the paradox of a religion of non-religion, or a theology without theos, also called a theology of the secular.[90]

To open up the horizon of a theology of religions, therefore, we must overcome not only orthodox-exclusivism, but also secular-rejectionism. With these two basic decisions, it might be said that Tillich has returned to the formulation of the problem facing a philosophy of religion which he had conceived forty years before. He reaffirms all the more strongly that there is no neutral, common ground, no privileged standpoint which could serve as the basis for a theological method which proceeds apologetically by way of a "correlation" of question and answer. More clearly than ever, Tillich is aware that even Secularism speaks of God, "however untraditional that language may be."[91] Secularism is, therefore, *also* a *religion*; indeed, it is one among many. If, then, the method of theology is still to be a method of "correlation," it can no longer be a correlation of question to answer, but of answer to answer; that is, a correlation of different but equal religions. Theology becomes of necessity a *theology of religions*. "This," Tillich maintains, "makes a serious affirmation of the history of religion possible."[92]

According to Tillich, the two basic decisions which open up the horizon of the theology of religions imply *five theses*, which together make up the methodological presuppositions of any theology of religions. Below, each of the five "systematic presuppositions" are stated and then followed by a commentary which shows how each is derived from the two basic decisions described above.

1. First, one must say that revelatory experiences are universally human. Religions are based on something that is given to a man wherever he lives. He is given a revelation, a particular kind of expe-

rience which always implies saving powers. One never can separate revelation and salvation. There are revealing and saving powers in all religions. God has not left himself unwitnessed.[93]

Commentary: If revelations were not given to all men and women, then it follows that they would be given either to some specially "chosen" group or groups, or to nobody at all. In the first case, where revelation is assumed to be given to a "chosen" people or peoples, we would have orthodox-exclusivism. For only those people would have access to God and Truth who belonged to this special group(s) and all other men and women would be excluded. These peoples would have to "convert" before they could participate in the truth. Their own religions would be mere superstition. If, however, as in the second case, revelations were given to nobody at all, we would have Secularism. For then there would no such thing as religion and faith. There would be no divine truth, but only that which all men and women, on the basis of their own powers, could know. Therefore, the two decisions to overcome orthodox-exclusivism, as well as secular-rejectionism, imply the thesis that revelatory experiences are given to all.

2. The second assumption states that revelation is received by man in terms of his finite human situation. Man is biologically, psychologically, and sociologically limited. Revelation is received under the conditions of man's estranged character.[94]

Commentary: This thesis means that there are no revelations which are fully transparent and comprehensible; that is, all revelations are *symbolic*. If it were so that *some* revelations were fully comprehensible, then they alone would be the standard of truth for all the others, and we would again have an orthodox-exclusivism. If, on the other hand, *all* revelations were conceptually transparent, then revelation as such would be *aufgehoben*, or sublimated into a conceptual language, as for example, in Hegel; and we would find ourselves within the bounds of secular universalism. Overcoming orthodox-exclusivism and secular-rejectionism, therefore, implies that all revelations are *symbolic*.

3. There is a third presupposition that one must accept. When systematic theologians assume the significance of the history of religions, it involves the belief that there are not only particular revelatory experiences throughout human history, but that there is a revelatory process in which the limits of adaptation and the failures of distortion are subjected to criticism.[95]

Commentary: This thesis implies that there is no revelation without *critique*. If the various revelations, in the way they are appropriated and interpreted, were not essentially subject to critique, this would mean that they were either held to be inviolable and sacrosanct mysteries, or that they were completely comprehensible, self-evident concepts. In the first case, since they are still considered *divine* revelations, they would be transformed into authorities standing above all criticism — which would lead directly to ortho-dox-exclusivism. In the second case, they would be taken up into a self-grounding conceptual system in which all questions are already answered. This would amount to nothing other than the claim of secular universalism. Thus, contrary to the self-understanding of orthodoxy as well as a certain secular polemic, critique belongs essentially to revelation. It holds revelation open and defends it against becoming fossilized in interpretations which are no longer questionable. Only in this way can revelation be, as Tillich says, a "revelatory process," and thus, essentially *historical*.

4. A fourth assumption is that there may be — and I stress this, there *may* be — a central event in the history of religions which unites the positive results of those critical developments in the history of religion in and under which revelatory experiences are going on — an event which, therefore, makes possible a concrete theology that has universalistic significance.[96]

Commentary: If, as we have seen, a religious tradition can only remain alive through the ever-renewed critical appropriation of its revelation (and in fact only in this way may a tradition be said to have a "history" in the authentic sense of the word), then this critical process must be directed towards absolute truth. This may be a veiled origin, or an eschatological event. There is, however, no history without movement, no movement without direction and no direction without a goal. Insofar as the different religions can at all be thought together, they must be thought within a common history. This presupposes that a "central event" be assumed as the goal of this common history. Tillich asserts here, neither that there *de facto* is such a thing, nor that *he* could say what it is, nor that it needs to be *named* at all; rather, he asserts only that it must be assumed as a methodological presupposition of a "concrete theology that has universalistic significance."[97]

With this assumption, a critical appropriation of revelatory experiences beyond the borders of any particular tradition becomes possible and indifferentism is overcome. The task of theological thinking, therefore, does not lie in the explication and preservation of the revelation given to one particular tradition; instead, theology must be responsible to *all* religions. This, in turn, implies that theology must proceed comparatively, constructively and critically toward an interpretation which is valid for all.

If, now, not *all* traditions were involved in this critical process, then those which refused to participate in mutual critical appropriation would degenerate into orthodox or secularistic forms — as was shown above in the commentary to thesis 3. If, on the other hand, this critical process had no "central event" as its goal, then it would *either* be transformed into an abstract, confessionless and *merely* comparative knowledge, which corresponds to the usual approach of the secular science of religions, *or* it would become a concealed apologetic for its own truth, which would correspond to an orthodox-exclusivism. Tillich's two basic decisions, therefore, are decisions *for* a critical process of appropriation which includes *all* traditions and aims at absolute truth.

5. There is also a fifth presupposition. The history of religions in its essential nature does not exist alongside the history of culture. The sacred does not lie beside the secular, but it is its depths. The sacred is the creative ground and at the same time a critical judgment of the secular. But the religious can be this only if it is at the same time a judgment on itself, a judgment which must use the secular as a tool of one's own religious self-criticism.[98]

Commentary: This fifth thesis claims that the sacred is the ground of the secular. Immediately it might be objected that this amounts to reviving the old apologetic struggle between orthodoxy and Secularism and quickly deciding the issue in favor of Christianity. Has Tillich, it might be asked, not given up the commitment to overcome orthodoxy? Where is there still to be found a possibility of criticizing religion, when critical reason is at the outset asserted to be grounded in the sacred? Have we not in this thesis, which apparently robs reason of its right to criticism, the most extreme form of orthodox-exclusivism imaginable?

These questions should make us more sensitive to the scope and significance of Tillich's new formulation of the problematic of theology. For if there is in fact no *neutral* position, if thinking has always already taken a *stand*, then Secularism can no longer naively identify itself with an allegedly universal and impartial reason. It must acknowledge that its own principle is grounded in a revelation. "The sacred," says Tillich, has not been "fully absorbed by the secular."[99] That is to say, it reappears within Secularism as soon as Secularism develops its own claim to universality. Within the realm of the secular, therefore, an absolute dimension distinguishes itself from the relative and conditioned — as its "creative ground." This "ground" is the "God" of Secularism, in whatever way it is there understood and whatever name it is given. "The sacred does not lie beside the secular," as Tillich says above, "but it is its depths."

Secularism is, therefore, not at all profane, but just as sacred as all other religions. Sacred and profane are distinctions which have validity and meaning only within a particular religious tradition and cannot be employed to determine the relationship between religions. In other words, Secularism is a religion which stands over against Christianity just as does Hinduism or Islam. It is not a profane area somehow within or without Christianity.

If this is the case, then the task of Christian theology, once it has acknowledged that other religions (including Secularism!) also contain authentic revelations, cannot lie in an apologetic against secular universalism, but rather, it can only lie in *dialogue*, which now is understood as dialogue with all religions. *The moment Christian theology abandons its apologetic approach to Secularism, a global horizon opens up and it becomes theology of religions.* Herein lies the significance of Tillich's new and radical reformulation of the question and task of theology. Thus he can say the following:

> Only if the theologian is willing to accept these five presuppositions can he seriously and fully affirm the significance of the history of religions for theology against those who reject such significance in the name of a new or of an old absolutism.[100]

From this point of view, we can better understand why Tillich was dissatisfied with the "liberal" theological program of Schleiermacher, Troeltsch, Harnack and others. Liberalism thought it could avoid the consequences of the continuity it admitted to exist between Christianity and all other religions by maintaining that Christianity was the "highest form" of religion. Whatever was "revealed" in other religions, therefore, was already perfectly developed and fully present in Christianity. Consequently, Christian theology had really nothing to learn from the religions of the world. This is a view from which Tillich only at the end of his life completely freed himself. In this respect he acknowledges his indebtedness to Mircea Eliade:

> I now want to return my thanks on this point to my friend Professor Eliade for the two years of seminars and the cooperation we had in them. In these seminars I experienced that every individual doctrinal statement or ritual expression of Christianity receives a new intensity of meaning. And, in terms of a kind of an apologia yet also a self-accusation, I must say that my own *Systematic Theology* was written before these seminars and had another intention, namely, the apologetic discussion against and with the secular. Its purpose was the discussion or the answering of questions coming from the scientific and philosophical criticism of Christianity. But perhaps we need a longer, more intensive period of interpenetration of systematic theological study and religious historical studies. Under such circumstances the structure of religious thought might develop in connection with another or different fragmentary manifestation of theonomy or of the Religion of the Concrete Spirit. This is my hope for the future of theology.[101]

There is no clearer expression of Tillich's definitive rejection of apologetics than in the wish that "the structure of religious thought" be transformed through dialogue with other religions. Nevertheless, we may ask where in all this does the possibility of critique lie. Everything seems to disintegrate into a myriad of different claims to absoluteness, each with the inviolable shield of the sacred before it and nowhere a weak flank where rational critique could find a point of attack. Tillich's answer is clear: The sacred can be the creative ground of Secularism and at the same time be "a critical judgment" of it, only when the sacred is "at the same time a judgment on itself." But how, we may ask again, can the sacred criticize itself? As cited above, Tillich answers that it must be "a judgment which must use the secular as a tool of one's own religious self-criticism."

The sacred, therefore, criticizes itself by means of its own plurality and diversity. Radical pluralism itself, on account of the internal tensions arising from conflicting claims to absolute truth, gives rise to a dynamic historical process in which the various religions mutually criticize and correct each other. Or, as Karl Marx rightly saw, "criticism of religion is the premise of all criticism." What he did not realize, however, is that the critique of religion is in fact the religion of critique.[102] This is a critique "of" religion in the sense that it is religion itself, in the form of the theology of religions, which performs the critique and not an allegedly neutral and objective science.

We are no longer standing upon the ground of a *merely* Christian theology. From here, the road leads in a completely different direction. We do not know, of course, how this road will look or where exactly it will lead us. But the horizon within which the road becomes visible has at least been opened. There remains the task of showing that this horizon and the way it would lead us are no mere illusions, no arbitrary inventions, but unavoidable presuppositions for any theology that would adequately deal with the problems of our *kairos*, our historical situation. It must be shown that the basic decisions and the methodological presuppositions which Tillich places before any theology of religions are not only possible but also necessary. Chapters 3 and 4 will be devoted to this foundational task. Before that, however, it is necessary to get a better idea of what the way itself looks like.

Tillich did not live to carry out the renewal of his systematic theology. We do not know how he would have accomplished this. The various suggestions which he put forward in his last works remain incomplete and preliminary. It would be a great risk to attempt to develop these proposals further. Therefore, we turn to the work of a man who has personally gone the way of a theology of religions; he is a man who thinks out of the praxis of the interreligious dialogue and from whose work we will be able to reconstruct the *method* of the theology of religions. This man is Raimundo Panikkar.

Let us briefly summarize what may be considered the result of this chapter. The horizon of a theology of religions is opened up by means of two basic decisions, which imply five theses; together these constitute the methodological presuppositions of the theology of religions.

Basic Decisions:

    I. The decision to overcome orthodox-exclusivism.

    II. The decision to overcome the secular rejection of all religion.

Theses Implied By These Decisions:

1. Revelatory experiences are given to all peoples. They are *universal*.
2. No revelation is fully transparent and comprehensible. Revelation is *symbolic*.
3. *Critique* prevents these symbols from becoming closed up in fixed and unquestionable interpretations.
4. Critique transcends the given borders of any particular tradition and aims at an *absolute truth*.
5. The sacred is not a separate realm alongside the secular, but the ground of the secular. Secularism is, therefore, itself a *religion* with sacred and profane elements of its own.

2

Method

If the encounter of cultures and religions had been a major impetus for a new orientation in the thinking of Paul Tillich, it is *the* determining factor in the life and thought of Raimundo Panikkar. Panikkar, whose father was Hindu and whose mother was Spanish Catholic, was indeed "born" into the encounter of cultures and religions. This is a destiny which became for him in his own words an "existential risk" and an "intellectual burden"[1] — that is, the existential risk of living within, or between, two different traditions and the intellectual burden of somehow thinking the two together in one coherent whole. The method of thought by which he proposes to accomplish this task he calls *diatopical hermeneutics*.

About the "existential risk" involved in the interreligious dialogue, he writes:

> It is not that I willfully consider myself both an Indian and a European, a Hindu and a Christian, or that I artificially declare myself to be a religious and a secular man. It is rather that I *am* by birth, education, initiation and actual life a man living from and sharing in the original experiences of the Western tradition, both Christian and Secular, and the Indian tradition, both Hindu and Buddhist. ... The mutual understanding and fecundation of the different traditions of the world may be accomplished only by sacrificing one's life in the attempt to sustain first the existing tensions without becoming schizophrenic and to maintain the polarities without personal or cultural paranoia.[2]

And about the "intellectual burden" of such an existence, he says:

> ... the thematic study of the relations among cultures has led me to develop what I call *diatopical hermeneutics*, which differs from the

morphological and diachronical kinds in that it takes as its point of departure the awareness that the *topoi*, the loci of various worldviews cannot be bridged using the tools of understanding from one tradition or culture alone. ... diatopical hermeneutics tries to bring together radically different human horizons.[3]

Of course one could ask whether such a method has any relevance for those of us who are not born into more than one culture and religion. To what extent can it be claimed that Panikkar's method for doing theology has universal validity? What relevance does his program possess for Christian theology as such?

We have seen that it is one of the essential characteristics of our time that the borders between cultures and religions are disappearing. The existential risk and the intellectual burden of the interreligious dialogue is, therefore, not merely the personal adventure of privileged individuals, but the very condition determining all relevant theology in our time.[4] In this context it is clear that Panikkar's "existential risk" is not the peculiar fate of one individual, but the situation in which we are all presently involved. What at first may seem the accidental destiny of one man is in fact a situation which is determinative in one way or another for all men and women; and therefore it also defines the proper task of theology in today's world.

After all that has been said, it should be clear why Panikkar claims that the encounter of religions "is today one of the most profound human problems."[5] He writes:

> To be sure, each tradition, seeing itself from within, considers that it is capable of giving a full answer to the religious urge of its members and, seeing other traditions from outside, tends to judge them as partial. It is only when we take the other as seriously as ourselves that a new vision may dawn. For this we have to break the self-sufficiency of any human group. But this requires that we should somehow have jumped outside our own respective traditions. Herein seems to lie the destiny of our time.[6]

Our question is: How can we consciously accept this destiny and approach the coming encounter of religions with methodological adequacy?

Panikkar has not yet published a systematic methodology for the interreligious dialogue. This does not, however, mean that he has neglected methodological concerns. No doubt, much of Panikkar's published work is primarily concerned with the concrete dialogue between Christianity and Hinduism. Still, there are important methodological reflections throughout these works, as well as major essays dealing specifically with methodological issues. Drawing upon these various sources, I will attempt a systematic *reconstruction* of Panikkar's method for conducting the interreligious dialogue. To state the result at the outset, the method will be found to consist of seven steps:

1. One begins with a faithful and critical understanding of one's own tradition — an understanding won with historical-critical, philological and phenomenological methods.
2. In the same way, an understanding of another tradition is acquired.
3. This understanding becomes conviction.
4. An internal, *intra*-religious dialogue begins between the two convictions.
5. The internal dialogue becomes an external, *inter*-religious dialogue with representatives of the other tradition.
6. Steps 1 through 5 are presupposed for all partners in dialogue.
7. New interpretations are tested for their "orthodoxy."

It should be noted that in the following discussion I will be primarily concerned with presenting a *method* not only specifically for interreligious dialogue, but also for intercultural encounter in general. The focus upon method necessarily implies a certain narrowness of vision with respect to the full body of Panikkar's thought. We cannot do justice to the entire philosophical and theological "system" which surrounds and, to a certain extent, grounds his method. Neither can we adequately answer the historical question concerning the development of his thought. As important and as justified as these questions may be in a study devoted exclusively to one particular thinker, they cannot make up the central concern of a systematic methodology such as I am here undertaking. For our concerns, it is not Panikkar the man and the thinker which is of central importance, but the method for interreligious dialogue which can be reconstructed from his work.

DIATOPICAL HERMENEUTICS

Panikkar places certain "indispensable prerequisites" at the beginning of the encounter of religions. These prerequisites consist of the following:

a deep human honesty in searching for the truth wherever it can be found; a great intellectual openness in this search, without conscious preconceptions or willingly entertained prejudices; and finally a profound loyalty towards one's own tradition.[7]

Already we have here the first two steps of the method which any interreligious dialogue must follow. The first step consists in obtaining a faithful and critical understanding of one's own tradition; and the second step requires that one acquire a similar understanding of another tradition.[8]

In order to make clear the procedures by which this is to be accomplished, Panikkar proposes to view human communication and thus intercultural understanding on the basis of a *diatopical model*. The diatopical model allows us to distinguish *three levels of discourse* upon which communication may take place. First, *within* a culture, tradition, worldview or religion, understanding is achieved by means of a first level of discourse which Panikkar calls "morphological" hermeneutics.[9] This refers to that language in which we make assertions about matters of fact in the broad sense. This is everyday language, the normal language in which we communicate and coordinate our practical as well as theoretical concerns. Whatever we say in this language is meaningful by reason of being either true or false according to commonly accepted criteria of truth and validity. These criteria form the lifeworld horizon, the set of taken-for-granted truths about reality which constitutes our "world." Within the horizon of shared criteria, the methods according to which we handle statements made on this level of discourse may be called methods of "verification."

When systematically developed, first-level discourse becomes the well-known methods of argumentation — formal, empirical, historical-critical and phenomenological — in which scientific inquiry is conducted. Panikkar refers to these methods as "morphological hermeneutics," for it is by means of them that the distance which separates us from understanding that which is strange or unknown, whether it be a natural phenomenon, a text, a work of art, or a social institution, is overcome. Morphological hermeneutics, therefore, makes understandable something which is *within the same cultural and historical context* as the interpreter. To take an example from everyday life, an expert explains the proper use of a computer to someone from his own culture who has a similar general education. The expert may presuppose a common language and form of thinking, and even a common worldview. It is presupposed that the person who is seeking information about the computer already knows, at least to a certain extent, what a "computer" is, what a "machine" is and what one does with such things.

The problem of explaining and understanding becomes very different, however, when it is a matter of obtaining information about something from the past, from a culture which lies far behind us in time. Imagine, for example, a text or artifact from ancient Rome or Greece. We can no longer presuppose a common language or worldview. The world has changed since then, and the context in which the text originally was written or the artifact produced no longer immediately determines our own view of the world. Understanding now requires that the context itself be reconstructed and mediated with our own present-day context or lifeworld horizon. This is a task which must be carried out upon a different level of discourse; namely, it demands a discourse which, since it cannot appeal to common criteria of truth or meaning, must itself express these criteria and thus "set boundaries" for our lifeworld horizon. Consequently, we may speak of this second-level discourse as *boundary discourse*. Panikkar calls boundary discourse "diachronic" hermeneutics because it overcomes distance and alienation of meaning *through time*. Specifically, it articulates itself as the retrieval of founding texts and events. A consequence is that it remains within *one* specific cultural tradition (e.g., Western culture). The understanding which it expresses by mediating horizons of meaning constitutes the historical continuity and cultural identity of a "tradition." As a systematically developed method of inquiry, boundary discourse becomes historical hermeneutics or dialectic.[10]

Both morphological and diachronical hermeneutics may be applied in the attempt to understand another culture. Such is the normal procedure in ethnology, anthropology and history and their respective applications in the science of religions. Nevertheless, says Panikkar, they are not sufficient to overcome the radical distance which separates different cultures from one another. For this reason, still a higher level of discourse must be postulated wherein these disciplines will be able to go beyond their present methodological borders. Only upon the basis of a discourse which opens up a *horizon of encounter* within which radically different contexts, or life-world horizons of meaning may co-respond with one another, does intercultural understanding become possible. Interreligious understanding has truly the character of a founding *event*, for at a certain point there occurs an appropriation of a *new horizon* of taken-for-granted truths. Such understanding is necessarily different from merely acquiring new information about something in the world, and it cannot, therefore, be carried out at the level of argumentative discourse, that is, by means of a merely historical or phenomenological comparison of beliefs. Furthermore, it cannot limit its horizon to the continuity of a single historical tradition and the retrieval of its founding texts or events. Therefore, it cannot be carried out upon the second-level boundary discourse of diachronic hermeneutics. It is for this reason that Panikkar has introduced a "third moment" into hermeneutics:

There is . . . a third moment in any complete hermeneutical process and the fact that it has often been neglected or overlooked has been a major cause of misunderstandings among the different cultures of the world. I call it *diatopical* hermeneutics because the distance to be overcome is not merely temporal, within one broad tradition, but the gap existing between two human *topoi*, 'places' of understanding and self-understanding, between two — or more — cultures that have not developed their patterns of intelligibility or their basic assumptions out of a common historical tradition or through mutual influence. To cross the boundaries of one's own culture without realizing that another culture may have a radically different approach to reality is today no longer admissible. If still consciously done, it would be philosophically naive, politically outrageous and religiously sinful. Diatopical hermeneutics stands for the thematic consideration of understanding the other without assuming that the other has the same basic self-understanding and understanding as I have. The ultimate human horizon, and not only differing contexts, is at stake here.[11]

If diatopical hermeneutics is to be possible, the "ultimate human horizon" is and must always remain a horizon of *encounter* rather than a horizon of *indifference* and *exclusion* as it is projected by first- and second-level discourse. The phenomenology of religion, for example, has its function in the identification and preliminary clarification of religious phenomena, but not in actually carrying out the dialogue between religions. This is because, as first-level discourse, it operates within a horizon of phenomenal *indifference*, or givenness which precludes the radical *discontinuity* between different religious traditions.[12] This is also true, according to Panikkar, for the philosophy of religion.[13] Philosophy of religion, as our discussion of apologetic universalism in Chapter 1 showed, operates, along with theology, upon the second level of discourse, which is concerned to establish specific criteria of meaning and truth as the encompassing boundary of a particular tradition.

From the methodological point of view, the first two levels of discourse, together with their respective systematic methods of inquiry, do not have the capability of constructively appropriating the moment of *praxis* which necessarily accompanies interreligious understanding — namely, the moment of becoming *convinced* of the truth of the other religion or worldview as a new possibility for one's own life. Although it is certainly *necessary* to study another religion or culture with all the methods which the various sciences place at our disposal before a meaningful dialogue can take place, it is not *sufficient*. This follows from the fact that the understanding of another culture or religion inevitably brings with it the disclosure of an entire world of meaning and value which includes new possibilities for human existence. The disclosure of such a world of meaning implies becoming convinced of its truth. Understanding upon this level is itself a "religious" event which in turn implies that we experience, with respect to the other religion, what can only be called a *conversion*.[14]

Of course this can and must be said for second-level boundary discourse also. To set the boundaries of a lifeworld is not to make assertions which may be either true or false according to given criteria, for boundary discourse expresses and "gives" the criteria themselves. Here also the pragmatics of discovering truth consists not in procedures of verification, but in processes of initiation, socialization and conversion. But the experience of conversion on the second level of discourse is limited to establishing the cultural identity and historical continuity of a single tradition *to the exclusion* of all others. Therefore, it is necessary to postulate a third level of discourse where conversion is not exclusive.

It is precisely this requirement which the various scientific disciplines cannot fulfill. The empirical sciences are bound to methodological abstinence from value judgments, whereas the hermeneutical and dialectical sciences are bound to a confessionally exclusive closure of the horizon of meaning which projects specific criteria as absolute. In order, therefore, to bring out clearly the implications of the problem of understanding on the level of interreligious encounter and also to explain what is involved in diatopical hermeneutics, Panikkar puts forth the following provocative thesis: "To understand is to be convinced."[15] This refers to the way in which truth is discovered on the level of a discourse that does not presuppose common, taken-for-granted criteria of meaning and reality. What is said within first level discourse is meaningful, as we said, precisely because it can be either true or false according to given criteria. What is said, however, upon those higher levels of discourse where it is not a matter of asserting facts about the world, but "proclaiming" the very boundaries of the world, is either meaningful or meaningless and its meaning *is* its truth.

This implies that, on the "religious" plane, understanding what a statement means is the same as acknowledging its truth. Or, put the other way round, on this level of discourse a false proposition cannot be understood at all. Panikkar says: "To understand something as false is a contradiction in itself."[16] This is because "Understanding produces conviction."[17] Panikkar summarizes his thesis so:

In the thesis lies the assertion that one cannot really understand the views of another, if one does not share them.[18]

How are we to understand this claim? Before looking more closely at how Panikkar seeks to establish this assertion, let us attempt to make clear just what is at stake. It is asserted that the historical, phenomenological and philosophical methods, with which we hitherto have understood our own and also other traditions, on the one hand, inevitably lead to conviction, whereas on the other hand, because of their ideals of value-free objectivity, they can neither consciously admit, nor adequately appropriate the "conversion" which accompanies all understanding. In a non-pluralistic situation characterized by relatively unquestioned agreement on basic values, the moment of conversion does not become explicitly problematical. Methods of understanding which are explicitly or implicitly intended to secure the cultural reproduction of a society are at first unproblematical; that is, they perform an enculturating function more or less adequately and actually do bring about understanding and belief in the basic values and truths of a society. We are usually unaware that we have been "converted" to our own cultural lifeworld and that such a conversion lies at the basis of almost all our beliefs and convictions.

As soon as this naive unanimity is broken, however, as it is in a radically pluralistic situation, methods of understanding which do not explicitly take the moment of conversion into account become counterproductive. The implicit convictions of the interpreters, as long as they are not raised to the level of methodological awareness and brought under control, cause polemical distortions and block understanding. What is at stake in Panikkar's claim, therefore, is the insight that the interreligious encounter requires its own method of understanding which *explicitly* includes the moment of conversion.

Let us now look at how Panikkar establishes his thesis. He offers the following example:

> Granted "A is B" means "Jesus is the Lord" and you, as orthodox Jew would not agree to the statement. Now you go further and say: "M is p," that is, "Christians believe that Jesus is the Lord." You ask yourself: How do they come to believe this? The reason: "M thinks that n is correct," that is, "Christians understand the Jewish Messiah to be the Lord and suppose that Jesus is this Messiah." You, however, do not believe that n is correct, that is, that Christ is the Messiah, although you admit that the Messiah is the Lord. You understand clearly that some men consider Jesus to be the Messiah and therefore say: "Jesus is the Lord" ("A is B"). But you will object that this is not correct, because the statement is grounded upon a false reading into the facts, namely, the identification of Jesus with the Messiah. Although you understand "M is p," you do not understand "A is B," because for you A is not the A which M means (Jesus, the Messiah), but A_1 (Jesus, a condemned Jew). This means that Jesus is not the Messiah for you so that the sentence "Jesus is the Lord" is for you unacceptable. You understand, therefore, the sentence "A_1 is B" and even "A_1 is not A" — and therefore you cannot perform the spiritual act of saying with meaning: "A is B." You understand what "they" say, and even why they say it, but you do not understand what they understand, and this precisely because you have another understanding of A (namely A_1).[19]

Since it is precisely the human sciences which formulate such sentences, namely, "M thinks that n is correct," or "M says, A is B," this argument shows the limits of a certain kind of scientific method. For if understanding of "what" the other says depends upon our insight into the truth of their statement, then the methodological ideals of value-neutrality and objectivity actually hinder the process of understanding in every situation where a common agreement about basic convictions cannot be presupposed. Not only is it unscientific for such methods to claim to be the only ones capable of yielding true knowledge, but such "scientific" ideals of knowledge tend to make dialogue impossible. In the first place they do not acknowledge other forms of thought as equally valid means of knowing, and in the second place they produce an interpretation wherein the other cannot "find himself." Panikkar writes:

> We investigate, for example, the customs of some "animistic" tribe and describe them in every detail, whereby we also show the logical connections between them, etc. We are able to reproduce "M is p"

almost like a photograph, but if we overlook the other (deeper lying) level, upon which the truth-claim arises, then we do not really attain to the thing which we are describing. In other words: The group M will not be satisfied with our purely phenomenological explanations, which have intentionally placed the question of truth, which to them is the most important question, in "parentheses." This means, "M is p" may indeed seem to me to be so, but the group M will not at all see itself in this statement.[20]

It is in this context that the full significance of *conversion* as the *third step* in the method for the interreligious dialogue becomes clear. Referring to the dialogue between Christianity and Hinduism, with which Panikkar has primarily been concerned, this means:

A Christian will never fully understand Hinduism if he is not, in one way or another, converted to Hinduism. Nor will a Hindu ever fully understand Christianity unless he, in one way or another, becomes a Christian.[21]

The concept of "conversion" must be taken seriously. Literally, the word, coming from Latin *convertere*, means "to turn about." It implies a change, which, because it occurs in the dimension of a person's basic beliefs, is a radical one involving the whole person, his or her vision of the world and the entire network of social relations in which the person is embedded. Traditionally, "conversion" has been *confessionally* understood in terms of a model of *rejection and acceptance*, that is, as a complete rejection of the "old" view and a similarly total and unquestioning acceptance of the "new." For this reason, it has become important in the theological rather than the philosophical or scientific traditions.[22]

Biblically, the idea of *metanoia* contains several moments: 1) a *total* disposition which involves the whole person and all of his or her abilities and powers; 2) a *religious* conversion, that is, the complete turning about which someone experiences when they "give up" their old way of life and "return" to a way of life in harmony with God; 3) not only a turning away from the old, but a turning into a *new orientation* for the future, which 4) implies a new and deeper *understanding* of God and his will; and finally, 5) all the above are seen as a *response* to God's call to reconciliation and his granting of the possibility of salvation through grace.[23] Psychological and sociological studies of conversion experiences yield a scenario of conflict, crisis of meaning and resolution of the crisis by means of a personal and social reorientation in which socialization processes, group support and institutional determinants play a decisive role.[24]

Summarizing these various moments, we may understand the *methodo-logical* concept of "conversion" — as opposed to the apologetic and exclusive *confessional* conversion — to denote a transformation of one's whole worldview—in its cognitive, affective and social dimensions—whereby the *turn away* from an inadequate and incomplete knowledge of truth, the *turn into* a true and valid order and the *turn towards* new possibilities for life and thought are all a function of genuine *communication* between religions rather than the result of an apologetic and defensive conflict. The significance of this idea for the general problem of understanding other cultures will become fully clear only in the discussion in Chapter 4 below. For the moment, we are interested in showing how conversion *functions* in the method for interreligious dialogue.

As we saw, the diatopical model allows us to distinguish between a second and third level of discourse so that the idea of a methodological conversion, as opposed to an exclusive, confessional conversion, becomes conceivable. But quite apart from the question of whether such an idea is adequately founded philosophically, a question we will take up in Chapters 3 and 4 below, there is the more immediate question of whether it is *theologically acceptable*. For at first sight it would seem that as a step in the method for interreligious dialogue, methodological conversion brings with it insurmountable theological problems.[25] The question arises whether dialogue must not be rejected from the very beginning in order to remain faithful to one's own religion. If understanding the other inevitably leads to some sort of conversion to what the other believes, as Panikkar claims, then the dialogue seems to demand that I be prepared to give up my own faith, which is, of course, neither theologically nor methodologically acceptable.

Panikkar attempts to solve this difficulty by means of a distinction between *faith* and *belief*.[26] Faith, for Panikkar, is a "constitutive dimension of man." Human existence is such only by virtue of an openness to transcendence, that is, to the absolute and unconditioned. If men and women did not have this possibility of openness toward the transcendent, then they could not distance themselves from the things around them and become aware of themselves as knowers of the world. Humans would not have the ability to become self-conscious at all and thus to become what a human being essentially is. The existential movement beyond oneself, however, must have a direction. This is the absolute as ground of being. For to go beyond oneself means nothing else than that a human being knows that he or she is *not* a thing in the world (see the *neti neti* of the Upanishads), but that existence is grounded in the mystery of the absolute and unconditioned.

It is the unconditioned ground of being which the Western tradition calls God. The constitutive self-transcendence of human existence is, therefore, nothing other than the ontological relation which a person has to his or her creator, to God. And since it is the relation to God which the Christian tradition has always called "faith," Panikkar feels entitled to use the properly theological term "faith" to denote this constitutive dimension of human existence:

Our thesis maintains that if creatureliness can be said to be simple *relation* to God, to the Source or whatever name we give the foundation of beings, faith is another name for the *ontological relation* to this absolute that characterizes Man, distinguishing him from all other beings. If beings as such are nothing but this relation (the creature neither is nor has its foundation in itself), Man is that unique being whose rapport with the foundation becomes the *ontological link* that constitutes him as Man. Thus faith is not the privilege of some individuals or the monopoly of certain defined groups, however large their membership. Faith is not a superfluous luxury, but an anthropological dimension of the full human being on earth.[27]

It follows from this that it is faith, and not, say, a common biological structure or purely natural reason which fundamentally unites humanity and makes communication and communion among men and women possible.[28] Faith, however, must not thereby be confused with *belief*, that is, the many expressions and formulations of faith. As Panikkar puts it, "faith is not in dogmas, but in the 'thing' expressed in and through them."[29] The "thing" which is here spoken of is "the ever inexhaustible mystery, beyond the reach of objective knowledge,"[30] which, therefore, we can only attain through a "real mysticism" that carries us "beyond—not against—formulae and explanations."[31]

Panikkar finds support for this view not only in the theological tradition, but also in philosophical reflection. For Christian theology, it is an axiom that humans can only be saved by faith. The problem thus arises of whether only those who have been reached by the Gospel and possess the *explicit* Christian faith may be saved, or whether God, out of his will to save all humankind, has not given every people always and everywhere an "implicit faith." Further, the ancient praxis of baptizing children could have no possible effect apart from faith—a faith, however, which is not dogmatically formulated or even consciously perceived. According to Panikkar, "both of these—the doctrinal insufficiency of the ignorant and the doctrinal incapacity of baptized infants" imply that "faith must be something common to Men, whatever their religious beliefs."[32]

As Panikkar is quick to add, however, this does not signify that faith is *not* a free, unearned gift of God's grace. One must distinguish between faith, which is given to all men as a condition of their existence—for how could the creature exist at all if not in some relation with his creator—and the conscious and explicitly formulated act of faith, which, because of human freedom and the different historical situations in which men and women find themselves, is enacted and expressed in different ways. If faith is not to be identified with some particular historically conditioned expression, then it must be constituted as indefinite openness, and it must function to ground the possibility that humans can always go beyond whatever conception they or their society may have of themselves.

Turning to philosophical reflection, Panikkar finds this confirmed. As we have seen, reason discovers human existence to be a finite being limited by space and time, but conscious of this finitude and thus co-conscious of the unconditioned and the infinite which is the ground of being. Humans exist as open towards being as such. Panikkar here finds that which he is looking for, that is, "something in Man that links him to transcendence":

We could describe faith as *existential openness toward transcendence* or, if this seems too loaded, more simply as *existential openness*. This openness implies a bottomless capacity to be filled without closing. Were it to close, it would cease to be faith. The openness is always to a *plus ultra*, to an ever farther, which we may call transcendence and in a certain sense transcendental.[33]

And he concludes:

Evidently this 'something' cannot belong to the purely doctrinal order since the world of concepts depends upon the possibilities offered by the different cultures through which it is expressed. In fact there is no universal culture in either time or space. And a concept is meaningful, and hence valid, only where it has been conceived.[34]

Free will and *questioning thought* are witnesses to this openness. In its unfinished state, humanity is *responsible* for its life and free to form this life not only according to pre-given patterns but according to new possibilities which it itself creates. Herein lies the ground of human historicity. Human existence is historical because, even though men and women may want to, they cannot realize and fulfill their longing for perfection in any inner-worldly situation. The desire for an *absolute good* continually drives humans beyond all which they have attained and ever will attain. The same is the case in the intellectual realm. Thought does not live from answers which silence it, but from questions which always impel it to seek further, indeed, to seek an *absolute truth*. Humans question because they do not know. Knowing that we do not know, *docta ignorantia*, keeps thought open for the unconditioned and prevents it from becoming imprisoned in an ideology of one sort or another. Panikkar concludes:

The quintessence of faith, then, reflects this aspect of Man that moves him towards fullness, this dimension by which Man is not closed up in his present state but open to perfection, to his goal or destiny, according to the schema one adopts. Faith is not fundamentally the adhesion to a doctrine or an ethic. Rather, it is manifest as an act that opens to us the possibility of perfection, permitting us to attain to what we are not yet.[35]

It is, therefore, upon this distinction between the universally human and religious dimension of faith on the one hand, and the various beliefs it gives rise to on the other, that Panikkar grounds the theological acceptability of the interreligious dialogue once it is admitted that all understanding implies conversion. The methodological significance of this distinction cannot be overestimated. We will do well, therefore, to pause here to consider some of its implications.

First, let us note that this distinction enables us to overcome the exclusivist truth-claims of both secular science and orthodox theology. Because science confuses faith with belief it must suppress the universality of the religious dimension. This compels it to assign belief to the aesthetic or affective realm of subjective opinion, which in turn allows it to base its own universal claims upon the methodological ideals of value-free objectivity. But, as we saw, scientific method cannot reach the level of knowledge upon which the interreligious encounter takes place. Conversely, because orthodox theology confuses belief with faith, it can only experience the moment of conversion, which all understanding on the interreligious level implies, confessionally and exclusively and thus as a threat to saving faith and not as a transformation, deepening and growth of belief. Consequently, it is in the distinction between faith and belief that the two basic decisions which Tillich placed at the beginning of any serious dialogue among religions, namely, the decisions to overcome orthodox-exclusivism and secular-rejectionism find their theological foundation.

A second important result of this distinction, which follows from the first, is that it allows a *horizon of encounter* to be opened up wherein all religions may meet. For once belief is distinguished from faith, it becomes clear that there exists a certain *similarity* between religions which can be articulated on a third level of discourse that is characterized neither by the mere comparison of phenomenal similarity nor by the apologetic projection of totality based upon a particular system of beliefs, whether it be orthodox-exclusivist or secular-rejectionist. Religions may thus encounter each other upon the basis of a *functional similarity*: for they are all expressions of a fundamentally human search for the absolute.[36]

On the one hand, this insight, as we noted above, delivers us from the impasse in which the science of religions currently finds itself, for it grounds the possibility of universalistic thinking upon a religious basis, instead of on the basis of the secular ideals of objective, value-free knowledge. On the other hand, it discloses a space of encounter and thus grounds the possibility that the different religions can enter into open and honest dialogue with each other without fearing that the conversion, which dialogue brings with it, will necessarily lead to the loss of saving faith.[37] It therefore serves to free religion from its exclusivistic aspects, its frequently sectarian and confessional character and from an apologetic universalism incompatible with the emergence of a global culture and universal human community.[38]

Thirdly, it is equally instructive to see what consequences follow for the interreligious dialogue when this distinction is *not* made and dialogue must occur upon a lower level of discourse. If faith is *identified* with belief, there arise certain *typical deformations* of thought. We have already discussed this question in Chapter 1, from a non-theological point of view, in terms of apologetic universalism and cultural pluralism as an existential problem. We have also spoken of the existential alternatives of "jumping-back" and "jumping-over" with which our present historical situation confronts us. Panikkar describes the same situation in terms of three *theological* programs or models: *exclusivism*, *inclusivism* and *indifferentism*. All three represent inadequate solutions to the problem of the interreligious encounter. They remain, nevertheless, typical theological approaches to this problem today. It is useful, therefore, to describe these programs briefly, in order to see what the interreligious dialogue is *not* before coming back to the question of how the third step of a methodological conversion is concretely to be carried out.

It is important at the outset of this discussion to keep in view the fact that although faith is distinct from its many expressions, there is still no such thing as a pure, expressionless faith:

> Faith cannot be equated with belief, but faith always needs a belief to be faith. Belief is not faith, but it must convey faith. A disembodied faith is not faith.[39]

This unique and indissoluble bond between transcendent faith and its inner-worldly expression will become important later on when we attempt to clarify the nature of the third level of discourse in terms of the religious symbol. For the moment I am interested in the fact that we must always begin from the formulations and doctrines of the tradition in which we stand. Panikkar never tires of pointing out that there is no neutral stand-point.[40] The three theological models for interreligious dialogue mentioned above arise from the different ways of reacting to this fact which are possible upon the second level of discourse.

Second-level discourse, we recall, is concerned with projecting the unity and totality of a lifeworld horizon, a tradition. On this level of discourse there are three possible relations to other traditions. First, our own symbols may be assumed to be the only valid ones and all others are rejected. Secondly, it is admitted that symbols other than our own are true, but only to the extent that they allow themselves to be integrated into our system of thought and belief. Thirdly, all traditions may be thought to be equally true, but with the proviso that they, for that very reason, cannot and should not have anything to do with one another. All of these positions may be developed into deliberate methodological models. The first represents an exclusivist model, the second an approach which may be termed inclusivism, and the third is indifferentism. Let us now examine these three models more closely.

Exclusivism

The positive side of this approach is its faithful commitment to its own tradition, which is never merely human contrivance, but contains real truth and authentic experiences of the holy. Nevertheless, there looms the danger of fanaticism. For the temptation is great, as the history of the missions gives witness, to consider other religions as false in relation to the truth of one's own, or as darkness in relation to one's own light, or as sinful in comparison to the salvation which one, as a member of a "chosen" people, has graciously received. Other exclusive oppositions with which this program attempts to deal with the problem of other religions are, for example, the "condemned" in comparison to the "saved," or a merely "natural" religion in comparison to "supernatural," "revealed" religion. In Panikkar's judgment, this model, based as it is upon such exclusive opposites, is neither historically, nor psychologically, nor theologically acceptable:

This solution is not only impracticable and utopian; it is also a religious and wrong and would create only disorder and confusion on both sides. A Christian "missionary" attitude desirous of undermining the foundation on which Hinduism rests would not only be dishonest and contrary to the principles of Christianity, but it would also be doomed to failure. Similarly, if a Hindu guru undermines or ignores the Christian background of Western disciples he not only violates such fundamental principles of the Hindu tradition as tolerance and openness, but is also doomed to failure. For psychology and history show that such radical (i.e., uprooting) conversions cannot last long unless a certain integration of both traditions takes place.[41]

In order to avoid the blatantly unacceptable consequences of this way of thinking, one may distinguish between different levels of truth, or between a subjective and an objective order of truth. Other religions, accordingly, need not be totally condemned or rejected; instead, they could now be considered either to be preliminary stages or first steps upon a way which leads to a full acceptance of one's own truth, or they could be excused of their objective falsity on account of the subjective "good will" of their individual followers. Such compromises lead directly into the program of *inclusivism*. But before we examine this position, which might seem the most suitable in the present situation, let us look at the third alternative, *indifferentism*. Thus we will have staked out on both sides the terrain in which the inclusivist program stands; first on the side of exclusivism which claims that only one religion is true, and then on the side of an indifferentism which claims that all are true, but disclaims the need for communication and consensus among them.

Indifferentism

In the face of the various religions one could take the position that all are true, but for that very reason they are completely incomparable. Furthermore, the religions do not at all *need* to be compared with one another. They are all supposed to be equally valuable and true ways of salvation. Different religions are like parallel lines, which meet only in infinity. One religion should not interfere in the internal affairs of the other. It is far more fitting for the followers of a religion to devote themselves to attaining the perfection which their religion grants them and to allow the followers of another religion to do the same. Such is the indifferentist position.

The positive side of this solution is that it staunchly avoids any sloppy syncretism and superficial eclecticism. On the other hand, the ideal of "peaceful coexistence" overlooks the realities of the undeniable historical interaction and mutual influence of religions and cultures. Furthermore, a forced condition of mutual indifference cuts off new possibilities of growth and development. One closes oneself up in a false self-sufficiency and contributes thereby to the fragmentation of humanity into many little worlds, thus hindering all convergence toward global unity.[42] Finally, it can be asked if such a position does not inevitably lead back into a *covert exclusivism*. Panikkar summarizes his objections to this program in the following reflections:

A simple peaceful coexistence . . . would at first sight seem a likely and practical solution, but it is shortsighted and superficial. Coexistence can only be lasting if there is a "coessence" to the two parties. A forced coexistence, adopted in order to avoid trouble, will dissolve the moment that one of the parties is convinced that the values they embody are of greater importance than the "trouble" in question. It will then appear worthwhile to break the "peaceful" *status quo*. True coexistence, as we have said, always implies a previous agreement on some form of coessence.[43]

Inclusivism

Between the extremes of exclusivism and indifferentism there is the middle way of inclusivism, which attempts to acknowledge the truth of other religions without placing its own truth into question. This program no longer works with static opposites, such as false/true, sin/salvation, darkness/light, but rather, it employs *dynamic* pairs, such as seed/fruit, potential/actual, preparatory stage/full realization. Despite positive acknowledgement of other religions, it is clear that all of these schemas tend to legitimate a covert exclusivism. For if one's own religion is the fruit, the fulfillment and so on, one is practically forced to see all other religions as inadequate ways to salvation, or what comes to the same, to disqualify them as ways of salvation altogether. Upon the basis of the legitimate obligation to give witness to one's own truth, one goes over to a more or less explicit rejection of the truth of other religions.

The result of this brief discussion of the three theological models of exclusivism, indifferentism and inclusivism seems to be that we are confronted with a decision, namely:

> Either [one] must condemn everything around him as error and sin, or he must throw overboard the exclusivistic and monopolistic notions he has been told embody truth — truth that must be simple and unique, revealed once and for all, that speaks through infallible organs, and so on.[44]

Here the methodological significance of the distinction between faith and belief becomes clear. For only after we have consistently carried this distinction through, not only theoretically but also existentially, will it become possible to "throw overboard" the presupposition of the monological unity, continuity and totality of truth lying at the base of all apologetics and thus overcome these three inadequate programs.

Our step-by-step reconstruction of the method for the theology of religions on the basis of Panikkar's work has so far led through the steps of a critical and faithful appropriation of one's own religion, a similar appropriation of another tradition and then directly into the problem of conversion as an unavoidable step in interreligious understanding. In order to show how such a methodological conversion may be conceived, we introduced a diatopical model of communication which allowed for the distinction between a second and third level of discourse. Second-level discourse, or what Panikkar calls diachronic hermeneutics, articulates religious understanding as an exclusive confessional conversion. Only upon the third level of discourse, which opens up a horizon of encounter wherein religions may appear as equally valid lifeworlds and enter into genuine communication with each other, does the notion of a "methodological conversion" become meaningful. To show that such a notion was also theologically acceptable, we appealed to Panikkar's fundamental distinction between faith and belief. We saw that upon the basis of this distinction to allow our beliefs to undergo transformation does not necessarily imply the loss of saving faith. Finally, we saw what consequences follow upon the failure to make this distinction, namely, the derailing of the dialogue into one or another of the inadequate programs of exclusivism, inclusivism or indifferentism. It remains now to show what that discourse is which claims to mediate radically different systems of belief while maintaining itself within a horizon of faith.

In order to answer this question we cannot avoid dealing with religious discourse, which up until now has been spoken of only in terms of faith and belief, in those terms in which it has traditionally been handled, namely, "mythos," "logos" and "symbol." A consideration of the essence and structure of the religious symbol in its relation to logical and mythological discourse will give us the opportunity to describe the third level of discourse and the form of "comparison" and understanding appropriate to it. For it is on the third level of a diatopical hermeneutics that the interreligious dialogue may actually take place.

Let us begin by returning to the remark with which we began the excursion into the various ways in which the interreligious dialogue should *not* be done, namely, the fact that although faith and belief must be distinguished, they cannot be separated; for there is no faith without belief of some sort, i.e., some expression, some *symbol*. The unique and indissoluble relationship between transcendent faith and its symbolic expression occasions, as we saw, not only the possibility of confusion between the two and consequently the distortion of the interreligious dialogue, but it also allows us to show how the three different levels of discourse which the diatopical model distinguishes can be described and related to each other.

The first two levels of discourse we have already discussed. It is upon these levels of comparison and understanding that those methods operate which Panikkar has termed morphological and diachronical hermeneutics. In terms of the religious symbol, it may be said that the first and most superficial level upon which religions may be compared is constituted by that side of the symbolic relation which appears as particular beliefs. Because religion appears as belief, it may be articulated in a "logical" discourse which speaks of religious phenomena, that is, about things religious as a certain class of entities in the world. On this level of discourse we have to do with the social-historical "clothing" which all religions wear. This is the system of practices and doctrines which are constantly changing, developing and fragmenting, but which, nevertheless, hang together to make up a cultural identity. It is on this level that historians and phenomenologists identify, describe and classify a myriad of different religious beliefs and practices. Of course, on this level of discourse we touch only the outer shell of a religion. Beyond merely talking *about* religion lies a second level of discourse which may be termed an essentially religious discourse, for it articulates the authentic *symbols* of a religion.

Symbols make up the actual center of a religion. They are the expressions of transcendent faith, without which there would be no experience of the transcendent at all. They are the *revelation* upon which a religion is based. It is from out of these symbols, these "articles of faith" that the various practices and doctrines which appear upon the first level of discourse have arisen. It is the authentic symbols which grant beliefs their unity, continuity and power to "circumscribe" or define an entire "world" of meaning and value. Revelatory symbols are much more resistant to change and external influences than their socio-historical "clothing," for they set the boundaries of the "world" within which any change may normally be perceived to occur. But when they do change, then there transpires one of those great historical earthquakes which fundamentally reshape the religious landscape of humanity. Examples of such changes on the level of basic symbols are the appearance of the ascetic "way of knowledge" of the Upanishads in relation to the old religion of sacrifice in India, or the appearance of philosophy and tragedy in ancient Greece in relation to the older religion of the cosmological myth.[45] It is because of changes on the level of revelatory symbols, which could be termed the *boundary discourse* of a religion or a culture, that a people may be said to have a religious history at all. The discourse in which this history is articulated is constituted as mythological narrative, a representation of collective identity and as a hermeneutical retrieval of founding texts and events. Consequently, this form of discourse, as we have seen, may be referred to as diachronical hermeneutics.

The symbols which make up the revelation are, however, *revelation*, and not mere mythology, only to the extent that they are "spoken" from out of a third and higher level of discourse, namely, the "transcendent divine reality,"[46] or that which Panikkar also calls the "existential truth."[47] This "reality" is that which the symbols, insofar as they are revelatory at all, actually *reveal*. Divine reality *is* only in its revelation, that is, only insofar as it is disclosed in the world. Panikkar writes:

It is not that this reality *has* many names as if there were a reality outside the name. This reality *is* many names and each name is a new aspect, a new manifestation and revelation of it. Yet each name teaches or expresses, as it were, the undivided Mystery.[48]

Consequently, we may speak of this third level of discourse as the level of *disclosure* which grants, grounds and encompasses the different boundary discourses circumscribing the systems of beliefs which found the various religious traditions.

Panikkar also speaks of the three levels of discourse in terms of "myth," "logos" and "symbol."

Myth is precisely the horizon over against which any hermeneutic is possible. Myth is that which we take for granted, that which we do not question; and it is unquestioned because, de facto, it is not seen as questionable. The myth is transparent like the light, and the mythical story — *mythologumenon* — is only the form, the garment in which the myth happens to be expressed, enwrapped, illumined.[49]

Myth *as such*, therefore, is neither objectifiable, nor questionable, for it is by definition what is taken for granted, what forms the horizon, the "space" within which questions can arise as meaningful. Consequently, if it is to be "spoken" at all, this must occur in a discourse which articulates itself not as assertions of matters of fact, but as *narrative*, as a story of founding events and also, seen from a religious point of view, as *proclamation*. As narrative and proclamation, or what Panikkar calls "mythologoumenon," myth has always already become a discourse of *closure*, for it "clothes," or "enwraps" the myth and thus sets the boundaries of a particular religious and cultural world. As we saw earlier, understanding on this level of discourse is the same as becoming convinced of the truth of what is proclaimed. Here to understand is to be converted. It is therefore not surprising that all second-level, mythological discourse articulates itself pragmatically as mission and is understood through processes of initiation, socialization and conversion.[50]

Mythological discourse, however, cannot become a question to itself. It becomes aware of itself *as such* and thus is questionable only at the moment of encounter with another mythology. At this moment, mythological discourse may become an "object" of thought and descend into the first level of discourse, the level of the *logos*. The interpretation of a myth, the moment it becomes aware of itself *as interpretation*, that is, as one possible understanding among others, as one system of beliefs among others, easily falls to the level of a "logical" discourse and is projected upon an indifferent field of givenness as a "religious phenomenon." The encounter of religions, however, opens up another possibility, namely, that our myth becomes "questionable" not with regard to its phenomenal structure, but with regard to its *disclosive universality*. The naive and exclusive *closure* of the lifeworld horizon is *dis-closed* by a discourse which recognizes *another* myth. As Panikkar puts it: "It is the other who discloses the myth I live, since for me it is invisible as myth."[51] The open space between lifeworld horizons or myths is neither the logical difference between entities, nor the mythological difference between cosmos and chaos, but what may be called the *symbolic difference* or the *discursive difference*.[52] For in it is articulated a discourse constituted by neither concept nor mythologoumenon, but by that which opens beliefs to the transcendent dimension of faith, namely, the symbol.

God, or whatever we have faith in, does not allow itself to be exhaustively expressed through mythological boundary discourse or logical argumentative discourse for which myths are at best particular systems of doctrine or theoretical bodies of knowledge. Were it not for the third level of discourse, humanity would long ago have become inescapably imprisoned in its various ideologies, and there would be no hope of freeing the mind from polemics and fanaticism. Accordingly, the "object" of diatopical hermeneutics is neither the myth, which hides behind a particular mythology and remains unquestionable, nor the logos, which does not point beyond itself toward the transcendent mystery; rather, the object of diatopical hermeneutics is the *symbol* which is articulated and expressed within a discourse of *disclosure*.

It is the singular achievement of symbolic discourse as a discourse of disclosure, as opposed to a logical discourse of phenomena or a mythological narrative of founding events, to keep belief open towards faith. Symbol is that which literally dis-closes the horizon of the transcendent, divine reality, Janus-like, as it were, with one face turned toward the absolute and the other face toward the world. Panikkar describes the peculiar nature of the symbol so:

> What expresses belief, what carries the dynamism of belief—the conscious passage from *mythos* to *logos*—is not the concept but the symbol. Symbol here does not mean an epistemic sign, but an *ontomythical* reality that *is* precisely in the symbolizing. A symbol is not a symbol of another ("thing"), but of itself, in the sense of the subjective genitive. A symbol is the symbol of that which *is* precisely (symbolized) in the symbol, and which, thus, does not exist without its symbol. A symbol *is* nothing but the symbol of that which appears in and as the symbol.[53]

The symbol, therefore, is not a *sign* for some inner-worldly thing, which we could just as well perceive without the sign or define with some other sign.[54] Symbolic, we might say, is only the *whole*. "My symbol is how I see the whole," says Panikkar, but he quickly adds that "others see it differently,"[55] which only means to say that the wholeness which symbol discloses is no indeterminate and empty abstraction. But if symbolic discourse discloses the whole, then it is also true that, despite concreteness, it cannot be a discourse of closure setting boundaries which cannot be transcended and which do not open onto a transcendent plane of being.[56]

When Panikkar speaks of the symbol as an "ontomythical" reality, he is referring to the fact that the way of being of the symbol is neither that of a thing in the world, an assertion about phenomena whose validity may be disputed; nor does symbolic discourse set the boundaries of the world by fiat, circumscribing the domain of being and non-being, meaning and meaninglessness without appeal, without opening onto a plane of transcendence beyond all closure. As becomes clear in the following citation, the symbol is a third dimension, neither merely ontic, nor ontological; neither natural, nor anthropological; but something higher than both and uniting the two:

> The symbol is neither a merely objective entity in the world (the thing "over there"), nor is it a purely subjective entity in the mind (in us "over here"). There is no symbol that is not in and for a subject, and there is equally no symbol without a specific content claiming objectivity. The symbol encompasses and constitutively links the two poles of the real: the object and the subject.[57]

In Chapter 4 we will return to this conception of symbolic discourse and show that it has its own specific pragmatics of validity which allow for a methodological conversion. We will see that symbolic discourse articulates itself by means of a pragmatics of *cosmotheandric solidarity*, that is, as a "cosmotheandric" event uniting God, humanity and nature.[58] For the moment, however, we are concerned with the fact that often the symbols of the different religions may *not* be understood and "compared" on the truly symbolic level of discourse, but either on the level of phenomena or on the level of conflicting proclamations. This, indeed, corresponds to the usual procedure of the science of religions on the one hand and the various theological approaches to interreligious dialogue on the other. Symbols are thereby either reduced to mere signs, or proclaimed mythologically, both of which strategies result in the collapse of the essential difference between faith and belief.

We have seen what this implies for the theological approach to other religions. There arises the inadequate programs of exclusivism, inclusivism and indifferentism. For the secular science of religions the consequences of the suppression of the symbolic difference are similar. Once understanding begins to operate upon the level of mere beliefs, one attempts to discover similarities and differences between various religions. Indeed, it is only upon this level that religions may be *compared* in the strict sense of the word. Above I have used the word "comparison" guardedly. Now we are in a position to see why the comparison of religions, as well as any discipline understanding itself as "comparative religions," cannot do justice to the problems of understanding encountered on the level of a real meeting of religions.[59]

The comparison of religions on the level of belief reduces symbols to mere signs. They become phenomena which can be understood either *univocally* or *equivocally*. One compares, for example, the system of Shankara with that of Thomas Aquinas by means of establishing a set of propositions of the sort "M is p," that is, "Shankara thinks/believes p," and "Thomas thinks/believes q." The term "knowledge," for example, which is important in both systems, may either be interpreted to mean the same in both systems, or it will be claimed that it has a completely different meaning, depending, of course, upon whether our methodological approach is exclusivist, inclusivist or indifferentist.

The decision for univocal meaning implies that we have not put our own concept of what knowledge is into question, but simply taken its present meaning as the only valid and acceptable one. The decision for equivocal meanings implies that we have, indeed, acknowledged another meaning and even learned something about it, but have kept our own meaning unquestioned; instead of confronting it with the other meaning, we have settled the problem by means of the indifferentist policy of peaceful coexistence. There has been neither mutual enrichment, nor further exploration of what "knowledge" might *really* mean, and therefore, no real *understanding*.

All this points to the fact that the proper approach to understanding religions cannot lie in the familiar attempt to discover similarities and differences. For even apart from the fact that religions are not mere things from which similar and dissimilar characteristics may be read off, we must ask how they could be seen to be similar or different apart from fixed criteria. And where are we to find such criteria, if we do not wish to condemn our symbols to univocity, and thus rob them of their specifically symbolic mode of being?

From the point of view of the specific mode of being of the symbol, it is only when we are prepared to let our symbols be understood *analogically* that dialogue becomes possible. Only when that which Shankara, for example, means by "knowledge" is not only objectively ascertained (the legitimate endeavor of morphological and diachronical methods), but accepted as *true for me*, without, of course, simply replacing my own traditional understanding of "knowledge" with a completely new and foreign one, do I really gain a new understanding of what "knowledge" is. My traditional understanding is enriched, deepened and purified. In fact, there is no concept or symbol which can avoid this autonomous process of *growth*, that is, if it is to remain a living symbol and not become a dead sign. Understanding which occurs upon the level of the true symbol always implies a *conversion* to a new and comprehensive horizon within which previous understanding is transformed and deepened. It is never merely a determination of similarities and differences by means of comparison.[60]

Summarizing what has been said; the task of diatopical hermeneutics is to go *through* the logos, as mere sign, *towards* the mystery *by means of* the symbol. Insofar as it goes through and beyond the self-understanding which a religion has of itself at any given time, diatopical hermeneutics comes into an area which is truly *between* the various religions and which may therefore be called a *horizon of encounter*. This area between the religions, which is the authentic place of dialogue and mutual understanding, however, can only become accessible when a new myth, or horizon, is disclosed within which the religions *can* meet each other. Diatopical hermeneutics is a movement of discourse *through* given beliefs, through the world-boundaries which systems of belief define *towards* a myth which transforms and unites them. In this context Panikkar speaks of a *dialogical dialogue*:

> The method in this third moment [i.e., diatopical hermeneutics] is a peculiar *dialogical dialogue*, the *dia-logos* piercing the *logos* in order to reach that dialogical, translogical realm of the heart (according to most traditions), allowing for the emergence of a myth in which we may commune, and which will ultimately allow under-standing (standing under the same horizon of intelligibility).[61]

We left off enumerating the steps of the method for interreligious dialogue at the difficult requirement of a "methodological conversion." We saw that understanding another culture and religion at a certain point becomes conviction and that this demands of us an authentic conversion to the truth of the other religion. This claim gave us occasion to distinguish between two kinds of conversion, confessional and methodological, for we had to face the objection that the requirement of conversion is not theologically acceptable. It would seem to demand of us a readiness to give up our own faith. We saw that the idea of a "methodological conversion," arising from a genuine communication between religions, could be grounded upon the distinction between faith and belief. We do not place our faith in question when we place our beliefs in question. Further, we saw what would happen to the interreligious dialogue — indeed, that which historically has happened to it — if this distinction is not made, namely, dialogue is deformed and channeled into the inadequate programs of exclusivism, inclusivism and indifferentism. Finally, we undertook an explication of religious discourse in terms of myth, logos and symbol in order to specify what sort of discourse diatopical hermeneutics is. Panikkar locates this discourse in the symbolic, analogical opening between mythos and logos, between faith and belief which is also the *horizon of encounter* between radically different worldviews and systems of belief.

This roundabout way was necessary to put us in the position to comprehend the fourth step in Panikkar's method. For it is not sufficient that I simply allow myself to be converted to another worldview. This is only the beginning of the real process of understanding. If the conversion experience is not to derail and become confessionally distorted into one of the above discussed inadequate responses to the encounter of cultures and religions, I must somehow bring the two convictions which I have within myself into harmony with each other. If the experience of conversion is to be sustained and I am not to break under the stress of conflicting loyalties, and the process of understanding is not to be forced back onto the second level of discourse and thus into a defensive, apologetic "jumping-back" or "jumping-over," then there must occur, as Panikkar says, a meeting of the two religions in myself:

> The meeting of two differing realities produces the shock of the encounter, but the *place* where the encounter happens is one. This one place is the heart of the person. It is within the heart that I can embrace both religions in a personal synthesis, which intellectually may be more or less perfect. And it is also within my heart that I may absorb one of the two religions into the other. In actuality religions cannot sincerely coexist or even continue as living religions if they do not "co-insist," i.e. penetrate into the heart of each other.[62]

Accordingly, the fourth step is what Panikkar calls the "intrareligious dialogue," that is, the en-counter and co-responding of two convictions in me. This is how the third level discourse of disclosure becomes concrete. Only at this stage can we begin to speak of dialogue in the full sense of the word:

The real theological task, if you will, begins when the two views meet head-on inside oneself, when dialogue prompts genuine religious pondering, and even a religious crisis, at the bottom of a Man's heart; when interpersonal dialogue turns into intrapersonal soliloquy.[63] . . . my intrareligious soliloquy will have to blend my earlier beliefs with those acquired later. . . . Here an alternative lies before me: Either I have ceased to be a Christian . . . or else I am able to establish a special kind of bond between the two that both religions, at least one of them, *can* acknowledge and accept (I do not say they already *have* accepted it).[64]

The *intra*religious dialogue is, therefore, the place where diatopical hermeneutics actually begins. For it is only when one finds oneself *between* two worlds, two *topoi,* that they become for the first time dis-closed and thus question-able. In the encounter with the other which occurs internally, as Panikkar says, within the "heart" of the person, our own myth loses its unquestioned taken-for-granted character and we become aware of its limits and thus also of its possibilities. It is through the other—and this is his or her great service to us—that we become capable of criticizing, renewing and deepening our own worldview; this is a critique which is desperately needed, if we are to realize the transcendental movement of faith. In this respect Panikkar writes:

Dialogue is, fundamentally, opening myself to another so that he might speak and reveal my myth that I cannot know by myself because it is transparent to me, self-evident. Dialogue is a way of knowing myself and of disentangling my own point of view from other viewpoints and from me, because it is grounded so deeply in my own roots as to be utterly hidden from me. It is the other who through our encounter awakens this human depth latent in me in an endeavor that surpasses both of us. In authentic dialogue this process is reciprocal. Dialogue sees the other not as an extrinsic, accidental aid, but as the indispensable, personal element in our search for truth, because I am not a self-sufficient, autonomous individual. In this sense, dialogue is a religious act par excellence because it recognizes my *religatio* to another, my individual poverty, the need to get out of myself, transcend myself, in order to save myself.[65]

It is, therefore, a presupposition of the internal intrareligious dialogue that our traditional symbols can be questioned without reducing them to mere signs and subsuming them under a non-religious, logical discourse which rejects revelation.

This does not mean, it must be emphasized, that we simply throw our tradition overboard, or that we must give up the idea of a *common language.* Were this the case all dialogue would be impossible. The very task of diatopical hermeneutics is fulfilled and the intrareligious dialogue realized only when a common language arises, wherein the two religions, which previously were perceived to exclude each other, now are seen to complement and mutually fecundate each other. Panikkar describes his program thus:

> I am attempting to speak a language that will make sense for the follower of more than one philosophical tradition — a risky task perhaps, but necessary if one is to do justice to a cross-cultural investigation.[66]

This claim immediately gives rise to serious questions: Where is such a *universal language* to be found? And if it could be found, how does it legitimate the claim it makes to speak for more than one tradition? Wherein is such a language grounded, if not in one religion/culture or another? Is a thinking not bound to any specific tradition at all possible? Would not such a "free-floating," culturally unconditioned thinking suffer from exactly the same illusion which Panikkar criticizes in the scientific ideals of objectivity and value neutrality? Do we not in the end have to decide *either* for a universalistic and thus *scientific* thinking, *or* for an inevitably exclusive religious *confession*?[67]

These are questions which we will have to face in the following chapters concerned with philosophical foundations. Here it is useful only to note once again how the two basic decisions, which Tillich placed at the beginning of the theology of religions, make all interreligious dialogue possible. For these decisions — to overcome orthodox-exclusivism as well as secular-rejectionism — force us to "jump-in-between" the religions and forbid us to "jump-back" or "jump-over" into a defensive commitment to one religion or the other. Whatever the sought-for universal language might be, it can certainly neither be the allegedly neutral language of science, nor the exclusively valid symbols of a particular confessional proclamation.

We must learn to think in and with the symbols of another tradition as with our own. Much depends upon whether we succeed in interpreting these symbols in connection with each other: first, the adequate appropriation of the conversion experience itself; secondly, understanding the other religion as well as our own (for we can, in the end, only understand our own religion *together* with the other);[68] and finally, upon the success or failure of our attempts to think the two traditions together depends our success or failure in avoiding the programs of exclusivism, inclusivism and indifferentism and thus in preserving the creative tension between faith and belief.

All this leads to the question of how different symbols can be thought together. Panikkar answers as follows:

> As an example of what is needed, we may use the notion of homology, which does not connote a mere comparison of concepts from one

tradition with those of another. I want to suggest this notion as the correlation between points of two different systems so that a point in one system corresponds to a point in the other. The method does not imply that one system is better (logically, morally or whatever) than the other, nor that the two points are interchangeable: You cannot, as it were, transplant a point from one system to the other. The method only discovers homologous correlations.[69]

An example of such an "homologous correlation," or as Panikkar also says, a "functional equivalence,"[70] may be found in *The Unknown Christ of Hinduism*.[71] In this book Panikkar attempts to bring the symbols Christ and Ishvara (the Lord) into correlation with each other through an analysis of their "functions" within their respective systems. He constructs the following analogy: *as* Christ constitutes the relation between God and the world in Christianity, *so* in Hinduism, a similar function is fulfilled by Ishvara. We cannot here examine how Panikkar substantiates this "comparison." Rather, let us note that he is uncomfortable with the term "analogy." Homology, he will say, is not identical to an analogy.[72] Nevertheless, Panikkar does not wish to dispense with the idea of analogy altogether:

Now a homology is not identical to an analogy, although they are related. Homology does not mean that two notions are analogous, i.e., partially the same and partially different, since this implies that both share in a 'tertium quid' that provides the basis for the analogy. Homology means rather that the notions play equivalent roles, that they occupy homologous places within their respective systems. Homology is perhaps a kind of existential-functional analogy.[73]

What is meant here by an "existential-functional analogy" we may perhaps discover by reflecting upon what is meant by a "system." In systems, symbols like Christ and Ishvara have a definite meaning. They function in a certain way and play a "role" which is defined in relation to all the other symbols, practices and doctrines of a religion. The question is whether a system, or a religion, is completely delimited and defined on all sides, or whether it is not rather the case that religious systems are essentially open, that symbols are never exhaustively interpreted, that their meaning is never completely defined and fixed once and for all. Can and must we not delve always further and always more deeply into the meaning of the revelation which has been granted us? Does not this growth in understanding belong necessarily to religious experience? And is the transformation of religious consciousness not much more than a mere increase of information, but rather, an existential and historical event which not only changes a man or woman, but also the "world" in which he or she lives? "At the very least," says Panikkar, "human consciousness is set in evolution"; and with it "the entire cosmos, all creation, reality."[74]

A religious system, therefore, insofar as it is part of a living religion, is not finished and closed, neither in its doctrinal *content*, nor in its conceptual *form*. For behind all formulations stands the mystery from which they spring forth. This is the goal of self-transcending faith. This is what third-level discourse of dis-closure expresses. Religions, again, are not things which can be compared in the same way that two chairs, for example, can be compared to see in what respects they are alike or different. Comparison and abstraction to the next higher generic concept is not a reliable method when it comes to religions, cultures and worldviews. Neither can we attempt to avoid the problem by apologetically projecting the closure of our own mythological discourse upon all other myths. The discovery of functional similarities, therefore, is neither an objective knowledge about something, nor an apologetic proclamation, but an existential event, a spiritual praxis and an authentic religious experience through which religious consciousness responds ever more deeply to the mystery of revelation. "Dialogue," Panikkar reminds us, "is not a bare methodology but an essential part of the religious act par excellence."[75]

What makes the discovery of functional similarities possible can be nothing other than the horizon of encounter opened up by the discourse of disclosure, or in other words, the ground of faith. For if it were not possible to discover such correspondences, the human spirit would either suffocate in an exclusivistic ideology, or it would disintegrate into a myriad of little "worlds," none of which would be capable of communicating with the others. But faith, as we saw, is precisely that which keeps human beings open to transcendence and thus guarantees spiritual unity. From the point of view of the discourse of dis-closure, that which is revealed in one religion cannot exclude what is revealed in another. From a Western-Christian standpoint, the ground of faith is the one "God" who is present in all religions. In this sense, Panikkar speaks of a "previous homogeneity" or a "certain presence" of one religion within the other:

> If the use of a concept foreign to a given cultural setup is to be made viable, if it is to be successfully grafted onto another system of thought (the Christian for example), it will succeed because it has somehow attained a certain homogeneity with the host cultural and religious world so that it may live there. If this is the case, it amounts to recognizing that its possible use depends on a certain previous homogeneity, on a certain presence of the one meaning within the other framework; otherwise it would be completely impossible to utilize the concept in question. In spite of the heterogeneity between the Greek and Christian conception of the *logos*, for instance, the former had to offer a certain affinity with the new meaning that would be enhanced once it was assumed.[76]

The full realization of such a functional similarity between the central symbols of two religions — in the cognitive as well as existential dimension —

implies a considerable rethinking of traditional Christian (and Hindu!) self-understanding. But it is precisely this "mutual fecundation"[77] which is "one of the primary tasks facing theology."[78]

Naturally, the intra-religious dialogue stands or falls with the discovery of those symbols which really are rooted in the transcendent ground of all religions and thus really do co-respond with each other over and beyond the socio-historical trappings in which they are clothed. Panikkar does not underestimate the difficulty here, and he is well aware that such symbols can neither be found lying about, nor simply invented, but must be *revealed*. This sets a clear limit to all methodology in the sense of prescribed rules of inquiry which guarantee objective knowledge. At this point in the encounter of religions and cultures there are no "controls," and we must admit that understanding is never continuous and progressive, but always discontinuous and surprisingly different from whatever we may have expected. As Panikkar puts it, "the continuation of the dialogue has to produce its own rules and categories."[79]

Supposing now that the sought-for categories and symbols have been found, namely, that the intra-religious dialogue has come to a preliminary conclusion, then the next step is to present this new understanding to a representative of the other religion.[80] At this point the intra-religious dialogue becomes a truly *inter*-religious dialogue:

> My partner in dialogue will then judge whether what I have learned ... is sound or not. I will have to give him an account of my belief and he will tell me whether what I say ... represents fundamental belief ... or not.[81]

The criterion of the correctness of my interpretation is the well-known hermeneutical rule that "the interpreted thing can recognize itself in the interpretation."[82] Panikkar writes:

> In other words, any interpretation from outside a tradition has to coincide, at least phenomenologically, with an interpretation from within, i.e., with the believer's viewpoint. To label a *murtipujaka* an idol-worshiper, for instance, using idol as it is commonly understood in the Judeo-Christian-Muslim context rather than beginning with what the worshiper affirms of himself, is to transgress this rule.[83]

And in another place he says that

> any genuine 'Christian' interpretation must be valid and true, and for this very reason it must also be acceptable to those who are being interpreted; a basic methodological rule for any interpretation. This means that no interpretation of any religion is valid if the followers of that religion do not recognize it as such.[84]

This rule not only firmly excludes reductionistic explanations of religion on the part of psychology and sociology, for example, but it also implies that both partners in dialogue must have gone through the same process up to this point. All the steps of the method which have been described up till now must be presupposed for both partners. This is itself an important methodological step. For "there must be *equal preparation* for the encounter on both sides, and this means cultural as well as theological preparations."[85] An exclusivist apologetic approach on either side would, of course, make all dialogue impossible.

Supposing, however, that both partners have gone through the intra-religious dialogue and have entered the inter-religious dialogue with "a set of propositions that may answer the requirements of orthodoxy on both sides,"[86] then they must be prepared to accept the judgment of the other whether their new interpretations are *orthodox* or not. This claim to ortho-doxy — not to be confused with the distorted "orthodoxy" of exclusivism! — constitutes the last step in the method of the interreligious dialogue. If I do not succeed, that is, if my new interpretation is not accepted by the representative of the other religion, then I am automatically sent back into the intra-religious dialogue, where I search for another, more adequate understanding.

Here it becomes clear that the method is circular, that the last step leads us back to the first. For in the methodological insistence upon orthodoxy exactly that is realized which was required by the first two steps of the method; namely, the appropriation of a faithful and critical understanding of one's own and of another tradition. "Faithfulness" to one's own and to another tradition is only to be secured by means of the principle of ortho-doxy, whereby "critique" of one's own and of another tradition can only be consequently carried through when understanding is no longer a one-sided apologetic for one particular tradition, but adequate to *both*. Therefore, it is only *through* the interreligious dialogue, and as it were, at its end, that we come back to a faithful and critical understanding of our own religion. Orthodoxy and critique do not exclude each other; rather, they complement each other, but only from the point of view of a truly *global* theology.

The method of the interreligious dialogue, and therefore also of the theology of religions, turns out to be a circular movement. The end leads back to the beginning. This circular structure of thought is typical of all genuinely *hermeneutical* methods.[87] It is hermeneutical in that it begins from an implicit fore-conception, or anticipation of meaning, not in order to go forward to new and unheard of results, but in order to come back to itself through the explication of what was already there. Methodical inquiry here, however, is not fundamentally limited in scope, as it is in the empirical, phenomenological and dialectical methods which Panikkar terms "morpho-logical" and "diachronical." Since it is only in the encounter with other forms of thought that our own becomes at all questionable to us, no her-meneutics which remains within one tradition can claim critical competence for itself without reservations.[88] Only diatopical hermeneutics (which operates in the realm *between* religions and cultures and aims at a universal horizon of encounter, or as Tillich would say, a universal "truth") fulfills the requirement of radical critique demanded of all thinking today, while at the same time remaining faithful (i.e., bound-back, *re-ligare*) to revelation and thus not giving up the claim to orthodoxy.

At this point we may note how Panikkar's method fulfills the demands of Tillich's five presuppositions for any theology of religions. First, it is clear that when, as Tillich proposes, revelatory experiences are universally human and present in all religions, then no method of understanding religion which is not itself essentially "religious" in the way diatopical hermeneutics is can be adequate to that which is being investigated. Further, it is only a method such as diatopical hermeneutics which takes full cognizance of the fact that the "object" it is dealing with has the mode of being of authentic symbols, which, as Tillich pointed out, all revelations are. Third, according to Tillich, symbols must be protected against being closed off in one-sided, ideological interpretations, a demand, which again, diatopical hermeneutics, as a discourse of dis-closure which goes beyond the boundary discourse of closure, fulfills.

Tillich's fourth stipulation was that understanding must be directed toward a transcendent, unconditioned or absolute truth in which all religions can find themselves. As we saw above, this is precisely the goal of diatopical hermeneutics. And finally, Tillich's fifth presupposition requires that the different traditions mutually correct and criticize each other — Panikkar would speak of "mutual fecundation." Diatopical hermeneutics satisfies this demand by consciously appropriating and explicitly contributing to what the historical process would otherwise blindly effect, namely, stripping the socio-historical peculiarities of a tradition from the real symbols and leaving them aside in an interpretation which unites religions.

In conclusion we should note that Panikkar always emphasizes that it is not the goal of the interreligious dialogue "to obtain agreement at the cost of fundamental . . . principles."[89] By means of an incessant mutual criticism and correction, the dialogue brings about an ever deeper understanding of what is revealed in the various religions. Panikkar closes his defense for a non-exclusive religiosity with this remark:

> I can only be free from a certain type of Christianity or Hinduism (and for that matter from a certain type of Buddhism and Secularism) if I become a better Christian and a better Hindu.[90]

In summary: On the basis of Panikkar's many important theoretical contributions to interreligious understanding we have reconstructed the following steps of a *method* for the theology of religions:

1. One begins with a faithful and critical understanding of one's own tradition — an understanding won with all reliable methods which we

have at our disposal: empirical, historical-critical, philological, phenomenological, etc.

2. In the same way, an understanding of another tradition is acquired.

3. This understanding becomes conviction. One experiences a genuine *conversion*.

4. An internal *intra*-religious dialogue begins between the two convictions. One searches for a *common language* which is capable of expressing the truth of both religions.

5. The internal intra-religious dialogue becomes an external *inter*-religious dialogue when one lays one's new interpretation before representatives of the other tradition.

6. Steps 1 through 5 are presupposed for all partners in dialogue.

7. New interpretations are tested for their "orthodoxy" in both traditions. If they are found inadequate, one returns to the level of the intra-religious dialogue and begins again.

3

Foundations

In Chapter 1 we argued that the present situation of radical pluralism was primarily a result of two factors. First, the rise and fall of colonialism opened up a global horizon in which no nation or culture could claim supremacy. International political and economic dependencies have become such that almost every major problem confronting contemporary humanity is a global problem which can only be solved by means of coordinated action based upon communication and mutual understanding. This global situation determines not merely international policy, but directly affects the personal lives of men and women everywhere who are existentially confronted with the encounter of cultures and find themselves forced in a variety of ways to make a decision either for or against dialogue.

At the same time, we saw that the two great traditions which Western culture has created, Christianity and Secular Humanism, are caught up in a polemical and apologetic struggle which makes communication and understanding impossible not only between each other, but also between Western and non-Western cultures. It was shown that Christian theology, on the basis of its historical development, could be understood as an *apologetic universalism*. Further, it was shown how modern Secularism, in its attempt to establish itself independently in opposition to Christianity, became an apologetic universalism of the same sort as Christian theology. Secular thinkers adopted the same apologetic method which Christian theologians had used against pagans and Jews a millennium earlier — a method which projects its own criteria of meaning, truth and reality as a horizon of unity, totality and continuity within which the *other* is neutralized, expropriated and incorporated. Furthermore, insofar as both Christianity and Secularism make similar universalistic claims, both could be called "religions." For centuries these two "religions" have contended with each other for exclusive possession of men and women's loyalty. Each proclaimed the other false. Each tried again and again to demonstrate how the other fits into its own system, while at the same time struggling to account for all reality within the limits set by its own premises.

As a consequence, Western humanity became "schizophrenic." Consciousness became divided into an enlightened, autonomous, rational intellect committed to the ideals of objective, value-free science and certain of its power and duty to create its own destiny, while another, private and subjective part of the Western mind clung to an "irrational" faith in a saving God. Religion became separated from science, church from state and the conflict between these two radically different claims to reality and truth settled into a troubled latency under the mantle of "tolerance." But the futility of polemics and the dangers of a schizophrenic division of the mind created by this conflict of irreconcilable universal claims could not remain repressed. In the first decades of our century, individual thinkers became aware that they were facing an unprecedented situation in which a plurality of absolute truth claims somehow had to be acknowledged.

In his early work on the philosophy of religion, Paul Tillich set out from the insight that *neither* traditional orthodoxy, *nor* Secular Humanism could maintain their claims to universality, for the apologetic projection of a horizon of unity constitutive for both prevents them from truly encountering each other. At first, Tillich sought a solution to this problem in a theological *synthesis* between the claims of revelation on the one hand, and reason on the other. This approach, which was essentially no different from traditional apologetics, remained decisive for Tillich's theology until shortly before his death, when the encounter with a foreign culture and religion revealed to him the full implications of his original question. It became clear to Tillich that the task of theology cannot lie in constructing a convincing *correlation* between biblical revelation and the "world," an approach which always carries with it the more or less explicit denial of the independent truth of the "world," but rather, on the basis of an open acknowledgement of a radically pluralistic situation, in the encounter of *all* religions and ideologies *on the same level.*

In order to carry out this task explicitly and open up a horizon of encounter which does not blind out and "repress" the *other* from the outset, Tillich posited two fundamental decisions as necessary presuppositions: first, the theologian must decide to overcome an orthodox-exclusivism, which denies all truth claims other than its own; and secondly, he or she must overcome the opposite alternative of a secular denial of all religious truth claims whatsoever. These two decisions carry with them five theses, which constitute the methodological presuppositions of a *theology of religions*:

1. That revelatory experiences are present in all *religions*;
2. that none of these revelations are fully comprehensible, that is, they are *symbolic*;
3. that symbols are in *need of critique* in order to protect them from "closed" interpretations;
4. that critique is constructively directed toward the *unity of all traditions*; and

5. that Secular Humanism is also a religion and that the critique of
religion is only possible as *religious critique*.

How these five theses are implied in the two basic decisions to overcome
orthodox-exclusivism and secular-rejectionism was discussed in Chapter 1.
But no attempt was made there to demonstrate that these basic decisions
were themselves necessary or even possible. As much as our present historical situation would seem to call for intercultural dialogue, it could be
that the exclusivist claims of orthodoxy and humanism alike, indeed of any
worldview, cannot be overcome and that on the level of worldviews there
is no alternative but decision and commitment. This would imply that a
global culture cannot emerge except by processes of domination and expro-
priation and that the history of humanity cannot be other than a history of
conquest.

Already in Chapter 1, it became clear that the problems of fundamental
theology in a pluralistic situation point toward a theology of religions. In
Chapter 2 we saw that an adequate method for intercultural and interreligious understanding calls for a *diatopical hermeneutics* which articulates
itself upon a level of discourse capable of expressing the truth of radically
different traditions and worldviews. It was shown 1) that diatopical hermeneutics derived directly from Tillich's presuppositions, 2) that such a
third-level discourse was a condition of the possibility of conceiving of a
methodological conversion, 3) that the idea of a methodological conversion
was theologically acceptable upon the basis of the distinction between faith
and belief, and 4) that a diatopical hermeneutics is neither mythical nor
logical but a symbolic discourse of disclosure. The question remains, however, wherein such a "universal language" is to be grounded. We will be
able to break out of the apologetic pragmatics which have heretofore structured Western thought in exclusivist/inclusivist models only when such a
universal discourse, or *discourse of disclosure* is shown not only to be needed
in a historical and existential sense, but also both *necessary* and *possible* in
the sense of philosophical foundations.

It falls to the lot of a philosophical and epistemological analytic, therefore, to show that a diatopical hermeneutics *can* — indeed, *must* — be
acknowledged. This raises the question which any attempt at philosophical
foundations in a radically pluralistic situation must face, namely, the suspicion of *ideology*. For universalist claims have become suspect of blinding
out or attempting to hide other aspects of truth. In order to show that a
universal "rationality" is possible, we will be forced to steer a course
between the Scylla of "objectivism" on the one side and the Charybdis of
"relativism" on the other. Our journey will take us through the various
domains in which the problem of the universality and relativity of thought
has been thematized, namely, the discussion surrounding ideology and a
possible critique thereof and the problem of understanding foreign cultures
in the methodology of the social sciences, especially ethnology and anthro-

pology. This will bring us to a position from which a philosophical foundation of diatopical hermeneutics as a *discourse of disclosure* will be possible.

THE PROBLEM OF IDEOLOGY

Thinking, so long as it is bound to a particular standpoint or tradition, while at the same time claiming universality, is necessarily *ideological* thinking, for it blinds out its own relativity. It does this by projecting its own criteria of meaning, truth and value as the common ground upon which the *other* is allowed to meet it. It commits itself thereby to an apologetic pragmatics which seeks to neutralize, expropriate and incorporate the *other* into its own frame. To speak of apologetic universalism as "ideology" is to assert at once that apologetic universalism is "untrue" *and* that ideology is more than merely "false consciousness," as it has often been understood to be. "Ideology" refers to a thinking which can only articulate its claim to universality in an apologetic way. Insofar as Western thought, both theological and secular, may be described as apologetic universalism, we are inevitably confronted with the problem of ideology.

If we have understood our inquiry up to this point as a methodology for a specific discipline called "theology of religions," then we now find ourselves forced to expand the scope of our investigation to include the question of whether truth is at all possible; that is, we are investigating the question of *knowledge as such*. The challenge of ideology forces the methodological foundations of the theology of religions beyond the borders of the discipline of theology into the properly philosophical domain of the theory of knowledge. But the reverse is also true; the task of epistemology to determine the nature, origin and limits of knowledge as such, once it has become clear that knowledge is historically, socially and culturally determined and that there is no neutral standpoint, can no longer be carried out apart from raising the question of the possibility of intercultural and interreligious understanding.

Following Richard J. Bernstein, we can say that we are faced with the problem of overcoming both "objectivism" and "relativism."[1] According to Bernstein, contemporary philosophy finds itself torn between two equally unacceptable alternatives. There is the view which goes back at least to Plato and which contends that it is the proper task of philosophy to ground truth and goodness in universal and therefore ahistorical certitudes. This tradition Bernstein calls objectivism:

> By "objectivism," I mean the basic conviction that there is or must be some permanent, ahistorical matrix or framework to which we can ultimately appeal in determining the nature of rationality, knowledge, truth, reality, goodness, or rightness.[2]

This school of thought claims that if a transcendent foundation of knowledge cannot be found, then there can be no truth at all, for all knowledge would be mere opinion, relative to person, place and time. Skepticism would be the result. This is precisely what the other tradition, known as relativism, proposes:

> In its strongest form, relativism is the basic conviction that when we turn to the examination of those concepts that philosophers have taken to be the most fundamental—whether it is the concept of rationality, truth, reality, right, the good, or norms—we are forced to recognize that in the final analysis all such concepts must be understood as relative to a specific conceptual scheme, theoretical framework, paradigm, form of life, society, or culture. . . . For the relativist, there is no substantive over-arching framework or single metalanguage by which we can rationally adjudicate or univocally evaluate competing claims of alternative paradigms.[3]

If we are not to fall into skeptical relativism on the one hand, or into an imperialistic objectivism on the other hand, we must face the problem of ideology squarely and ask whether and how a *new universalism* which is not apologetical is possible. This means that we must search for an answer to the following questions:

1) If there is no thinking free of ideological distortions, how can ideology be criticized? From which perspective, or standpoint, can one question the perspectivity of all thinking? How can falsity, illusion, and meaninglessness be discovered and exposed, if such concepts have a clear and binding meaning only within a specific framework, paradigm, religion, or culture?

2) What counts as an argument, as rational discourse, if the criteria of meaning, truth, and reality are different in different traditions and cultures? What is thinking, if there can be a radically different kind of thinking? Does thought have a unity at all? And if not, how are we to think its disunity?

3) How is communication and mutual understanding in a global situation at all possible?

In the light of these questions which, as we shall see, are at once questions of epistemology *and* of intercultural hermeneutics, it becomes clear why the crisis of apologetic universalism must be recognized as the *crisis of reason itself*. For once the implications of our pluralistic situation have been grasped, it becomes doubtful whether *any* language or *any* form of thought is capable of mediating universal meaning and truth. What is at stake in the methodological foundations of a theology of religions is therefore nothing less than a fundamental reordering of the structure of the Western "episteme."[4]

The concepts "ideology" and "critique of ideology" are today used in so many senses that a preliminary clarification of the sense in which these terms are here being used is unavoidable. This will also serve as an introduction to the problems with which the following sections will be concerned.[5]

In everyday usage, "ideology" has the connotation of being a *lie* which serves the *purposes* of a particular group or class within society.[6] This definition implies, first, that there is a *true* description of reality which one can discover above or behind ideology and which one can then use to *criticize* ideological thinking and expose it for what it is. Further, it implies that not all men and women are liars, but only particular individuals or groups, who think ideologically because this serves their interests—that is, because they *want* to. In short, it is presupposed that critical knowledge is possible and that certain individuals or groups are capable not only of *theoretically* knowing the truth, but also of *practically* carrying out the critique.

In the definition given above there is further implied the possibility of distinguishing between a "partial", psychological form of ideology and a "total," sociological form. Accordingly, ideological thinking can be either *conscious* and *intentional*, as was religion in the opinion of the Enlightenment thinkers who saw it as an instrument of oppression in the hands of wicked priests and kings; or, it can be *unconscious*, as in Marx's theory that the bourgeoisie *and* the proletariat both believed in the fiction of a "free" market because the forces of production and the structure of society erected upon them (base-superstructure) determined them to think in this way.[7] In the view of the Enlightenment, the "purposes" which the ideological "lie" serves are the particular, subjective and conscious interests of evil individuals. In the Marxist view, they are objectively given in the structure of society. Marx says:

> In the social production of their life, men enter into definite relations that are indispensable and independent of their will, relations of production which correspond to a definite stage of development of their material productive forces. The sum total of these relations of production constitutes the economic structure of society, the real foundation, on which rises a legal and political superstructure and to which correspond definite forms of social consciousness. The mode of production of material life conditions the social, political and intellectual life process in general. It is not the consciousness of men that determines their being, but, on the contrary, their social being that determines their consciousness.[8]

It was on the basis of Marx's insight into the social conditionedness of thought, that the *sociology of knowledge* at the beginning of the 20th century postulated the *necessary* nature of ideology as a condition of all thinking. With this development we are approaching the concept of ideology which is relevant for the problem of intercultural understanding. Karl Mannheim writes:

Only in a quite limited sense does the single individual create out of himself the mode of speech and of thought we attribute to him. He speaks the language of his group; he thinks in the manner in which his group thinks. He finds at his disposal only certain words and their meanings. These not only determine to a large extent the avenues of approach to the surrounding world, but they also show at the same time from which angle and in which context of activity objects have hitherto been perceptible and accessible to the group or the individual.[9]

Although Mannheim situated knowledge within the tension between a conservative clinging to the past and a progressive and visionary project for the future and thus opposed "ideology" to "utopia," the concept of ideology gains with the sociology of knowledge a certain *positive* connotation. For humans cannot live without some view of reality as a whole which allows them to orient themselves in an otherwise chaotic environment. Thinking is unavoidably, though for the most part implicitly, universalistic. A *worldview* is always bound to a particular historical and social situation and, therefore, never really capable of claiming universal validity, nonetheless it *must* do so as a necessary condition of its existence.

This insight has important consequences for how the problem of ideology is to be understood. Once it becomes clear that there is a plurality of different views of reality, the fundamental question for philosophy and theory of knowledge becomes *how* these various claims can be adjudicated and *how* the unity of thought and consciousness can still exist:

It is with this clashing of modes of thought, each of which has the same claims to representational validity, that for the first time there is rendered possible the emergence of the question which is so fateful, but also so fundamental in the history of thought, namely, how it is possible that identical human thought-processes concerned with the same world produce divergent conceptions of that world. And from this point it is only a step further to ask: Is it not possible that the thought-processes which are involved here are not at all identical? May it not be found, when one has examined all the possibilities of human thought, that there are numerous alternative paths which can be followed?[10]

This point of view leads directly to two further problems which are decisive for all following attempts to criticize ideology. First, the *suspicion* that thinking may be ideological is necessarily *reciprocal*. I cannot suspect another of ideological thinking without at the same time formally acknowledging his or her right to suspect the same of me. And secondly, since *all* thinking is in some respect ideologically distorted, there can be no absolute truth. The last words science speaks are *skepticism and relativism*. Mannheim writes:

> Today . . . we have reached a stage in which this weapon of the reciprocal unmasking and laying bare of the unconscious sources of intellectual existence has become the property not of one group among many but of all of them. But in the measure that the various groups sought to destroy their adversaries' confidence in their thinking by this most modern intellectual weapon of radical unmasking, they also destroyed, as all positions gradually came to be subjected to analysis, man's confidence in human thought in general. The process of exposing the problematic elements in thought which had been latent since the collapse of the Middle Ages culminated at last in the collapse of confidence in thought in general. There is nothing accidental but rather more of the inevitable in the fact that more and more people took flight into skepticism or irrationalism.[11]

Ideology now becomes a problem on the level of *meaning*. The question is no longer a question of true versus false consciousness, which is a question that can be answered only *within* a given horizon of meaning, or what is called a "lifeworld," where there are commonly accepted criteria of what counts as real and true. Instead, the issue is now *meaning versus meaninglessness*. In the face of the threat that our very criteria of meaning and truth are corrupted by the contradiction of claiming universality while in fact being a mere projection of totality invented by the collective mind, there arises a *crisis of meaning*. But it is precisely upon this level that the sociology of knowledge did not meet the challenge. This would only have been possible by abandoning the level *of discourse* and concerns of an inner-worldly search for truth and raising the discussion to the level of a general theory of meaning.

Despite its insight into the "situational determination" (*Seinsgebundenheit*) of *all* thinking, the sociology of knowledge nonetheless excepted itself and set about the task of achieving objective universal knowledge by means of scientific methods. Truth was to be attained by discovering and describing the social and historical conditions determining *every* worldview. This task was to fall to the lot of a specific class of men and women, a "free-floating intelligentsia" (*freischwebende Intelligenz*), who had taken a purely scientific attitude, and had thus become detached from their social conditionedness. These scientists were supposed to be able to view the whole of human history and society impartially and to judge whether or not a certain worldview corresponds to reality better than another. Obviously the entire problem of worldviews is here located within a discourse which the diatopical model would call a first-level discourse of phenomena, that is, talk about matters of fact. This level of discourse presupposes a horizon of factuality, an "indifferent" field of givenness wherein worldviews appear and become accessible to a discourse of argumentation and verification. It cannot, therefore, convincingly show that it itself is not an ideological projection of criteria and that a truly "value-free" position is at all attainable. The outcome was that the sociology of knowledge could not make good its claim to universal validity and objectivity and ended in *relativism*.

The recognition of the perspectival nature and relativity of thought, coupled with the inability to reestablish a convincing universalism on the plane of theory, led Lenin to consider ideology inevitable, but nonetheless useful, for the problem of *unity* could be settled by means of revolutionary *praxis*. Inherent in Marx's conception of ideas as a reflection of the economic basis was the further assumption that ideas can change reality through revolutionary praxis. Once it was understood that "theory" also was an ideology, the way was open for Lenin to make ideology into an instrument for educating and forming the consciousness of the masses. In advanced capitalistic societies, wherein the economic conditions alone do not intensify the conflict between the classes to the point where the proletariat may develop a revolutionary consciousness by itself, it becomes necessary that an elite of professional revolutionaries form a party which takes over the leadership of the masses. It is the task of this avant garde to educate the proletariat to revolutionary consciousness.

Ideology, in the sense of false consciousness, applies only to the ideology of the political opponent. Ideology, in the sense of "scientific socialism," however, is true knowledge of society. And insofar as it is also a means of forming the consciousness of the masses, it becomes a weapon in political conflicts. Thinking becomes here a tool of totalitarianism, for Lenin claims, as did Marx before him, that the interests of the proletariat are identical with the interests of all humanity, but he adds that it is the function of the party to make men and women aware of this.

In view of the totalitarian misappropriation of science and philosophy, for which Stalinist Russia and Nazi Germany were examples, thinkers returned to the tradition of the Enlightenment (Critical Rationalism) and to the early Marx (Critical Theory) in order to develop a *critique of ideology* which would be able to avoid both the praxis-crippling relativism of the sociology of knowledge on the one hand, and the dangers of a totalitarian subjection of truth to "revolutionary" praxis as Lenin had proposed on the other. For the positivistic-oriented Critical Rationalism (Popper, Topitsch, Albert),[12] "ideology" is understood as the attempt to present statements of value in the form of statements of fact. Consequently, all ideas which are not subject to empirical falsification are suspect of being ideological. For what other way is there of distinguishing between products of subjective evaluation and true knowledge than the test of experience? Men and women must orient themselves on what is *given* (positivism); and the given is not a product of imagination, but that to which empirical science alone has access (empiricism).

For the critical sociology of the Frankfurt School (Adorno, Horkheimer,

Habermas),[13] it is precisely the claim of the "positivists" to possess objective, value-free knowledge of society that is suspect of being an ideological legitimation of a society dominated by instrumental and technological rationality.

It was the valuable insight of the Frankfurt School, following Max Weber, that science and technology—that is, the very forces which hitherto had been thought to free humanity from domination and insure progress toward freedom and happiness—actually function in modern industrial societies as means of oppression. Domination of nature implies domination of human beings, once instrumental rationality begins to govern not only the relation of humanity to nature, but also those relations constitutive of human community. According to this school of thought, methods of empirical falsification cannot expose and criticize ideology, for knowledge gained by the objectivizing empirical sciences can only be knowledge enabling technical control over its object. It is precisely this sort of knowledge which, because it blinds out the intersubjective dimension of ethics and politics, has enslaved men and women in modern "rationalized" society and turned them into manipulable objects of a "social technology" which sets system-immanent goals of functionality above critical reflection on whether or not such goals are legitimate. Only by means of "reflection" upon the whole of society, including the ideological function of sub-systems of instrumental and systemic rationality, can humanity gain a view of those factors which condition it and thus potentially free itself for practical action. From the point of view of Critical Rationalism, however, this claim to total knowledge amounts to a reversion to metaphysical thinking and totalitarian assertions of absolute truth.

Both views have one thing in common, namely, the conviction typical of the early stages of the discussion of ideology that a non-ideological thinking is possible and, of course, that they themselves are the ones who possess it and are, therefore, able to put it into politically effective practice. All in all this amounts to a regression to a conception of the problem of ideology which was already in principle overcome by the sociology of knowledge. Once the insight into the situational character of *all* thinking has been gained, it is no longer acceptable to claim that one's own thinking is not ideological, even if this may appear to solve the problem of the crippling separation between theory and practice which the sociology of knowledge had left unanswered.

The lack of self-critical awareness endemical to these theories is a legacy of the sociology of knowledge itself insofar as it failed to carry discussion onto a higher level of discourse where the question of *meaning* could be placed, and insofar as it continued to strive for an objective, value-free, indeed, "scientific" truth. The model which all these conceptions share is that of meaning constituted by the referential relation of words and statements to entities and of truth as correspondence to external, objective reality, *adequatio intellectus et rei*. Ideology, whether understood as "false consciousness" or as inevitable perspectivalism is still considered to be a thinking which does not *adequately correspond to reality*. Whether "objective reality" be conceived as *physical* (Critical Rationalism) or *social-economical* (Critical Theory), thinking is true (non-ideological) or false (ideological) to the extent that it more or less adequately reflects a pre-given reality. It is for this reason that none of the approaches so far discussed allow themselves to be affected by the general and total suspicion of ideology which was the major discovery of the sociology of knowledge. They remain bound to the program of "objectivism," that is, the supposition of a permanent, solid foundation for all knowledge.

Once science itself, however, in its very claim to objectivity and value-neutrality, has been exposed as ideological, then critique can no longer consist in an allegedly value-free discovery of the "true nature" of, say, the forces of production in a given society, and then in the *comparison* of this reality with false views which disguise structures of domination. The question can no longer be, Which view of reality is true? for they are all "true."

This is an insight common to many contemporary thinkers who have proclaimed the "end" of modern Western philosophy and thus have come to be called *postmodern*.[14] For these thinkers, relativism is as far as we can go. Richard Rorty, for example, proclaims the demise of objectivism and sees "the Platonic tradition as having outlived its usefulness."[15] But he does not go on to offer an alternative to relativism. Instead, he proposes what he calls a "post-Philosophical culture,"[16] in which we would give up "the impossible attempt to step outside our skins — the traditions, linguistic and other, within which we do our thinking and self-criticism — and compare ourselves with something absolute."[17] According to Rorty, it is misguided to think that

> the intuitions built into the vocabularies of Homeric warriors, Buddhist sages, Enlightenment scientists, and contemporary French literary critics are not really as different as they seem — that there are common elements in each which Philosophy can isolate and use to formulate theses that it would be rational for all these people to accept, and problems which they all face.[18]

Instead, Rorty offers us an interpretation of pragmatism appropriate for a post-Philosophical culture which openly admits that "knowledge is power, a tool for coping with reality."[19] Rorty writes:

> In such a culture criteria would be seen as the pragmatist sees them — as temporary resting places constructed for specific utilitarian ends. On the pragmatist account, a criterion (what follows from the axioms, what the needle points to, what the statute says) *is* a criterion because some particular social practice needs to block the road of

inquiry, halt the regress of interpretations, in order to get something done.[20]

And he concludes:

> The question of what propositions to assert, which pictures to look at, what narratives to listen to and comment on and retell, are all questions about what will help us get what we want (or about what we *should* want).[21]

But of course there is no guarantee that "what we want" is indeed "what we *should* want." For in Rorty's view there can be no criteria of truth and rationality other than those which we establish for our own purposes. Despite Rorty's liberal disclaimers, one cannot escape the feeling that "what we should want" boils down to whatever serves "our" (that is, whichever group, party, nation or culture we happen to belong to) will to power.[22]

Here is the point at which we may note how indebted postmodern thought is to Nietzsche. For it was Nietzsche who most radically and consistently accepted the consequences of the relativistic insight that all thinking is ideological. If, in fact, there is no objective reality against which we can measure our opinions, then we must face the fact that our views of reality are products of our own *will*.[23]

For Nietzsche, and the postmodern thinkers who follow him, ideas are not derived from and tested against our experience of reality; rather, we create them and impose them upon the world, others and ourselves. From the point of view of the adequation theory, this can only mean that truth, as Nietzsche says, is a lie:

> Truth is the kind of error without which a certain species of life could not live.
>
> That the value of the world lies in our interpretation (—that other interpretations than merely human ones are perhaps somewhere possible—); that previous interpretations have been perspective valuations by virtue of which we can survive in life, i.e., in the will to power, for the growth of power; that every elevation of man brings with it the overcoming of narrower interpretations; that every strengthening and increase of power opens up new perspectives and means believing in new horizons—this idea permeates my writings. The world with which we are concerned is false, i.e., is not a fact but a fable and approximation on the basis of a meager sum of observations; it is "in flux," as something in a state of becoming, as a falsehood always changing but never getting near the truth: for—there is no "truth."[24]

This does not imply that our views of reality are merely arbitrary, since our very existence depends upon them. We see the world in the way we want because *what* we want is to affirm our own being. Thinking is an expression not merely of will, but of *will to power*. The problem of a *plurality* of such views in conflict with each other is, therefore, a problem which cannot be solved by a synthesis based upon some neutral and common standard, but only by the external imposition of unity through power. In the realm of ideas, as in nature, it is a question of survival of the "fittest." Overcoming fragmentation and achieving unity is only possible when one worldview dominates over the others. Meaning is thus reduced to a function of power.[25]

Postmodern, relativist theories propose, in effect, to solve the problem of ideology by declaring that there is no problem. If everything is ideology, nothing is ideology. Critics have been quick to point out that this solution carries with it the danger of imperialism and nihilism because it is a "relativism" which in fact denies any real "relation" to and acknowledgment of the *other*. We have no choice but to conquer or be conquered. If we do not stop at postmodern relativism, however, the question becomes to what extent different views of reality, indeed different "realities," are capable of *communicating* with each other and being *integrated*.

Granted that the criterion of "truth" can no longer be an objective reality with which worldviews can be *compared*, if there is to be universal truth at all, then it must lie in the extent to which different and apparently conflicting realities can be brought into harmony with each other. This means that the task of critical thinking must shift at this point from *comparing* to *integrating*, and the level of the discussion concerning ideology must change from either a first-level discourse which searches for the truth argumentatively, or a second-level discourse which posits *the* truth imperialistically to a third level of discourse which fully acknowledges the *otherness of the other* and searches for a form of meaning and rationality in which radically different articulations of "reason" and "knowledge" can encounter each other and enter into dialogue. This corresponds to the requirements of the *diatopical model* of human communication discussed in Chapter 2, which postulates a third level of discourse, a *discourse of disclosure* beyond the first two levels which either presuppose shared criteria of meaning or proclaim such criteria absolutely. If the critique of ideology and a universal language which does not suppress otherness is to be possible, then what is required is a theory of meaning which sets itself the task of discovering the *conditions for coherence and consensus beyond shared lifeworld horizons*. This is the way the problem of the universality and relativity of thought has been posed in the methodology of those social sciences whose task it is to understand other cultures.

OBJECTIVISM VERSUS RELATIVISM IN INTERCULTURAL UNDERSTANDING

If the entire discussion surrounding ideology in the West has achieved nothing else, at least it has become clear that neither objectivism nor relativism can adequately conceive of the *other*. Equally apparent is the seeming inevitability of speaking out of either one or the other of these two positions. For if we do not assert relativity and plurality, then it would seem that we must automatically defend some form of objectivist universalism. Consequently, the discussion of ideology has not provided us with a solution, but rather with a more clearly defined problem; for it remains to be shown that a third alternative is possible. In order to take another step toward solving this problem and answering the question of a possible critique of ideology and universal form of thought, we must now enter into the discussion concerning the *possibility of intercultural understanding* in the social sciences.

From the objectivist point of view, it can be claimed that understanding foreign cultures is something obvious and unproblematical. Is there not a universal human nature upon which cultural differences are but variations on a theme? Do not all human beings, just as animals, have the same basic biological, psychological and social needs; they must all sleep, eat, propagate and care for their young, organize themselves in such a way as to insure survival of the group, etc. Can such behavioral patterns not be *explained* with the same methods of observation and generalization which explain the behavior of animals? And is not the human mind constituted by the same structures no matter where and under what conditions men and women live?

Although there are different languages, the objectivist may further argue, it seems that they may easily be translated into each other. Do not all speak of the same objective reality? Do they not all express the same human worries, joys and aspirations? Is this not sufficient to guarantee the unity of the human race and to serve as an *objective* basis upon which intercultural understanding can occur? From an objectivist standpoint one could even ask if there really is such a thing as *another* culture. What makes a foreign culture "other"? Wherein lies its "otherness"? And why is this otherness a problem?

In the face of such questions it becomes necessary not only to say clearly *how* it is possible to understand another culture, but even before this, to explain *why* we have to ask the question at all. It must be shown that talk of "other" cultures has a legitimate meaning and marks a real problem. This necessitates broadening the discussion so as to include the question of the *other as such*. As we shall see, understanding foreign cultures is problematical *only* when it can be assumed that they do not have merely *other views* — that is, other information about the *same objective reality*, which can be communicated and verified within the horizon of a presupposed universal rationality — but have radically other forms of thought and consequently access to other realities than we. This "relativist" assumption, should it prove to be well founded, allows us to place Western science's methodological presupposition of intersubjective unity as a guarantee of objectivity into question and thus also its claim to universal validity. On the other hand, we shall see that, when properly understood, it shows us a way beyond the skeptical consequences of postmodernism by reestablishing the universality of thought upon a different basis than objectivism has been able to provide—namely, upon a real acknowledgement of the *other*.[26]

It is thanks to Peter Winch that this problem can be approached from the point of view of the philosophy of language.[27] Winch was among the first to raise the question of the objectivity of the human sciences on the basis of the insights of the later philosophy of Ludwig Wittgenstein, and thus to raise the discussion in the methodology of the social sciences to the level of a theory of meaning. It is no accident that Winch thereby focuses on the problem of intercultural understanding and deals with ethnology as representative of all the social sciences. In his classic essay, "Understanding a Primitive Society," Winch develops his analysis of the conditions for intercultural understanding in critical dialogue with the social anthropology of E. E. Evans-Pritchard.

In the following discussion I will not primarily be concerned with whether Winch's critique of Evans-Pritchard is justified; that is, I will not question if Winch has correctly understood Evans-Pritchard. Instead, I will accept Winch's portrayal of Evans-Pritchard's methodology as an example of an approach typical for an objectivist attempt to understand another culture and concentrate on Winch's analysis of the *problem* of intercultural understanding. This will lead us into a more detailed examination of Wittgenstein's thought, which is the basis of many of the current relativist theories. This discussion will show that Wittgenstein need not be interpreted as a postmodern, skeptical relativist. Instead we will see that it is possible to understand Wittgenstein's philosophy as founding a discourse of disclosure upon a theory of meaning which equips us to answer the questions raised by the problem of ideology and by the task of understanding other cultures.

Winch's relation to Evans-Pritchard is complex, for Evans-Pritchard seems readily to admit the relativist principle which Winch wishes to defend, namely, that forms of thought are culturally determined. Evans-Pritchard writes:

The fact that we attribute rain to meteorological causes alone while savages believe that Gods or ghosts or magic can influence the rainfall is no evidence that our brains function differently from their brains. It does not show that we "think more logically" than savages. ... It is no sign of superior intelligence on my part that I attribute rain to physical causes. I did not come to this conclusion myself by observation and inference and have, in fact, little knowledge of the meteorological processes that lead to rain. *I merely accept what everybody else in my society accepts*, namely that rain is due to natural causes. Likewise a savage who believes that under suitable natural and ritual conditions the rainfall can be influenced by use of appropriate magic is not on account of this belief to be considered of inferior intelligence. He did not build up this belief from his own observations and inferences but adopted it in the same way as he adopted the rest of his cultural heritage, namely, *by being born into it. He and I are both thinking in patterns of thought provided for us by the societies in which we live.*[28]

The Western scientific view of reality is, therefore, just as much a function of our culture as the "magical" view of reality is a function of the culture which the ethnologist studies. Neither form of thought, it seems, can claim universal validity. With this insight, Evans-Pritchard wishes to discredit the thesis of Lévy-Bruhl that members of traditional societies have a "primitive mentality," or an illogical way of thinking. Nevertheless, Evans-Pritchard still wants to practice *anthropology*; that is, he still wants to make the beliefs and practices of primitive peoples *understandable* to himself and to his readers. This implies, as Winch points out, that he must "present an account of them that will somehow satisfy the criteria of rationality demanded by the culture to which he and his readers belong. . . ."[29] What criteria are these? These are the criteria of rationality characteristic of modern Western scientific culture. Here the danger is great that the ethnologist could commit a methodological mistake, which, as Winch claims, Evans-Pritchard, in a fashion representative for ethnology as a whole, actually did commit. In his well-known book, *Witchcraft, Oracles and Magic among the Azande*,[30] Evans-Pritchard asserts that the oracle practice of the Azande — indeed, their entire magical system of beliefs — does not correspond to "objective reality," while the scientific view does. Here is where Winch's critique sets in:

> I think that Evans-Pritchard is right in a great deal of what he says here, but wrong, and crucially wrong, in his attempt to characterize the scientific in terms of that which is "in accord with objective reality." . . . Evans-Pritchard, although he emphasizes that a member of scientific culture has a different conception of reality from that of a Zande believer in magic, wants to go beyond merely registering this fact and making the differences explicit, and to say, finally, that the scientific conception agrees with what reality actually is like, whereas the magical conception does not.[31]

The difficulty with asserting that Western science is "in accord with objective reality," whereas the Zande view is not, arises from the fact that the very concept of "reality" is culturally determined. If Evans-Pritchard had stuck to his (and Winch's) principle, namely, that different cultures have different forms of thought and thus also different conceptions of what reality is, then he could not have said that "reality," in the sense in which *we* use this concept *within* the context of Western scientific culture, is valid *outside* our culture. When we transfer concepts which are valid only within our culture to other cultures, then we inevitably end up making assertions of the sort which Evans-Pritchard and many other ethnologists make.

Winch disputes the validity of such statements, not because he denies the existence and applicability of criteria of reality and truth of any sort — for without such criteria one cannot think at all — but because such assertions overlook the fact that criteria of reality, truth and meaning are different in different cultures, and that we cannot *uncritically* assume our own to be the only valid ones. In order to support this "relativist" contention against the opposing universalist contention that scientific thought is indeed generally valid, Winch refers to the later philosophy of Ludwig Wittgenstein. From Wittgenstein Winch derives the following thesis:

Reality is not what gives language sense. What is real and what is unreal shows itself *in* the sense that language has.[32]

What, then, is the "sense" which language "has"? Winch writes:

If then we wish to understand the significance of these concepts [e.g., reality, truth, meaning], we must examine the use they actually do have — *in* the language.[33]

An example of such an investigation of language would be the comparison of the use of the concept "reality" in religious language, say, in the story of Job, who praises the reality of God's great deeds; and in the use of the concept of "reality" in scientific discourse, where, for example, the results of an experiment reveal the "real" state of affairs. The point of such a comparison is that concepts such as "reality," "truth" and "objectivity" are not defined by means of simply *pointing* to God's great deeds on the one hand, or to the results of an experiment on the other. This sort of ostensive definition merely involves one in a circle, where that which is supposed to be demonstrated by means of pointing is already presupposed as known; namely, it is presupposed that one already has an understanding of this or that thing *as* real.

Upon a certain level of discourse, both religious as well as scientific, the reality of those things about which one speaks is simply presupposed. *In between* the two, however, the meaning of reality is completely undetermined. What is real for one may well be unreal for the other. It is precisely this *in between* which is the area wherein are located ethnological discourse, as the understanding of other cultures, and the discourse of the social sciences in general (as the understanding of alien and alienated meaning). If this may not be a discourse which presupposes criteria of reality, then what sort of discourse is it? "We have then to ask," Winch concludes, "by reference to what established universe of discourse, the use of those expressions *is* to be explained. . . ."[34] And according to Winch, it is this question —

that is, the question of a *universal discourse* —which Evans-Pritchard, representative for ethnology and the social sciences in general, has failed to ask and to answer.

This critique, of course, would not be damaging if it should be the case that there were no such things as "other" cultures in the radical sense which Winch gives this term. In order even to raise intelligibly the question of a universal language within which the understanding of other realities could become a problem and a task for the social sciences, Winch must ask:

> Is it in fact the case that a primitive system of magic, like that of the Azande, constitutes a coherent universe of discourse like science, in terms of which an intelligible conception of reality and clear ways of deciding what beliefs are and are not in agreement with this reality can be discerned?[35]

If it should turn out that this is so, and that, therefore, there is a real need to understand other cultures, then immediately there arises the second, properly methodological question, What are we to make of the possibility of understanding primitive social institutions?[36]

Winch makes the answer to the first question dependent upon the answer to the second. For if it were not possible to understand other cultures, there would "be" no such thing for us. The very existence of radically other forms of thought rests upon the possibility to recognize them as meaningful in the first place. The seemingly empirical question of whether or not there exist other forms of thought reveals itself to be the "transcendental" question of whether or not the conditions of meaning as such allow this. Consequently, Winch pushes the inquiry back to its philosophical roots in a theory of meaning and asks, "What criteria have we for saying that something does, or does not, make sense?"[37] For only after the question of the criteria of meaning in general has been answered, that is, only after we know what it is that makes language have sense at all and where the bounds of sense and nonsense are, only then can we decide whether or not concrete cases of other uses of language do indeed have a specific meaning which we must try to understand.

To pose the question of understanding other cultures on this most basic level of a theory of meaning implies that if Winch is to be able to answer the question concerning the existence of radically different forms of thought in other cultures affirmatively, he must first demonstrate that the possibility of there being *other forms of thought* is *a condition of the possibility of meaningful speech as such.* Were this not the case, it would be impossible even to raise the question of whether this or that belief or custom of *another* culture is meaningful, since the bounds of meaning would exclude radical otherness. If, therefore, the understanding of other cultures is to be a possible task at all, it must be shown that the possibility of a *radically different thinking* belongs to the very conditions of the meaningfulness of our own thinking. It is in order to demonstrate precisely this that Winch turns to the philosophy of Wittgenstein. For, as we shall see, it was Wittgenstein who showed that the objectivist conception of meaning and validity in terms of "agreement with reality" holds only for a certain level of discourse. This is a discourse which itself becomes meaningful only when it is embedded within higher levels of discourse upon which criteria of reality are not already presupposed as fixed and given, but are first established and transformed.

Before we examine Wittgenstein's thought more closely, however, we must consider one way of answering the question of the criteria of meaning which would seem to solve the problem without further ado and at the same time settle the dispute in favor of the scientific universalist. Even if we cannot use the criterion of agreement with a supposedly objective reality, the scientific universalist could still claim that there remains the *logical* criterion of *non-contradiction*, or *internal consistency*:

> A partial answer is that a set of beliefs and practices cannot make sense insofar as they involve contradictions.[38]

Accordingly, if it can be shown that any given system of beliefs is internally inconsistent, then we have proof that it is irrational. *Formal logic* is, according to this contention, a universal basis upon which intercultural understanding may take place, and upon which other forms of thought may be criticized.

On the basis of Evans-Pritchard's account of the Azande oracle practice, a critique of this sort could be made with some plausibility. As Evans-Pritchard reports, among the Azande witchcraft is thought to be inherited. To discover a witch in a clan would then be sufficient evidence to conclude that all the members of that clan were witches. If there were only one witch in each clan, then everybody would be a witch; and vice versa, if there were one who was not a witch in each clan, then nobody would be witch. Evans-Pritchard remarks that the "Azande see the sense of the argument but they do not accept its conclusions. . . ."[39] Winch writes:

> It might now appear as though we had clear grounds for speaking of the superior rationality of European over Zande thought, insofar as the latter involves a contradiction which it makes no attempt to remove and does not even recognize: one, however, which is recognizable as such in the context of European ways of thinking.[40]

The contradiction here is so blatant that Evans-Pritchard feels he must offer an explanation of how it is possible that human beings can hold such beliefs. But as far as Evans-Pritchard is concerned, the answer does not exonerate the Azande view from the charge of irrationality; it merely attempts to show how such ideas may persist in the face of logic. He says that thinking does not occur in a vacuum, but is embedded in the entire context of personal and social life. The system of beliefs of a culture are not merely an "argument" which may be tested for formal-logical consistency, but a "world" in which questions concerning the meaning and destiny of life, moral value and personal and social identity may be asked and answered. On the level of a discourse which articulates worldviews, formal-logical problems alone do not amount to decisive criticisms. In the words of Evans-Pritchard:

> Azande observe the action of the poison oracle as we observe it, but their observations are always subordinated to their beliefs and are incorporated into their beliefs and made to explain them and justify them. Let the reader consider any argument that would utterly demolish all Zande claims for the power of the oracle. If it were translated into Zande modes of thought it would serve to support their entire structure of belief. For their mystical notions are eminently coherent, being interrelated by a network of logical ties, and are so ordered that they never too crudely contradict sensory experience but, instead, experience seems to justify them. The Zande is immersed in a sea of mystical notions, and if he speaks about his poison oracle he must speak in a mystical idiom.[41]

Even if one is inclined, contrary to the intention of Evans-Pritchard, to take this as a *justification* for the Azande view and not merely an explanation of it, it may still be claimed that a worldview which resists criticisms raised against it is less rational than one which is capable of *self-criticism*. If self-criticism is considered to be one of the special characteristics of modern Western culture, then again we have here a universal criterion of "rationality" from which the superiority of scientific culture may be deduced.[42] Against this objection, and in order to focus in on the important philosophical issue, as well as to reassert the relativist thesis, Winch offers the following parody of the remarks of Evans-Pritchard cited above:

> Europeans observe the action of the poison oracle just as Azande observe it, but their observations are always subordinated to their beliefs and are incorporated into their beliefs and made to explain them and justify them. Let a Zande consider any argument that would utterly refute all European skepticism about the power of the oracle. If it were translated into European modes of thought it would serve to support their entire structure of belief. For their scientific notions are eminently coherent, being interrelated by a network of logical ties, and are so ordered that they never too crudely contradict ... experience but, instead, experience seems to justify them. The Eur-

opean is immersed in a sea of scientific notions, and if he speaks about the Zande poison oracle he must speak in a scientific idiom.[43]

The moral of the story is not only that the accusation of internal inconsistency is always a criticism which can be turned against the accuser, but more importantly, that formal-logical consistency is a criterion of rationality only upon a specific level of discourse. It is *not* a sufficient criterion of rationality *as such*. What is rational and what irrational is not decidable upon the level of worldviews by means of formal-logical criteria. For what worldview does not have its internal contradictions? Couldn't the Azande ask the "enlightened" European how it is possible for humans to be free, autonomous and rational, when they obviously are everywhere in chains, always bound to their desires, and fully incapable of being happy? Or could not the Azande ask the Christian missionary how, upon the premises of Western thought itself, God can be human? Is such a concept not just as self-contradictory as a round square? Further, how can it be possible that we supposedly have been saved by the coming of Jesus Christ two thousand years ago, but still today are "waiting" for salvation? And finally, must not the Western scientist admit, upon logical grounds, that the project of formal-logical consistency cannot be radically carried through, for there is no form of thought which can be completely formalized, even mathematical logic, which itself must be rooted in a non-formalized meta-language?

In summary: If Western critics find the beliefs of another culture "irrational" on formal-logical criteria, then, as we saw, these critics must at least admit that their own worldview is also open to this criticism. They may, of course, readily do this and say in their defense that they, in fact, are open to criticism from other cultures, that they are even willing to "learn" from other cultures, and above all that they are "self-critical"—whereas members of traditional societies are not; and again, that it is precisely *this* which makes their worldview *rational* as opposed to that of the other. This would, however, only beg the question, by assuming to be universally valid the specifically Western scientific meaning of "self-criticism." If they do not make this assumption, then they must say what criteria of rationality they *are* relying upon in order to determine what is meaningful and what is not in another culture. Winch makes this point very well in terms of the conflict between religion and science within Western culture itself:

criteria of logic are not a direct gift of God, but arise out of, and are only intelligible in the context of ways of living or modes of social life. It follows that one cannot apply criteria of logic to modes of social life as such. For instance, science is one such mode and religion is another; and each has criteria of intelligibility peculiar to itself. So within science or religion actions can be logical or illogical: in science, for example, it would be illogical to refuse to be bound by the results of a properly carried out experiment; in religion it would be illogical to suppose that one could pit one's own strength against God's; and so on. But we cannot sensibly say that either the practice of science itself or that of religion is either illogical or logical; both are non-logical.[44]

Here it would seem that there are only three choices: either the anthropologist "jumps back" into his or her own form of rationality, or "jumps over" to the form of rationality in the other culture, or "jumps in between" the two cultures and claims that rationality is not merely *given* here or there, but is "something" which both cultures must *attain* in and through the encounter with each other. Jumping in between in this way, however, cannot mean merely accepting a third form of rationality unrelated to the other two.

But to state the problem in terms of these three decisions is not to have already solved it. For even if we may find the third alternative the only desirable one, since alternatives one and two inevitably lead to misunderstanding, the question remains whether such a way out is at all *possible*. To illustrate this question we may use an example which Wittgenstein was fond of, the "duck-rabbit":[45]

Diagram 1 — Duck-Rabbit

Either we see a duck, *or* we see a rabbit, but not both at once. In terms of the problem of intercultural understanding Winch wishes to pose, it would seem that we *must* either stand within the Azande worldview, where magical practices are meaningful, or within the Western scientific worldview, where such practices are meaningless and irrational, but not within both at once — for the two mutually exclude each other not only in content (because for us witches don't exist), but also in form (because they are worldviews encompassing the *whole* of reality). The question, therefore, seems to boil down to the question of *whose* criteria of rationality we are using when we attempt to understand and to criticize the rationality and meaningfulness of worldviews. According to Winch, the answer cannot be that we merely accept the one or the other as fixed and given. For this can only lead to misunderstanding on the theoretical plane and, as we shall presently see, to still worse consequences on the practical level.

Let the following account of an intercultural encounter — typical under present-day conditions of worldwide development and industrialization —

illustrate the problem we are facing on the practical level. In 1968 natural gas was discovered in Prudhoe Bay in Alaska. Corporate and government developers from the United States and Canada proceeded to make plans to build a pipeline to transport gas across northern Alaska and the Yukon down the Mackenzie river valley to southern Canada and the United States. The government appointed the Honorable Mr. Justice Thomas R. Berger to preside over an inquiry into the social and environmental impact of the project. During the hearings, which were one of the rare occasions when members of traditional societies have been allowed to speak concerning what the industrial nations do "for" them, the following testimony was recorded from one of the spokesmen for the Indian tribes who were to be affected by the pipeline:

> For many years before we heard about the white man, our people, who lived in what is now called the Yukon, lived in a different way. We lived in small groups and moved from one place to another at different times of the year. ... Sometimes we gathered together in larger groups to fish and relax after a hard winter. We had our own God and our own religion that taught us to live in peace together. This religion also taught us how to live as part of the land. We learned how to practice what you people call multiple land use and conservation and resource management. We have something to teach white men if they will listen to us.[46]

Gibson Winter, who reports this testimony in his foundational work on religious social ethics in the global situation, *Liberating Creation*, is careful to point out that one must not read these statements with a romanticizing intention. The native people of the Northwest know very well that their traditional life style must come to terms with the modern world. The important question is which "paradigm" or "root metaphor" of the world is going to inform, guide and give meaning to this social and technological change. For the Indian, it was clear that the Western secular worldview was inadequate. At one of the hearings where representatives of the interested corporations were present, an Indian spokesman, Frank T'Seleie, made the following remarks:

> Obviously Mr. Blair, president of Foothills (who is present) and his friend Mr. Horte, president of Gas Arctic, want to see us destroyed. Maybe Mr. Blair, that is because you do not know us or understand us. Or maybe money has become so important to you that you are losing your own humanity. ... I only know you are a human being. There must be times when you too think of your children and their future. I doubt that you would knowingly destroy what is valuable to them. Why are you asking us to destroy our future? ... Mr. Blair, there is a life and death struggle going on between us, between you

and me. Somehow in your carpeted boardrooms, in your paneled office, you are plotting to take away from me the very center of my existence. You are stealing my soul. Deep in the glass and concrete of your world you are stealing my soul, my spirit. By scheming to torture my land you are torturing me. By plotting to invade my land you are invading me. If you ever dig a trench through my land, you are cutting through me. . . . It seems to me that the whole point of living is to become as human as possible; to learn to understand the world and to live in it; to be part of it; to learn to understand the animals, for they are our brothers and they have much to teach us. We are a part of this world.[47]

The clash of two worldviews is here expressed with a pathos and urgency which cannot be ignored. We Westerners are no longer certain that our scientific and technological project of domination of nature and rationalization of society is unquestionably the way to build heaven on earth. We can no longer easily repress the temptation to "see" the world in the way Winter describes that the Indians see it; namely, as an "organicist world of interdependence, communal participation, and commitment to the sacredness of the world."[48]

Recalling the problem of the duck and the rabbit, could it not turn out that the other view is right? Could it not be that what we actually always *meant* by a rational and humane life is exactly that which *they* now say it is, and that we have simply not "seen" in the right way what we ourselves were all about? What then *is* the *meaning* of life? How shall we name our vision of the "whole?" Is it a "duck" or a "rabbit," or something else altogether, for example, a "dabbit"? *How* do we know? And if we don't have any binding criteria of meaning which tell us what it is, then meaning is whatever *we* say it is — we who have the *power* to enforce our view on the rest of the world.[49] Truth becomes, as Marx and Nietzsche said it was, the "lie" of the mighty. This is, in fact, what happens in most of the Third World today.

After having seen that formal-logical criteria of meaning are inadequate for criticizing worldviews — our own included! — and that the problem of the encounter of worldviews is not a merely theoretical preoccupation, but perhaps one of the most pressing problems of our time, we may return to the philosophical problem with which Winch is concerned.

We spoke above of three alternatives between which anthropologists may choose when they wish to understand another culture. They may choose the standards of rationality given in their own culture and worldview, or they may choose those of the culture they are trying to understand, or they may try to jump in between worldviews by choosing another, third set of criteria given in neither of the two cultures, but allegedly adequate to both. In order to identify clearly the philosophical issue involved here, we may formulate these three alternatives in terms of a *trilemma*.

Ethnologists have only three choices, but, as we shall see, none of them are acceptable. If they choose *their own* standards of rationality, then they must judge the other culture, insofar as it is "other," and thus in need of understanding at all, to be irrational and meaningless and thus, paradoxically, incapable of being understood. If they choose the standards of the other culture, they must reject much of what is rational in their own culture and thus find themselves in the embarrassing position of not being able to "understand" in the sense of making something intelligible to members of their own culture. And if they choose *some third set* of criteria, they must either show how they are in continuity with the rationality of both cultures, and thus capable of making both cultures intelligible, or condemn both cultures to irrationality. Now, if they wish to show that their new criteria are in continuity with both cultures, then they must say what criteria allow them to say this, their own, the other's, or again, a third set — and so on into infinity. In none of these choices — all of which are generated upon a level of discourse constituted by the presupposition of fixed critera of rationality — is there a possibility of actually *understanding* another culture. Winch puts the problem in the following way:

> it cannot be guaranteed in advance that the methods and techniques we have used in the past — e.g., in elucidating the logical structure of arguments in our own language and culture — are going to be equally fruitful in this new context. They will perhaps need to be extended and modified. No doubt, if they are to have a logical relation to our previous forms of investigation, the new techniques will have to be recognizably continuous with previously used ones. But they must also so extend our conception of intelligibility as to make it possible for us to see what intelligibility amounts to in the life of the society we are investigating.[50]

And he concludes:

> Seriously to study another way of life is necessarily to seek to extend our own — not simply to bring the other way within the already existing boundaries of our own, because the point about the latter in their present form, is that they *ex hypothesi* exclude each other.[51]

The possibility of understanding and criticizing other cultures — as well as our own! — stands or falls with the possibility of showing that there is a level of discourse upon which standards of rationality are not presupposed, but can change, be extended and transformed, and that this *transformation is itself rational*. This brings us back to the problem of the criteria of meaning and rationality in general. As we saw, if the understanding of other cultures is to be possible at all, then it must be shown that the possibility of a *radically different thinking* belongs to the very conditions of the meaningfulness of our own thinking. This is the point where the philosophy of Wittgenstein becomes important. Wittgenstein shows that a discourse of disclosure, which breaks open the closure of rationality within fixed criteria, is both possible and necessary.

CAN THERE BE A UNIVERSAL DISCOURSE?

The assertion that meaning is based upon a given reality which grounds the claim to objectivity and universal validity of the scientific worldview finds its exemplary expression in Wittgenstein's early work, the *Tractatus Logico-Philosophicus*.[52] In his later "language-game" philosophy, Wittgenstein discarded this thesis for the view that meaning is use and that language has a plurality of "grammars." In the later work the meaning of language does not come from a given, fixed world of objects and its logical structure, but lies in the *use* which language has in various "forms of life." Just as language has different uses, so there are different criteria of meaning, truth and reality. That these are all different uses *of language*, however, and not radically different languages completely unrelated to each other, implies that any given set of criteria are not closed, but are open to other criteria and tô transformation. Thus it comes to the thesis put forth by Winch:

> Reality is not what gives language sense. What is real and what is unreal shows itself *in* the sense that language has.

In the following I will argue that the development in Wittgenstein's thought is to be understood as the move from a *realistic semantics* to a *pragmatic semantics*, and that the question of an intercultural hermeneutics, as the question of a universal discourse, can only adequately be placed from the point of view of a pragmatic theory of meaning of the sort that Wittgenstein developed in his later work.[53]

I will begin with a brief portrayal of Wittgenstein's early thought in the *Tractatus* and of the problems of the realistic theory of meaning which he there proposes; then I will discuss the language-game theory of the later work with the intention of showing how the pragmatic theory of meaning developed there lays the foundation for a discourse of disclosure within which intercultural understanding might occur.

Language as a Picture of Reality

Language, for the early Wittgenstein, consists of sentences, or propositions (4.001). All propositions can be *analyzed* into elementary propositions (4.221). The elementary propositions are combinations of names (4.22). Names immediately refer to objects (3.203). Objects exist in the world. They are simple and cannot be further analyzed (2.02). They can only be named (3.221). An elementary proposition is the most simple combination of names possible and, therefore, a *picture* of the most simple possible combination of objects (4.21). This most simple possible combination of objects, Wittgenstein calls a "state of affairs" (*Sachverhalt*), or merely a "fact" (*Tatsache*) — also translated as an "atomic fact" (2.01). The atomic facts come together to compose states of affairs of varying complexity, just as the elementary propositions come together to form sentences of varying complexity. The "world" consists, according to Wittgenstein, of the totality of facts (1.1), just as language consists of the totality of the sentences which picture these facts (4.001). Language is, therefore, a *picture of reality* and has the function of *describing* the world (4.021).

At the basis of this conception of language lies the "picture theory" and the "truth functional theory." The picture theory asserts that, "A proposition states something only in so far as it is a picture" (4.03). This presupposes that language and reality are somehow so *co-ordinated* that it is possible for a constellation of names to re-present, or picture a constellation of objects. What coordinates language with reality is "logical form."

Logical form is, speaking with Kant, the condition of the possibility of propositions, as well as of the facts, i.e., the objects of knowledge.[54] For it is only on the basis of this *a priori* common structure of language and reality that we can, as Wittgenstein puts it, "picture facts to ourselves" (2.1).

Once we have made a picture of the facts, then we can proceed to compare the picture with reality and thus decide if it is a *true* or *false* picture.

A picture agrees with reality or fails to agree; it is correct or incorrect, true or false. (2.21)

In order to tell whether a picture is true or false we must compare it with reality. (2.223)

The *possibility* of comparing, that is, of demonstrating the truth or falsity of a proposition by seeing if it corresponds to reality, is that which gives a proposition its *sense*. A sentence becomes meaningful the moment it becomes *possible to decide*, by means of comparison, whether or not it is true. In the formulation of this idea which became important for the famous "principle of verification" of logical positivism, Wittgenstein says:

To understand a proposition means to know what is the case if it is true. (One can understand it, therefore, without knowing whether it is true.) (4.024)

But let us immediately add that one can *not* understand it without the *possibility* of comparing it to the world. For only in this way can one find out whether it is true. Therefore, every meaningful sentence is *either* true *or* false; that is, it must always be possible to compare it to the world.

This possibility depends, however, not only on a common logical form or structure which *a priori* coordinates language and reality. It must also be possible to compare *a posteriori* the *content* of a sentence to the world. Imagine a world without trees. In such a world the sentence, "The tree stands in front of the house," would be *formally* comparable to reality but not according to its *content*. For in this world there just happens to be no such thing as a tree. Because there is a name used in this proposition which refers to no object, we could not *decide* whether the sentence in question was true or false.

Words are meaningful insofar as they denote objects in the world. These are *names*. Here the *realistic semantics* and the nominalism of Wittgenstein's early thought is clearly expressed. Words are exclusively understood in terms of their reference function. Meaning is reduced to the reference relation between a simple name and a simple object:

A name means an object. The object is its meaning. (3.203)

It is important to note that the metaphysical thesis of the world being made up of simple objects is a requirement of the realistic theory of meaning which needs a fixed external reality with which sentences can be compared.

Objects *must* be simple in order that the names denoting them have a single univocal meaning. And the names *must* have a univocal meaning, for without such a univocal meaning we would not know how, or with what we were supposed to compare the sentence. The question of its truth or falsity would be unanswerable. If there were no such simple objects functioning, as it were, as basic elements making up, as Wittgenstein puts it, "the substance of the world" (2.021), then we could make no picture of the world. The picture theory, therefore, *implies* the theory of truth functional analysis of sentences—that is, the capability of *analyzing* all complex sentences into elementary propositions consisting of the most simple possible combinations of names.[55] For it is an axiom and not merely a desiderative that

Everything that can be thought at all can be thought clearly. Everything that can be put into words can be put clearly. (4.116)

If, however, there were a sentence whose *words* did not refer to any *objects*, it could not picture any state of affairs at all. The sentence would, in that case, not be a sentence at all. It would be merely senseless noise. Since only objects within the world can give names a *clear* meaning, all sentences speaking of otherworldly objects such as God, the soul, the good and the beautiful must be meaningless. The positivist *critique of meaning*, which Wittgenstein here definitively formulates, aims at excluding all propositions of metaphysics, ethics, theology and aesthetics from the realm of rationality. Such sentences refer to "the mystical" (6.522), about which, as the famous closing sentence of the *Tractatus* puts it, we "must pass over in silence" (7).

We know today that Wittgenstein was no positivist in the sense in which the Vienna Circle, for example, wished to understand him.[56] For him, "there are ... things which cannot be put into words" (6.552). This is what he called the "mystical." It is not a matter of claiming that such things are mere nonsense. He was concerned, rather, to clearly segregate the realm of discourse about matters of fact from that of inescapable existential responsibility and to protect the latter from becoming an indifferent object of scientific inquiry on the one hand or the victim of the idle talk of academic philosophers on the other. His purpose was preeminently ethical.[57] This remains the fundamental intention of his thought throughout all the changes of the later period.

Just as fundamental for an understanding of the continuity and significance of Wittgenstein's philosophy is his program of *critique of meaning*. For if philosophy is to have a task apart from the clarification of scientific methodology (philosophy of science), it can only lie in the area of a critique of meaning and not in formulating the logical requirements of empirically falsifiable hypotheses. Beyond showing philosophy the way from the question of truth to the more primary question of meaning,[58] the significance of his critical program consists in revealing the basic problems any critique of meaning must face, and in the fact that he definitively formulated these problems for any attempt to ground a discourse claiming universal validity.

Let us now look at two of these difficulties. First, a major problem for any critique of meaning is the status of its own propositions. For the early Wittgenstein, this difficulty arises from the fact that it is not only the otherworldly objects of metaphysics, ethics and aesthetics which cannot be pictured by the descriptive language of the empirical sciences — that language which alone is meaningful according to the *Tractatus* — it is also the very conditions of the possibility of language, the logical form, which cannot be described:

Propositions can represent the whole of reality, but they cannot represent what they must have in common with reality in order to be able to represent it — logical form.
In order to be able to represent logical form, we should have to be able to station ourselves with propositions somewhere outside logic, that is to say outside the world. (4.12)

What then of Wittgenstein's own sentences which speak about logical form and the nature of language? Do they also belong to the ineffable? Wittgenstein does not shrink back from this conclusion. He openly admits that anyone who understands his propositions must find them "nonsensical" (6.54). To a certain extent, this paradox is lessened by the important distinction between that which may be *said* and that which can only be *shown*:

Propositions cannot represent logical form: it is mirrored in them. Propositions *show* the logical form of reality. (4.121)

What *can* be shown, *cannot* be said (4.1212).

But this only lessens the paradox and does not remove it entirely, for it does not save his sentences from being labeled nonsensical.

Here it is important to note that Wittgenstein distinguishes between "sense," "nonsense" and the "senseless."[59] Sentences within the clearly demarcated domain of fixed criteria of validity, that is sentences of the "sciences," have *sense*. The sentences of metaphysics, ethics, aesthetics and theology, because they attempt to speak of what is beyond the limits of discourse about matters of fact are *nonsense*; they are "mystical." *Senseless*, however, are the propositions of philosophy, whose task it is to set the very boundaries of sense and nonsense. Can that which is "senseless" be meaningful? If it is not, then how can it set the limits of sense? And if the "senseless" somehow does have meaning, where does it draw its meaning from, since meaning is that which must. first be established by it?

Hidden behind these rather torturous logical gymnastics lies a problem which has haunted modern philosophy from the very beginning. For according to the principle of autonomy, secular thought has taken over the task of determining itself.[60] It is a thinking which claims to be self-grounding and thus to set its own limits, but which, in the very moment when it binds itself also unbinds itself and sets itself "outside" the world in the place of the arbiter of meaning. Furthermore, it is *the* problem of any thinking structured by a principle of closure, of exclusion and inclusion, which, in the very moment that it asserts its own universality, is forced to recognize an "other" beyond itself, which can only appear as the "mystical," or "irrational."

A second major problem arises from the inherent universality of meaning. In the *Tractatus* this is expressed in the definition of language as a picture of the world. According to this definition, the boundaries of language are at the same time the boundaries of the world:

The limits of my language mean the limits of my world. (5.6)

It is important here to note that the logical limits of the world have two important characteristics; first, they are *univocal*, because they consist of pure definitions or tautologies, and secondly, they are *universal*, because they are the conditions of the possibility of all meaningful speaking and thinking. Therefore, there can be no subject who speaks a logically different language than I. There is only *one* language, or as we would say today, there is only one form of rationality. And because it is the language in which we all already agree, there is really only one subject, that is, one form of rational knowing.[61] Accordingly, Wittgenstein can say that the limits of *my* language are at the same time the limits of *the* world. There is no individual who could speak a language other than the *one, univocal,* and *universal* language which describes the world; that is, there is no subject who *could* speak a language other than the language of matters of fact.

The speaker of this one, univocal, universal language of science cannot be an existential, historically and socially conditioned individual or group. It is a *metaphysical subject* or a logical subject which itself is nothing other than the logical limits of language and reality:

The subject does not belong to the world: rather, it is a limit of the world. (5.632)

Here it can be seen that solipsism, when its implications are followed out strictly, coincides with pure realism. The self of solipsism shrinks to a point without extension, and there remains the reality coordinated with it. (5.64)

The philosophical self is not the human being, not the human body, or the human soul, with which psychology deals, but rather the metaphysical subject, the limit of the world — not a part of it. (5.641)

The "subject" is a pure observer without prejudices, values, feelings or interests. It does not belong to any human community or any historical culture. This is the subject who alone is capable of "objective" scientific knowledge. The subject of objective, universally valid knowledge is a *logical subject*, a pure function, a role which any individual anywhere at any time can fulfill.[62] On the level of discourse about matters of fact, the concrete existential subject, for whom its own existence is, as Heidegger says, an "issue"; the individual, who in a particular cultural and historical situation seeks a "meaning" of life and of the world as a whole does not "exist." For according to the early Wittgenstein, the only language such a subject could speak is one in which a "meaning" of life, a worldview, or religion could not be meaningfully formulated. All attempts to do so end in utter nonsense, or in a less critical formulation, in mere opinion. In the face of the one, objective, universally valid language of the logical subject, the ambiguous, perspectival and pluralistic languages of *existential interpreters* must be silent.[63]

The existential interpreters are, therefore, not subjects of *rational knowing*, but rather, of an *irrational willing*. This means that all worldviews are grounded in an individual and non-linguistic *decision*.

The view that science agrees with reality, however, is itself a worldview of this sort; for it boils down to the meta-scientific assumption that *all knowledge is hypothetical*.[64] This assertion, however, cannot itself be a hypothesis. It is an *a priori* decision. For there is no conceivable experience which could falsify it. Every counter instance would only serve to reaffirm that it is in principle falsifiable and thus a hypothesis like all others. Consequently, the philosophical critique of meaning which sets the limits of language in such a way that only empirically falsifiable hypotheses have meaning, can, because of its own meaninglessness, be grounded only in an irrational *decisionism*.[65] Here positivism and existentialism join forces. They are not mutually exclusive opposites, as is usually supposed, but complement each other.[66] The idea of an interest-free, purely theoretical, scientific subject, together with the world it knows and describes, turns out to be itself an existential interpretation; indeed, it is *one among many*. In a pluralistic situation, in which the problem of the universal validity of knowledge is intertwined with that of intercultural understanding, the assertion that the only meaningful form of discourse is that of matters of fact blinds out the possibility of rationally (i.e., discursively) criticizing that form of discourse which sets the boundaries of meaning. Such an assertion can amount to nothing more than covert cultural imperialism imposing one particular form of human consciousness and experience upon all the others.

This brings us back to the problem Peter Winch was concerned with in his critique of Evans-Pritchard, who, for Winch, represents the views of the *Tractatus*. Winch sees the *Tractatus* as a prime example of the scientific worldview. The conviction that only discourse which describes matters of fact is meaningful expresses itself in the typical assumption of Western ethnologists that the scientific view of reality corresponds to what reality *really* is, whereas the views of other cultures do not.

We have seen how this assumption, when carried to its logical consequences, leads to serious difficulties. First, as we saw, there is the problem of a thinking which attempts to set its own limits. How can thinking limit itself without at the same time, paradoxically, setting itself beyond those limits? Further, if it is logically impossible for thought to avoid absolutizing itself, since the "other" of reason is always unreason, then how can it nonetheless adequately acknowledge and understand its limitedness? Must not the limit and ground of thought consist in an irrational decisionism which would lead us directly into Nietzsche's Will to Power and the various postmodern relativist theories? That Wittgenstein was fully aware of these problems and of their implications for an intercultural hermeneutics, may be seen from the following citation from *On Certainty*,[67] which seems made to order to illustrate Winch's point:

Is it wrong for me to be guided in my actions by the propositions of physics? Am I to say I have no good ground for doing so? Isn't precisely this what we call a "good ground"? (608)

Supposing we met people who did not regard that as a telling reason. Now, how do we imagine this? Instead of the physicist, they consult an oracle. (And for that we consider them primitive.) Is it wrong for them to consult an oracle and be guided by it? — If we call this "wrong" aren't we using our language-game as a base from which to *combat* theirs? (609)

And are we right or wrong to combat it? Of course there are all sorts of slogans which will be used to support our proceedings. (610)

Where two principles really do meet which cannot be reconciled with one another, then each man declares the other a fool and heretic. (611)

I said I would "combat" the other man, — but wouldn't I give him *reasons*? Certainly; but how far do they go? At the end of reasons comes *persuasion*. (Think what happens when missionaries convert natives.) (612)

The problematic status of that discourse which sets boundaries is here no longer blinded out by simply declaring it to be "nonsensical." Instead, the question of the validity and relativity of boundary discourse comes glaringly to the fore. It is a widely held misinterpretation of Wittgenstein's thought, however, to suppose that in his later work he gave up the ideal of a universal language which had inspired his early work for the sake of a radical relativism.[68] In the early work, so goes the interpretation, there is the one, universal, world-describing language of science, and in the later work there is instead a plurality of different and independent *language-games*, each circumscribed by its own rules, its own criteria of validity. Further, it is claimed that since Wittgenstein goes so far in his later work as to completely deny the possibility of general theoretical statements about language, his thinking ends in relativism.

It would be more adequate to the *continuity* of Wittgenstein's thought, however, to see things the other way round. Wittgenstein, according to the view I wish to propose, never gave up the ideal of a universal language; rather, he saw the difficulties of his attempt, in the *Tractatus*, to base such a language upon a *realistic semantics* and, therefore, attempted, in the later work, to solve these problems from the point of view of a *pragmatic semantics*. Once the tie with objective reality is no longer constitutive of meaning but rather the embeddedness of language in practical forms of life, it becomes possible to ascribe meaning also to those levels of discourse lying beyond assertions of matters of fact, that is, those levels of discourse in which criteria of validity are first established and in which questions of the meaning of the "whole" are addressed. The goal remains the same; the methods, however, are radically different. For relativism is not a consequence of understanding language in terms of a plurality of language-games; rather, it is the outcome of the attempt to derive the meaning of language from reference to a fixed external reality. As we saw, this line of thought ends by grounding meaning in an arbitrary and irrational decisionism. If we are to look for the source of relativism it is to be found here. For one decision is as good as another, and every decision is merely externally related to every other as a brute fact. Furthermore, if basic decisions of this sort do come into contact with each other, their relations can only be of an "agonistic," that is, apologetic and polemical nature. Here it is Nietzsche who has the last word.

When, however, language does not receive its meaning from an external and non-linguistic reality, then what does ground the meaning which language has? It is with this question in mind that we turn to an examination of Wittgenstein's philosophy of language-games.

Language-Games

The *Philosophical Investigations* (1953) is generally taken to be the most representative of Wittgenstein's later works.[69] It is here that the conception of language as consisting of many semi-independent patterns of meaning and action — or, as Wittgenstein puts it, "language-games" — receives its fullest exposition. The work begins with a long citation from St. Augustine, which "gives us a particular picture of the essence of human language":

When they (my elders) named some object, and accordingly moved towards something, I saw this and I grasped that the thing was called by the sound they uttered when they meant to point it out. Their intention was shewn by their bodily movements, as it were the natural language of all peoples: the expression of the face, the play of the eyes, the movement of other parts of the body, and the tone of voice which expresses our state of mind in seeking, having, rejecting, or avoiding something. Thus, as I heard words repeatedly used in their proper places in various sentences, I gradually learnt to understand what objects they signified; and after I had trained my mouth to form these signs, I used them to express my own desires. (*Confessions*, I. 8)

This is the picture which lies at the basis of the realistic semantics of the *Tractatus*. Now, however, Wittgenstein calls it "a primitive idea of the way language functions" (2); and he finds it only "appropriate" (*brauchbar*) for a "narrowly circumscribed region," but not as a portrayal of the "whole," that is, of "everything that we call language" (3). The meaning of words is not once and for all determined by a given reality; rather, meaning depends upon how words are *used*. Naming is *one* use of language among others. The realistic semantics of the early work turns out to be a generalization of one particular use of language.

Wittgenstein demonstrates this by showing that *ostensive definition*, which allegedly connects a name to an object and thus, according to a realistic semantics, stands at the beginning of all meaningful speech as the meaning-giving act par excellence, itself has presuppositions and previous conditions of meaning.[70] No object can be named, and no name can be given an object, if one does not previously know what the act of pointing is supposed to do. Words can only be defined, that is, given a meaning when the *language-game* in which they are to play a role is *already known*:

> So one might say: the ostensive definition explains the use — the meaning — of the word when the overall role of the word in language is clear. Thus if I know that someone means to explain a colour-word to me the ostensive definition "That is called 'sepia' " will help me to understand the word. (30)

If I do not already know that the person is pointing at the color and wishes to tell me its name, then I cannot understand the definition. Wittgenstein offers another example to clarify this point:

> Consider this further case: I am explaining chess to someone; and I begin by pointing to a chessman and saying: "This is the king; it can move like this, . . . and so on." — In this case we shall say: the words "This is the king" (or "This is called the 'king' ") are a definition only if the learner already "knows what a piece in a game is." That is, if he has already played other games, or has watched other people playing "and understood" — *and similar things*. Further, only under these conditions will he be able to ask relevantly in the course of learning the game; "What do you call this?" — that is, this piece in a game. We may say: only someone who already knows how to do something with it can significantly ask a name. (31)

But what if we don't already know how to do something with it, that is, what if we don't have the *concepts* such as "game," or "piece in a game"? These concepts cannot be explained by ostensive definitions without themselves presupposing still other undefined concepts, such as "human activity," or "thing," and so on. Where then do our concepts come from, if not from the definitions we give them? What, after all, gives language its meaning?[71] If we can only ask for and understand an ostensive definition when we *already have certain concepts*, where then do these concepts come from if not from the objects? Merely pointing to the king and uttering the sentence, "This is the king," can only be an explanation if we *already know* what is being pointed at, namely, at a piece in the game of chess. This in turn we can only ask about, if we *already know* what a game is and what it means to play and so on. The objectivist would ask: Where does the explanation end? One definition seems only to lead to another and this in turn to yet another; words are simply replaced by more words. When do we ever reach solid ground, a fixed meaning? Wittgenstein replies by posing the question: What does it mean here to *already know* something?

What does it mean to know what a game is? ... Isn't my knowledge, my concept of a game, completely expressed in the explanations that I could give? That is, in my describing examples of various kinds of game; shewing how all sorts of other games can be constructed on the analogy of these; saying that I should scarcely include this or this among games; and so on. (75)

My knowledge of what is a game is neither a clearly delimited definition, nor some simple object out there in the world which I could point to, but the fact that I know "how to do something" with that which I call "game"; that is, I can use the word together with certain *activities*. When I explain the word to someone who does not know how to do something with it, I do nothing more than attempt to teach that person how to play a game. Think of the way a child first learns to play a certain game. We teach by showing how to do it; that is, we go through the various "moves" and encourage the child to do *the same*. At a certain point the child does as we do and can even go on without our guiding him. At this point we usually say he has understood. Wittgenstein claims that learning a language is no different. At a certain point we can go on *in the same way* as those who are teaching us.

It is on the basis of this insight that Wittgenstein makes a very important comparison. Learning to understand and speak a language is, he concludes, like learning a game in that both are *rule-governed activities*. The logic and the grammar of a language are "normative" in the same way as the rules of a game. Both constitute the meaning of a particular activity. Playing a game, speaking a language and thus also *thinking* are, therefore, activities constituted by rules. It is only within such an activity that we can have *concepts* at all. And this is so for even the most abstract concepts of philosophy and mathematics, for example, even for the very concepts with which Wittgenstein himself wishes to explain what a rule is, namely, the words "same," "uniform" and "regular":

Then am I defining "order" and "rule" by means of "regularity"? — How do I explain the meaning of "regular," "uniform," "same" to anyone? — I shall explain these words to someone who, say, only speaks French by means of the corresponding French words. But if a person has not yet got the *concepts*, I shall teach him to use the words by means of *examples* and by *practice*. In the course of this teaching I shall shew him the same colours, the same lengths, the same shapes, I shall make him find them and produce them, and so on. I shall, for instance, get him to continue an ornamental pattern uniformly when told to do so. — And also to continue progressions. And so, for example, when given: . .. ... to go on: .... I do it, he does it after me; and I influence him by expressions of agreement, rejection, expectation, encouragement. I let him go his way, or hold him back; and so on. Imagine witnessing such teaching. None of the words would be explained by means of itself; there would be no logical circle. And when I do this I do not communicate less to him than I know myself. (208)

But what, it may be asked, do I myself "know"? Wittgenstein answers that knowledge is a kind of practice, a technique:

> The grammar of the word "knows" is evidently closely related to that of "can," "is able to." But also closely related to that of "understands." ("Mastery" of a technique.) (150)

Or again:

> To understand a sentence means to understand a language. To understand a language means to be master of a technique. (199)

That which I teach and, therefore, what I myself "know" is nothing other than that which I can *do*. To be able to do something, to be master of a technique, implies that I am able to distinguish between actions which are *correct* and those which are *incorrect*. Uses of language, like games and all techniques, have *rules* according to which what is correct can be distinguished from what is incorrect. To understand a word or a sentence means to be able to *use* it *properly*, that is, to use it within a specific language-game. This is what I must "know" when I set about to teach someone the meaning of a word.

It is important to note at this point that "knowledge" of the rules of a language-game cannot be understood as an *explicit* or *theoretical* knowledge *about* the rules. For if playing language-games depended on theoretical knowledge of the rules, one could always ask the question of the meaning of a rule, and the rule could always be further interpreted. Just as was the case when we were asking for the meaning of a word we never came to an end of words, one would never come to an end of interpretations. The same difficulty would repeat itself as in the case of ostensive definitions. According to Wittgenstein, the problem is that "whatever I do is, on some interpretation, in accord with the rule" (198) and thus, we may add, on some interpretation, in conflict with the rule. If we were to identify the rules of our language-games with our interpretations of the rules, then the difference between correctness and incorrectness disappears and with it every notion of a rule. Explicit interpretations of the rules, therefore, cannot ground meaning; otherwise, there would be no possibility of ever deciding which interpretation is right, or of arbitrating between conflicting interpretations. Interpretations must come to an end somewhere, but this does not mean, as Rorty seems to think, that anywhere they come to an end is as good as anywhere else. Thus, rules do not make language meaningful in that we explicitly interpret them, but rather, in that they are embedded in a *praxis* which we *cannot get behind*:

> This was our paradox: no course of action could be determined by a rule, because every course of action can be made out to accord with the rule. The answer was: if everything can be made out to accord with the rule, then it can also be made out to conflict with it. And so there would be neither accord nor conflict here. It can be seen that there is a misunderstanding here from the mere fact that in the course of our argument we give one interpretation after another; as if each one contented us at least for a moment, until we thought of yet another standing behind it. What this shews is that there is a way of grasping a rule which is *not* an *interpretation*, but which is exhibited in what we call "obeying the rule" and "going against it" in actual cases. (201)

> And hence also "obeying a rule" is a practice. And to *think* one is obeying a rule is not to obey a rule. Hence it is not possible to obey a rule "privately": otherwise thinking one was obeying a rule would be the same thing as obeying it. (202)

Here there are two points which, for the purpose of understanding the relevance of Wittgenstein's philosophy for intercultural hermeneutics, are of major significance. First, there is the *pragmatic turn*. The meaning of language is grounded in a bedrock of *praxis*. Secondly, there is at the same time the opening up of a *universal horizon*. For basic praxis cannot itself be limited by merely subjective, irrational and therefore exclusive decisions without implying that "thinking one was obeying a rule would be the same thing as obeying it." The praxis which gives language meaning, therefore, cannot be *private*; rather, it must be *intersubjective* and *communal* and the community in which praxis takes place cannot be limited. These two criteria of meaning are inseparable or, as we may say, equiprimordial. Together they constitute the conditions of the possibility of any discourse claiming universality.

The pragmatic turn and the opening up of a universal horizon make an intercultural hermeneutics possible in two ways. On the one hand, they allow for the genuine relativity of all thinking, which mitigates against objectivist claims that there is one, universally valid view of reality. On the other hand, they allow us at the same time to avoid the difficulties of relativism by binding thought to a *universal community of discourse*.[72] If the rules of language were mere conventions, which could be arbitrarily determined, this would amount to putting an *interpretation* of the rules in the place of the rules themselves. One cannot save conventionalism by setting up a *collective subject* in the place of the individual subject of existentialism. For, from the *global* perspective, exactly the same decisionist difficulties recur at the level of the collective "subject." Therefore, Wittgenstein emphasizes that even before all conventions there lies a fundamental "agreement" in praxis, or as he says, in *forms of life*. Only within this original "agreement" are decisions (individual or collective) concerning the interpretation of rules at all possible:

> "So you are saying that human agreement decides what is true and what is false?" — It is what human beings *say* that is true and false; and they agree in the *language* they use. That is not agreement in opinions but in form of life. (241)

Or, as he says in another place:

> What has to be accepted, the given, is — so one could say — *forms of life*.

The question of the criteria of meaning ends, for the later Wittgenstein, as little in an arbitrary decisionism of the sort which relativism proposes as in some sort of extra-linguistic "reality" which objectivism insists upon. This is nowhere more clearly apparent than in Wittgenstein's famous *private language argument*.

The argument against the possibility of a private language, that is, against the language of a solipsistically closed subject (individual or collective!) is one of the central concerns of the *Philosophical Investigations*. According to some, the entire book is a long, many sided attack upon the major tenets of modern epistemology and metaphysics; namely, methodological solipsism, epistemological idealism and empiricism (which complement each other), the exclusive alternatives of *a priori* and *a posteriori*, and the ideal of disinterested, value-free knowing.[73] This thesis is certainly correct when one views Wittgenstein's work within the context of modern philosophy. For from Descartes to Husserl, it is practically an axiom of modern theory of knowledge that the knowing subject can only know with *certainty* the contents of its own consciousness, be it sense data or transcendental concepts.

Wittgenstein's critique of modern epistemology and of the metaphysics of the absolute subject amounts to turning this thesis around: If it is meaningless to suppose that one can think (know) other than one's own thinking, then, argues Wittgenstein, it is equally meaningless to think that one can *only* think one's own thinking. The point of the argument is that language-games are meaningful only to the extent that they are open to correction from without. Recognition of another language-game thus becomes a condition of the meaningfulness of our own.

In formulating the question of a private language, Wittgenstein is careful to emphasize that it is not a matter of a language which we speak with ourselves, but rather, of a language which we can *only* speak with ourselves, since others are in principle excluded from understanding it:

> The individual words of this language are to refer to what can only be known to the person speaking; to his immediate private sensations. So another person cannot understand the language. (243)

In various ways and with different arguments, Wittgenstein tries to show that a solipsistic metaphysical subject like that of the *Tractatus*, whose knowledge is a knowledge of objects which it alone knows, and whose language is a language which it alone speaks and understands is absurd. We will follow only two of the many lines of argumentation Wittgenstein develops: first, the argument against private objects, and second, the argument against a private logic, or private rules.

To begin with, Wittgenstein argues that even if there were such things as private objects to which words could refer, these would play no role whatsoever in the actual use of language and would be completely superfluous. One could, as he puts it, "divide through" by such things; they "cancel out," whatever they may be. In the following example, he discusses the allegedly private sensation of pain:

> If I say of myself that it is only from my own case that I know what the word "pain" means—must I not say the same of other people too? And how can I generalize the *one* case so irresponsibly? Now someone tells me that *he* knows what pain is only from his own case! — Suppose everyone had a box with something in it: we call it a "beetle." No one can look into anyone else's box, and everyone says he knows what a beetle is only by looking at *his* beetle. — Here it would be quite possible for everyone to have something different in his box. One might even imagine such a thing constantly changing. — But suppose the word "beetle" had a use in these people's language? — If so it would not be used as the name of a thing. The thing in the box has no place in the language-game at all; not even as a *something*: for the box might even be empty. — No, one can 'divide through' by the thing in the box; it cancels out, whatever it is. That is to say: if we construe the grammar of the expression of sensation on the model of "object and designation" the object drops out of consideration as irrelevant. (293)

One could object that this is no argument against a metaphysical subject; for an absolute subject does not need to speak *with others*, since they, by definition, do not exist. The solipsist does not need to use his word "beetle" in a language-game with others. According to the presuppositions of a private language, he speaks only with himself. Here is where the second line of argumentation begins. Wittgenstein claims that the solipsist must

still *follow a rule*, that is, use the *same word in the same way*, if the word is
to have any sort of *use* at all. And if the solipsist is not *using* the word, then
it can be no word and no part of a language, not even of a private language.
For a word that can be neither correctly nor incorrectly used, cannot be
used at all. If it should turn out that a private language can only consist of
such words, then such a language is absurd:

> It might be said: if you have given yourself a private definition of a
> word, then you must inwardly *undertake* to use the word in such-and-
> such a way. And how do you undertake that? (262)

> Let us imagine a table (something like a dictionary) that exists only
> in our imagination. A dictionary can be used to justify the translation
> of a word X by a word Y. But are we also to call it a justification if
> such a table is to be looked up only in the imagination? — "Well, yes;
> then it is a subjective justification." — But justification consists in
> appealing to something independent. — "But surely I can appeal from
> one memory to another. For example, I don't know if I have remem-
> bered the time of departure of a train right and to check it I call to
> mind how a page of the time-table looked. Isn't it the same here?" —
> No; for this process has got to produce a memory which is actually
> *correct*. If the mental image of the time-table could not itself be *tested*
> for correctness, how could it confirm the correctness of the first mem-
> ory? (As if someone were to buy several copies of the morning paper
> to assure himself that what it said was true.) Looking up a table in
> the imagination is no more looking up a table than the image of the
> result of an imagined experiment is the result of an experiment. (265)

> A definition surely serves to establish the meaning of a sign. — Well,
> that is done precisely by the concentration of my attention; for in this
> way I impress on myself the connexion between the sign and the
> sensation. — But "I impress it on myself" can only mean: this process
> brings it about that I remember the connexion *right* in the future. But
> in the present case I have no criterion of correctness. One would like
> to say: whatever is going to seem right to me is right. And that only
> means that here we can't talk about "right." (258)

When whatever seems right to me is right, then there is no longer any
distinction between right and wrong. Where there is neither right, nor
wrong, neither correct, nor incorrect, there is also no such thing as the *use*,
or *application* of a word. For to use a word is to *do* something with it,
something which can be taught and learned and which, therefore, must
allow of a right way and a wrong way. A private language is, therefore, an
absurdity, as is also the idea of a solipsistic subject, whose language constitutes the limits of the world. An absolute subject is in the privileged

position that whatever seems right to it is right, which only amounts to saying that such a metaphysical subject cannot set the bounds of meaning as it was supposed to. For the arbitrary decisionism of a solipsistic subject, there can be no rule, no border between sense and nonsense, meaning and meaninglessness.

What remains after the destruction of the idea of a private language? There remains only the ambiguous, perspectival languages of a plurality of existential interpreters. The meaning of these languages, however, is not grounded in their character as projects of a free and autonomous subjectivity, but rather, in their dependence upon each other; that is, in their necessary openness toward each other and their need for *mutual correction* and *intersubjective control*. Corrigibility and with it openness to another, to a principally unlimited *community of discourse* is, therefore, a condition of all meaningful speaking and thinking.[74]

It is important to see here that this community of discourse can itself not be closed, say, at its social, historical and cultural boundaries—we may imagine a "cultural solipsism"—without the difficulties of a private language returning all over again.[75] For the same reasons that there can be no private speakers, there can be no completely closed community. For meaning requires as a condition of its possibility an open horizon. In other words, *the only linguistic community there really is is a universal community*. What practice, what "form of life" such a universal community must have if it is not itself to become a sort of metacultural and metahistorical private speaker, is a question which will occupy us in the following chapter. At the moment let us note that Wittgenstein's thesis is that there is no meaningful speaking and thinking, be it ever so widely spread across the face of the earth and extended through history, which is not principally open to correction from without. To be, we might say, is to be capable of being other.

Philosophy as a Universal Discourse of Disclosure

In the *Tractatus*, philosophy had the task of showing the logical structure of the one, univocal and universal language which describes the world. Since, however, the logical form of description can itself not be described, Wittgenstein had to declare his own thinking to be nonsensical. Philosophy ended in a self-denying, positivistic critique of meaning:

The correct method in philosophy would really be the following: to say nothing except what can be said, i.e., propositions of natural science—i.e., something that has nothing to do with philosophy—and then, whenever someone else wanted to say something metaphysical, to demonstrate to him that he had failed to give a meaning to certain signs in his propositions. Although it would not be satisfying to the other person—he would not have the feeling that we were teaching him philosophy—*this* method would be the only strictly correct one. (*Tractatus* 6.53)

In the *Philosophical Investigations* Wittgenstein says:

We see that what we call "sentence" and "language" has not the formal unity that I imagined, but is the family of structures more or less related to one another. — But what becomes of logic now? Its rigour seems to be giving way here. — But in that case doesn't logic altogether disappear? — For how can it lose its rigour? Of course not by our bargaining any of its rigour out of it. — The *preconceived idea* of crystalline purity can only be removed by turning our whole examination round. (One might say: the axis of reference of our examination must be rotated, but about the fixed point of our real need.) (108)

In order to understand correctly Wittgenstein's later thought, it is important to note that the "examination" which is here spoken of is the *philosophical* examination; and that "our real need" to which Wittgenstein refers, is the need of *philosophical* thinking. For, in contrast to the *Tractatus*, it is no longer a matter of attempting "to reform" (132) our ordinary, non-philosophical language by means of constructing an ideal language. Wittgenstein now says:

Philosophy may in no way interfere with the actual use of language; it can in the end only describe it. For it cannot give it any foundation either.
It leaves everything as it is. (124)[76]

The "real need" which philosophy must satisfy is to keep *philosophy* itself from undertaking imperialistic reforms of language of the sort of which the *Tractatus* is a prime example. Its real critical task is no longer directed against ordinary language, but against philosophical abuses of ordinary language. This is "our real need."

We do not need to change ordinary language. Problems arise when we do not leave it as it is. That we do not leave language as it is, but always attempt to reform it in service of our own interests, is the source of "philosophical problems," not, as Rorty's pragmatism claims, the solution. Ideology, as we saw above, is a problem *in* thinking itself with which thinking alone can deal.

In the same way that the Augustinian picture of language, which Wittgenstein cites at the beginning of the *Philosophical Investigations*, inspired the attempt of the *Tractatus* to reform language according to a certain model, so, says Wittgenstein, all "philosophical problems" arise from attempts to *absolutize* a particular model of how language is used:

A *picture* held us captive. And we could not get outside it, for it lay in our language and language seemed to repeat it to us inexorably. (115)[77]

It is only as a philosophy which is eminently *self-critical*, that Wittgenstein's later thought can be properly understood:

What is your aim in philosophy? — To shew the fly the way out of the fly-bottle. (309)

For this reason there can be no *theory* of language-games. This would be no more than another attempt to reform language:

Our clear and simple language-games are not preparatory studies for a future regularization of language — as it were first approximations, ignoring friction and air-resistance. The language-games are rather set up as *objects of comparison* which are meant to throw light on the facts of our language by way not only of similarities, but also of dissimilarities. (130)

This does not imply, as might first appear, that there is simply no such thing as philosophy any more. There is, indeed, a specifically philosophical thinking, even if Wittgenstein does not allow us to call it *theoretical*. Wittgenstein does offer us, if not a "theory," then a "worldview." But it is a quite different worldview than that of the absolutized language-games which he criticizes; for these are nothing other than *ideologies*. Philosophy, therefore, is a thinking which *dis-closes* limits. Consequently, it is not boundary discourse which sets up a particular model of rationality and meaning as the only valid one. But neither is it a relativism which gives up its responsibility towards a universal linguistic community. Philosophy is the attempt to free itself, and thus the community as well, from its imprisonment in particular "pictures." Only in this way can a universal language be realized in a pluralistic situation.

Therefore, we may say that "philosophy," as it is understood by the later Wittgenstein, is the attempt to realize a universal language as a discourse of *dis-closure*.

RATIONALITY, IRRATIONALITY, AND OTHER-RATIONALITY

Any attempt to philosophically ground a universal discourse must confront and overcome the suspicion of ideology, not on the level of truth or falsity, but on the level of meaning. This is precisely what Peter Winch proposed to do for that discourse which claims to understand other cultures. If the understanding of other cultures is to be possible at all, then it has to be shown that the possibility of a *radically different thinking* belongs to the very conditions of the meaningfulness of our own speaking and thinking.

Winch's critique of the methods of the social sciences was that they covertly absolutize a discourse of matters of fact. This, however, is a discourse which necessarily presupposes fixed, objective criteria of reality and validity. Winch argued that the possibility of understanding another culture cannot be separated from the possibility of *criticizing* standards of rationality — theirs as well as our own! — and that the possibility of critique stands or falls with the demonstration that criteria of validity themselves can change, be extended and transformed, and that this transformation must itself be carried out discursively and rationally and not result from an irrational, non-discursive decision. If it cannot be shown that there is a level of discourse beyond that which articulates matters of fact within the horizon of fixed criteria, then the entire project of understanding in the social sciences ends in the trilemma of neither being able to use one's own criteria of rationality, nor those of the other culture, nor some third set of criteria belonging to none of the parties concerned. There would be no alternative other than the absurd and dangerous claim that whatever *we* say is right is right, a claim which constitutes apologetic universalism.

In his early thought, Wittgenstein carried out the critique of meaning by distinguishing between a discourse of matters of fact, a discourse which sets the boundaries of meaning and a discourse which expresses what lies beyond these boundaries. But because he was committed to a realistic semantics at that time, only discourse of matters of fact could be meaningful. He thereby excluded not only "mystical" statements, but also his own philosophical discourse from the realm of rationality. The critique of meaning paradoxically became its own victim and abolished itself. Rationality turned out to be grounded in an irrational decisionism.

If language does not receive its sense from reality, but rather from the uses which words have in various forms of life, then the critique of meaning must investigate forms of *communicative action*. It is no longer necessary to exclude philosophical and "mystical" discourse from the realm of meaning. Instead, we are led to investigate the *pragmatic* conditions of validity for different forms of discourse. The question becomes, What are the pragmatic conditions of validity for the various levels and forms of discourse? This is the question I will take up in the following chapter. Now I am concerned with formulating those categories in terms of which Wittgenstein's later thought may be said to have grounded the possibility of a universal discourse on the level of a theory of meaning.

With regard to the problem of categories in terms of which a theory of meaning grounds intercultural understanding, the important results of Wittgenstein's later philosophy may be formulated in the following way. Intersubjective corrigibility, which is *the* condition of the possibility of all rule following, and thus of all meaningful thinking and speaking, implies first that *rationality* is always complemented by its opposite, by the possibility of *irrationality*, and secondly, that rationality is always complemented by the possibility of an *other-rationality*, that is, by the *possibility* to learn that our interpretation of the rules is not the right one, that they can be followed in a different way, that they are not as we thought them to be. These three principles are constitutive of all meaning: *rationality*, *irrationality* and *other-rationality*.[78] These principles allow different levels of discourse to be distinguished and open up a global horizon. Consequently, they may be said to ground the diatopical model of communication and thus also the possibility of a discourse of disclosure as a universal discourse carrying rationality beyond the limitations imposed by logical and mythical discourse.[79]

The significance of Wittgenstein's thought for us is that it grounds the possibility and the necessity of a discourse which is capable of acknowledging other forms of thought; i.e., other ways of making the distinction between rational and irrational. Every language-game, every form of life, every culture has already made this distinction in its own way.[80] We cannot presuppose that our way of making this distinction is universally valid and proceed to apply it to another culture, without offending against the criterion of corrigibility and other-rationality. The result of applying our own standards to another culture can only be misunderstanding of the other; for, if we consider a language-game (= culture) as being constituted like a perimeter *around* a certain separation of the rational from the irrational, and then impose one circle upon another, rather like the duck upon the rabbit, the result is that certain sectors of reality which *for the other* are rational would fall automatically into sectors which *for us* are irrational. This can be represented in the following way:

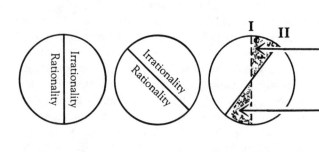

Part of what is rational for culture II falls into the area of irrationality for culture I.

Part of what is irrational for culture II falls into the area of rationality for culture I.

Culture I   Culture II   Imposition of I upon II

Diagram 2 — Imposition of Standards of Rationality

According to this method of applying standards of rationality, other cultures can only appear irrational. It is exactly this sort of mistake which

Winch accuses Evans-Pritchard—who exemplifies a typical form of ethnology and the social sciences—of having committed.

The category of other-rationality not only prevents us from imposing our standards upon other cultures, but more importantly, it opens a *horizon of encounter*, it *overcomes relativism* and it grounds, as we shall see in the following chapter, a diatopical hermeneutics in a *pragmatics of cosmotheandric solidarity*. For if other-rationality is a constitutive moment of our own thinking, we are ourselves only *rational* to the extent that we are prepared *to change* our interpretation of the way in which rationality is distinguished from irrationality. Language-games are so many different interpretations of meaning, *all* of which are mutually dependent upon each other for correction, if, that is, they are not to fall into the meaninglessness of a private language.

A *universal horizon of encounter* opens up—we are neither closed in upon ourselves in cultural solipsism, nor locked in competitive conflict with other cultures and religions. According to Winch, this is what ethnology and the social sciences, as a consequence of their decision for the exclusive validity of the scientific worldview, have not yet realized. Western secular science is, therefore, in danger of becoming an ideological private language. The same, of course, must be said for Christian theology. Winch's (and Wittgenstein's) argument strikes at the heart of secular and Christian universalism alike. At the same time, however, it grounds the possibility of a mutual appropriation of theology and secular universalism in a *new universalism*.

But again, Wittgenstein's *pragmatic* semantics has shown us that the possibility of non-ideological knowledge in a pluralistic situation, that is, of a truly *global* thinking, cannot be grounded in mere theory. The criterion of meaning which would allow us to determine if *other* systems of thought constitute, as Winch puts it, "a coherent universe of discourse like science," is a *global form of life*. For global thinking is a function of a *global praxis*. It remains now to specify what the *pragmatics* of such a global form of life may be.

4

The New Universalism

We saw in Chapter 1 that the internal fragmentation of the Western mind caused by the split between Christianity and Secularism and the external relativization of Western convictions of cultural supremacy caused by the opening up a global horizon has forced "theology" (no matter whose!) to admit that it can no longer realize its universal claims apologetically. In the global situation, theology cannot claim to speak to all men and women without first grounding and legitimating its right to do so. This changes the very nature of the task which theology had always set itself, namely, the "correlation" of revealed truth with the world. As we saw in the discussion of Paul Tillich, the question facing theology today is no longer how it can correlate its "answer" with the "question" found in the world, but rather, how it can correlate its answer to the many other answers which the history of religions presents. This requires an entirely different form of thinking from that required by the apologetic universalism which theology had become.

The attempt to found the possibility of a new, non-apologetic universalism, however, had to face the problem of ideology. For the collapse of apologetic universalism affects not only theology, but every general interpretation of reality. Universalist claims have become suspect no matter who makes them. The critique of ideology in its most radical form has undermined the self-evident validity of any world horizon, of any projection of unity, continuity and totality within which all entities have their being. The demonstration of the situational and historical conditionedness of thinking has established finitude, historicity, fallibility and relativity in the place of eternal, absolute being and truth and has definitively dispersed human projects of meaning into a situation of "radical pluralism."

In a radically pluralistic situation truth can only be discovered and guaranteed by universal *communication*. We do not first somehow come to possess *the* truth and then attempt to communicate it by whatever means prove most successful. This is the model underlying exclusivist, inclusivist and indifferentist programs for interreligious encounter. Instead, we enter into dialogue in order to arrive at the truth. Communicative action suddenly receives an epistemological priority and a foundational significance heretofore reserved for subjective experiences of insight, revelatory events and monological procedures of reality testing.

The idea of universal communication, as we saw in Chapter 2, may be explicated in terms of a *diatopical model* which allows us to distinguish *three levels of discourse*. The first level of discourse mediates communication *within* the boundaries of a particular lifeworld horizon, a particular culture or religion. Communicative action upon this level takes the form of "argumentation" about matters of fact. With regard to interreligious understanding, it conveys information *about* religion according to historical, phenomenological and comparative methods.

The second level of discourse establishes the boundaries of a lifeworld. Here communicative action sets criteria of meaning and validity, but cannot go beyond them. It limits itself to establishing the unity and continuity of a historical tradition by means of the retrieval of its founding texts and events. Panikkar calls this "diachronical" hermeneutics. As a model for interreligious dialogue, this form of discourse articulates itself in those theological programs which begin with the dogmatic priority of their own traditions and seek either to exclude or somehow include other traditions within the boundaries established by their own symbols and doctrines.

There is a third level of discourse, however, which operates within the space of encounter between different lifeworld horizons. It is upon this level of discourse, if at all, that universal communication and thus also interreligious dialogue may be possible. Panikkar refers to the mode of understanding which takes place upon this third level of discourse as "diatopical" hermeneutics, and I have termed it a discourse of "disclosure."

The diatopical model with its three levels of discourse received its philosophical foundation in Chapter 3 from the later thought of Ludwig Wittgenstein. Following Wittgenstein's pragmatic semantics, meaning may be seen as a rule-governed activity or a language-game. This implies, as Wittgenstein showed with regard to the possibility of a "private language," that linguistic meaning is consitituted by three distinct, but interdependent levels. First, there is the level of speech acts which make up the game being played at any given time and place; second, there is the level of the rules or criteria of validity which define the game; and third, since *believing* one is following a rule is not, and cannot be, the same as actually following the rule, there is a still higher level of discourse which compares, corrects and moves between language-games. With the critique of a private language Wittgenstein opened up the horizon of a rationality other than our own and thus the possibility of a discourse located *in between* lifeworlds, religions and cultures.

The idea of "rationality" no longer presents us with the image of a homogeneous, unified field surrounded on all sides by the irrational. There is now a third category, which necessarily constitutes the meaningfulness of every language-game, namely, "other-rationality." Other-rationality means, quite simply, that there is always another way of distinguishing rational from irrational, i.e., other rules and other forms of life. This other way of thinking, however, is not something exotic; rather, it is one of the necessary conditions of the meaningfulness of our own speaking and thinking—indeed, of all communication whatever.

A language-game is structurally similar to a cultural "code" or a world-view and thus we may say that just as no language-game is closed to rein-terpretation of its rules, so is no religion or culture a universe closed in upon itself. So long as it is meaningful at all, it is constituted by a level of discourse which articulates the possibility of it being "played" differently. In terms of the problem of objectivism verses relativism in intercultural understanding raised by Peter Winch, it is because a language-game, and thus also by analogy a religion or culture, is *internally* open to other-ration-ality that it is possible for us to *learn* other language-games (religions, worldviews), to *participate* in them and, through participation, to extend and reinterpret our own. The idea of other-rationality is, therefore, not merely a name for a *problem*—that is, the problem of alien and alienated meaning—but also a *solution* to the problem in the sense that it grounds the possibility to understand a radically different lifeworld.

From the discussion of Wittgenstein's pragmatic semantics it also became clear that understanding depends upon communicative *practice*. We can say something only because we also *do* something when we speak. Indeed, once it has become clear that the meaning of what we say is not grounded in a reference relation to an objective world, it also becomes clear that meaning cannot occur except as *communicative action*. A realistic semantics allows a private speaker to know how a statement might be ver-ified monologically—that is, independent of intersubjective corrigibility—reducing thereby what is right to whatever such a speaker says (to himself) is right. In a pragmatic semantics meaning is founded in communicative actions and these activities are the *pragmatic conditions* of meaning.

The "pragmatic turn" in the theory of meaning implies not only the aforementioned methodological priority of communication, but also an epistemological priority of *praxis*. In a foundational sense, therefore, think-ing is acting. Thus we become obliged to specify the ways enactment must occur if discourse is to be meaningful, communication possible and knowl-edge well-founded. The task of grounding intercultural communication and the interreligious dialogue is fulfilled, therefore, only when the *pragmatic conditions* of a universal discourse have been specified. This means that the demonstration of the possibility of a discourse of disclosure needs now to be completed by showing the *pragmatic conditions*, which, in Wittgensteinian terms, make up a global form of life.

We must begin from the insight that if a universal discourse in which different cultures and religions may communicate is at all possible, it will be grounded neither in subjective certainties nor in objective reality, but in the pragmatic conditions of a global form of life. As we saw in the discussion of Wittgenstein's later philosophy, concepts are learned when one is taught a practice, a technique, a way of doing things. This links language-games with concrete social institutions and takes them out of the ethereal realm of Platonic ideas. As Wittgenstein points out in *Philosophical Investigations*:

> It is not possible that there should have been only one occasion on which someone obeyed a rule. It is not possible that there should have been only one occasion on which a report was made, an order given or understood; and so on. — To obey a rule, to make a report, to give an order, to play a game of chess, are *customs* (uses, institutions). (199)

To say that human actions cannot be done only once is to say that they are constituted by rules, patterns and scripts which enable repetitions. Indeed, apart from constant reproduction in human action, such "things" as games and institutions would not exist at all. To say, furthermore, that they are rule-governed activities is to admit the possibility of errors as well as corrigibility, which, as we saw in Wittgenstein's critique of a private language, necessarily implies interaction among a plurality of speakers. Meaningful actions are therefore necessarily communicative actions, or at least, are embedded in contexts of communicative action. For the possibility of correction from without rests upon the possibility of communication. How can an actor follow a rule, commit an error and be corrected apart from communicative interaction?

Every society is made up of an entire network of rules, customs, institutions, situation definitions and "frames" of action which are, as Wittgenstein points out, never enacted merely once, but are repeated and reproduced under conditions of intersubjective corrigibility in daily life.[1] Together they make up that implicit, unthematic "knowledge" which serves as the background against which the various activities of everyday life may take place. Even if we are not playing a game of chess or making a report at the moment, we "know" what it means to play a game and what sort of action counts as making a report; that is, we know what is expected of us and what we expect of others when we are engaged in these activities.

We may speak of this background knowledge as the *horizon* of our lifeworld. It is within this field of possible activities that the language-games which belong to our cultural world are located and held-in-ready for the occasion when we need them. In our everyday communicative interactions we are aware of the lifeworld horizon as a self-evident, undifferentiated and all-encompassing worldview. We are also, as we have seen in the discussion of other-rationality, more or less aware of the possibility of transcending the boundaries of this worldview, of speaking and understanding in completely new and unforeseen ways, although this awareness is usually repressed and when manifest, then often as a vague source of anxiety.[2]

In all speech acts the implicit knowledge of the lifeworld horizon is not only presupposed but also more or less explicitly communicated and "enacted." Consequently, normal linguistic interactions of everyday communication serve not only to meet our immediate needs by transferring information and coordinating action among individuals, but more generally and deeply they reproduce an entire cultural "reality." Communicative actions perform educating, socializing, enculturating and legitimating functions. For it is by means of communicative action that individuals are provided with opportunities and patterns for the development of a personal identity and for integration into social groups. Furthermore, in order to insure the solidarity of the group as a whole, individuals are brought to participate in the communicative reproduction and transmission of a general cultural identity, a "tradition." Becoming a psychologically mature person, a member of a society, understanding what is being said and in turn being able to speak in a variety of personal and social contexts is, therefore, a matter of participating in communicative action not merely upon the level of the transfer of information, but also upon levels of socialization, social integration and cultural reproduction. Communication, therefore, is a multileveled practice of *participation*.[3]

Just as participation in a game of chess, for example, means that one is able to perform certain activities, so does participation in communication have its pragmatic conditions. And just as participation in a game of chess also means participating in the general activity of "playing a game," so does participation in any particular language-game imply the performance of communicative activities of a more general nature. My thesis is that the general pragmatic conditions of communicative action, that is, those activities in which we must participate if we are to communicate at all, are patterned according to the three levels of discourse which the diatopical structure of language-games articulates.

Before more is said about the general pragmatic conditions of communication, some terminological clarification is necessary. I have spoken of "levels of discourse," "language-games," "speech acts" and "communicative actions." How are these the same and how are they different? Meaning, as Wittgenstein tells us, is use. A word, a sign, a gesture, an object are not meaningful in themselves, but only within a rule-governed activity. As rule governed, such activities are internally related to the possibility of error and correction and thus to communication. This is communicative action. This is also what is called a language-game. Within communicative action, or a language-game, the smallest unit of meaning may be termed a speech act. As meaningful, rule-governed, communicative activity, every speech act is, however, also a language-game, although a language-game may consist of many speech acts. Every promise, for example, is a language-game, but any particular game of promising may consist of many different speech acts. What I have called a *level of discourse*, however, is not itself a language-game. It is a general structure constitutive of all speech acts. This does not mean that under certain conditions it cannot also become a language-game in its own right. Whenever a level of discourse becomes *thematic* in concrete speech acts it is also a language-game—for example, the game of argumentation, of proclamation or of disclosure.

With this terminological clarification in mind, let us return to the task of explicating the pragmatic conditions of universal communication. As we have seen, every language-game consists first of a set of "moves," secondly, of the rules which govern those moves. The rules define what is rational and irrational for any language-game and serve as criteria according to which speech acts made within that game can be considered valid. Third, a language-game is also constituted by the possibility of transforming its rules in the encounter with other language-games. On a certain level of generality, therefore, it may be said that every speech act, regardless of what language-game is being played, participates in all three levels of discourse. Explicitly and implicitly communicative action makes claims about states of affairs, proclaims boundaries and opens up a universal horizon of encounter and disclosure.

As action, it was said, communication is governed by rules which may be termed pragmatic conditions, as opposed to merely formal, cognitive conditions of meaning. It is by means of the pragmatic conditions that what is said upon the three levels of discourse becomes not only meaningful but also *convincing*, for they function as criteria of validity. Therefore, in the following discussion of the pragmatic conditions of communication I shall speak of a "pragmatics of convincement." I choose, following Panikkar, the old word "convincement" in order to make clear that I am not referring merely to that subjective state of mind known as being convinced, but rather to the fact that the subjective state of *being convinced*, and the intersubjective procedures for *becoming convinced and convincing others*, and also that which is held to be true, *conviction* itself, all hang together in specific modes of participation which make up the pragmatic conditions for the three levels of discourse constitutive of communicative action.[4]

Different discourses are convincing in different ways and lead to different kinds of conviction. Internal, logical discourse, for example, presupposes pragmatic conditions of convincement in terms of, among other things, procedures for verification. What amounts to a convincing "argument"—regardless of whether it is an argument about empirical matters of fact or formal consistency—may be fully unconvincing in another form of discourse—for example, in mythical discourse, where the kind of participation constituted by "argumentation" has no meaning. The reason for this is not that the argument isn't sound, but that the pragmatics of convincement in these forms of discourse are different. Whereas one partner in communicative interaction may be playing the game of argumentation, the other may be concerned with the proclamation of the very boundaries of discourse, as, for example, in the case of the so-called non-verifiability of metaphysical, ethical and aesthetic statements, a problem which plagues philosophy still today. Asymmetry in the pragmatics of convincement and consequent failure of communication depends, therefore, less upon *what* is being said then upon *how* it is being said. Much confusion could have been avoided if this "discursive difference" had not been "forgotten."

To illustrate this, let us recall the example of the ethnologist faced with talk about witches among the members of the ethnic group he or she is investigating. Within a certain worldview it is understandable that a misfortune, such as the sudden collapse of a house, can be attributed to witchcraft. In this society we may assume that there is also a relatively fixed set of procedures by which the assertion that someone is a witch can be verified – for example, by means of an oracle. Speakers making assertions about such matters and attempting to ascertain what is the case, can be said to participate in a community of argumentation constituted by procedures of verification. Structurally and pragmatically the game of argumentation they are playing is no different from that of anyone in any culture who is concerned with settling matters of fact and coordinating action for the satisfaction of everyday needs. It is also in principle no different from the activities of the Western scientist who employs the refined methods of verification (perhaps better termed "falsification") which his or her culture provides.

The transcultural, structural generality of the game of argumentation accounts at once for the fact that when it comes to many aspects of everyday life members of different cultures can readily "understand" one another, as well as the fact that upon a certain level understanding breaks down. Confronted, for example, with the objection of the anthropologist that the entire language-game of determining who is a witch is meaningless, since magical causes do not exist and since it is demonstrable that the house collapsed because mice had eaten through the supporting ropes, only elicits the further question of why mice ate through the ropes of this particular man's house at this particular time. The anthropologist might respond that this particular constellation of events is to be accounted for by the climatically conditioned scarcity of the normal food sources for mice and also by the proximity of this particular house to the forest and so on. The native might accept all these facts but not see their explanatory value, for it can still be asked why they all occurred at this particular time and place.

Clearly, at a certain point in the discussion about matters of fact participation in the game of argumentation breaks down and the presuppositions of a worldview in which magic, witches and oracles have a place, or do not, become explicitly thematized. When this happens the level of discourse changes from an internal, logical discourse governed by practices of argumentation to a mythical, boundary discourse governed by practices of proclamation and conversion. The irresolvable conflict which manifested itself within the game of argumentation thus reveals itself to be rooted in the structural embeddedness of argumentative pragmatics within boundary discourse. Participation in this discourse is that of participation in a cultural tradition, a community of narration, proclamation and witness. For whether they intend it or not, both anthropologist and native would soon find themselves attempting to *convert* the other to their respective worldviews.[5] The fact that conversion is possible and is practiced implicitly or explicitly in almost all intercultural encounters is, again, based upon the cross-cultural, structural generality of second-level boundary discourse.

If the discussion concerned more serious matters as, for example, in the case mentioned in the previous chapter of the Native Americans of the Northwest in their dispute with government and industry over development and exploitation of natural gas in the Yukon, the discourse of conversion, the clash of worldviews, would quickly become a dangerous test of power between communities and/or nations. Communicative solidarity breaks down and, as the history of colonialism has shown, the only way to avoid a violent conflict of cultures at this point lies in opening up a third level of discourse wherein conversion may be experienced and practiced as a method of understanding and attaining consensus. Participation in this third level of discourse is, I will argue, that of an unlimited, or *cosmotheandric* solidarity constituting a universal community of communication.

This is a thesis, however, which must be argued for because every language-game is structured by all three levels of discourse. Therefore it is possible for one level of discourse to become thematic while the others melt into the background. This allows universalist claims to be made for argumentative and proclamative discourse as well as for disclosive discourse. In the place of the naive objectivism of the sort Winch criticized, there has arisen a more sophisticated attempt to universalize argumentative discourse upon the basis of Wittgenstein's pragmatic semantics itself. With the theory of communicative action of Jürgen Habermas and the ethics of discourse of Karl-Otto Apel, first-level discourse about matters of fact again becomes the model of all meaningful speech. For proclamative boundary discourse, on the other hand, universalist claims have been proposed by the philosophical hermeneutics of Hans-Georg Gadamer. The task of grounding intercultural communication and the interreligious dialogue in the pragmatic conditions of a universal discourse requires, therefore, answering the question of whether or not the pragmatics of argumentative or of proclamative discourse can in fact be universalized; or if it is not much rather upon the basis of a discourse of disclosure alone that communicative universality is to be achieved.

Since the diatopical model leads us to postulate only disclosive discourse as universal, the demonstration of the *limitations* of argumentative and proclamative discourse by means of a *critique of the programs of an ethics of discourse and a philosophical hermeneutics* will ground the application of this model to problems of interreligious communication. I will argue that the universalist claims of the ethics of discourse and philosophical hermeneutics are untenable and that although argumentative, proclamative and disclosive discourses are structurally constitutive of all communication, they are not equally universal, but are related to one another in such a way that the very meaning of argumentation depends upon proclamation, whereas the meaning of proclamation in turn depends upon disclosure. My thesis is that global communication can only be grounded upon the level of disclosure.

THE UNIVERSALITY OF ARGUMENTATION

Much of our everyday communication is meaningful because it stands in relation to reason giving or *argumentation*. Common sense tells us that what we say is rational because it can be argued for; that is, it may be supported by giving reasons or grounds when it is criticized. Indeed, the activity of doing so is precisely what we mean by a rational activity. If we follow Habermas, "argumentation" may be defined as:

> that type of speech in which participants thematize contested validity claims and attempt to vindicate or criticize them through arguments. An *argument* contains reasons or grounds that are connected in a systematic way with the *validity claim* of a problematic expression. The "strength" of an argument is measured in a given context by the soundness of the reasons; that can be seen in, among other things, whether or not an argument is able to convince the participants in a discourse, that is, to motivate them to accept the validity claim in question. Against this background, we can also judge the rationality of a speaking and acting subject by how he behaves as a participant in argumentation . . . . there is, on the side of persons who behave rationally, a willingness to expose themselves to criticism and, if necessary, to participate properly in argumentation. In virtue of their criticizability, rational expressions also admit of improvement; we can correct failed attempts if we can successfully identify our mistakes. The concept of *grounding* is interwoven with that of *learning*.[6]

Argumentative discourse, as it is here defined, is constituted by a series of pragmatic conditions the first and most general of which may be said to be that speech acts are meaningful because they can be either true or false, right or wrong, correct or incorrect, authentic or inauthentic, or in general either valid or invalid. Discourse articulated between these dyadic opposites inevitably has the performative function of *raising a claim to validity with regard to a specific criterion*; for example, with regard to the criterion of truth, or the criterion of normative rightness, or the criterion of authenticity. Apart from criteria of validity, *which themselves are not the object of dispute*, it would be impossible to decide whether a given utterance is valid or not. But it would be equally impossible to raise and settle a claim to validity, if the criteria were not *commonly accepted* and the same for all parties to the dispute.

For this reason it is justified to refer to argumentation as that discourse *internal* to a specific language-game. For it is only *within* the established framework of a rule governed activity that criteria are unproblematically given. Therefore, Habermas can say that "Participants in interaction cannot carry out speech acts that are effective for coordination unless they *impute* to everyone involved an intersubjectively *shared* [emphasis added] life-world."[7] And in another place Habermas defines "communication" as the relation between a speaker and hearer "who coordinate their plans for action by coming to an understanding about something in the world," and who consequently "move *within* the horizon of their *common* lifeworld" [emphasis added].[8] Furthermore, that criteria become effective in communication through arguments is the reason why this discourse may be termed *logical*. For logic is concerned with the validity of arguments, although in this context concern is much less with the formal consistency of propositions, which indeed is one form of argumentation, than with the pragmatic conditions of argumentative discourse in general, that is, with what might be termed an "informal logic."[9]

Argumentative discourse makes claims to validity, claims which can be criticized, vindicated and, if need be, modified. These claims, however, are made not only with regard to criteria of *truth* for what is said, but also for the *correctness* of the way it is said—that is, the normative rightness of the particular "move" within the language-game which is being played, and also for the *authenticity* of the intention of the speaker.[10] Any speech act whatever—for example, "The cat is on the mat," or "The universe is governed by physical laws"—claims not only that what is said is true with regard to criteria of truth, but also correctly said with regard to the normative rules of the language-game being played at the moment, and finally, sincerely said with regard to the intention of the speaker.

Apart from raising constative, normative and intentional claims to validity, argumentation is constituted secondly by pragmatic procedures of criticizing and vindicating these claims—that is, by what I shall term *procedures of verification*. Claims may be contested, criticized and vindicated by means of giving reasons. Depending upon the context and upon what is said, the procedures of verification may be very different.

Depending upon whether the statement "The cat is on the mat" occurs within actual experience or within a novel, it must be validated in different ways. In one case this is done by simply pointing to the cat and in the other by means of textual analysis. In the case of the statement that the universe is governed by physical laws, still other means of criticism and validation are required. It is obviously no longer sufficient merely to point to the "regular" movements of the heavens; nor is a textual analysis, say of the holy scriptures, appropriate. Here sophisticated theoretical and empirical methods must be employed.

With regard to the normative claim of the speech act in question, to say that the cat is on the mat is appropriate and meaningful only within certain language-games. Disputes about just what game is being played or should be played are, upon a certain level of generality, disputes about the definition of the situation, of the "frame" of communicative action. To criticize claims of this sort and to vindicate them requires other procedures than simply pointing to facts or testing empirical hypotheses.

Finally, it is always possible that a speaker is lying or otherwise disguising his or her intentions, even if this occurs unconsciously. Contesting and vindicating claims to authenticity require, therefore, still different procedures; for example, behavior consistent with a claim over a long period of time or even a lie-detector test. If someone declares their love for me, I might be disposed to accept this without further ado, or in case of doubt, to wait and see if they consistently act in a caring, supporting and affectionate way. In sum: Argumentative discourse may be said to be that discourse constituted by the making of claims to cognitive truth, normative rightness and subjective authenticity; claims which are subject to procedures of verification.

Beyond making contestable validity claims within the framework of shared criteria and procedures of verification, argumentative discourse thirdly is made possible by the pragmatic condition of being action undertaken with the *aim of establishing consensus* or agreement. To give reasons for what one says when criticized is an altogether different activity from applying force in order to secure acceptance. It belongs to the pragmatics of argumentation that one takes a step back from the pressure of action. One takes up a hypothetical attitude wherein the rejection of an argument is met, countered and overcome not by the use of coercion or violence, but only by means of another argument. Achieving consensus, therefore, is a result of insight into the validity of the claims and not the result of any external forces which might appear to bring about "unity."

A fourth pragmatic condition of argumentative discourse arises from the fact that validity claims are revised in light of the "facts." As we saw, critique and vindication of claims to validity are carried out in procedures of verification which might be called "reality testing." This gives argumentative discourse a specific *temporal orientation towards the future* and a specific dynamic of *progressive learning*. Past knowledge is revised in terms of present experience with a view towards future "completion." There occurs an accumulation of experience and knowledge. This teleological orientation may become thematic and raised to the level of myth, as in the case of modern Western scientific rationalism with its myth of progress, but it must not be forgotten that it is a condition of argumentative discourse as such operative also in cultures which do not believe in "critique" and "progress."

The fifth pragmatic condition of argumentation—namely, that claims to validity must be made against a potentially *universal community of communication*—follows from the fact that argumentation cannot secure truth apart from achieving a consensus. Once a naive objectivism has been overcome and it has become clear that there is no court of appeal outside language, objective reality manifests itself as agreement within language.

As Peter Winch put it, it is not reality which gives language sense, but what is real and what is unreal shows itself *in* the sense that language has. This well-known result of the linguistic critique of objectivism would carry with it the relativistic and even solipsistic consequence that truth is whatever we say it is, were it not for the proviso that "we" involves all possible partners in communicative interaction and not merely our group, party, nation, culture or age. Consensus may be said to guarantee truth only when it is achieved within an unlimited or "ideal" community of communication. For only in terms of such a community is the criterion of intersubjective corrigibility respected.

The requirement of universal communicative solidarity follows also from the fact that since argumentative discourse is progressive learning and thus open to revision and modification of claims, no partial consensus at any given time and place can claim truth pure and simple. In order to avoid relativism and denial of the very meaning of truth as universal validity, it becomes necessary to postulate that the pragmatic procedures of the actual discourse we are at any given time involved in are such that what is claimed and agreed to by means of them is subject to critique and vindication within a universal community of communication.

On the basis of these five pragmatic conditions of argumentative discourse, Habermas and Apel have asserted that argumentation is the only truly *rational* and *universal* form of discourse. For there is nothing which cannot be made the subject of a claim to validity and no action which cannot be argumentatively criticized and legitimated. Furthermore, since argumentation necessarily presupposes shared criteria of validity, any attempt to place the criteria themselves in question reaffirms what it wishes to deny and thus contradicts itself. This leads to the conviction that to speak at all is to speak argumentatively. And since argumentation is constituted by pragmatic rules, these offer themselves as the norms of an *ethics of discourse* prescribing those actions which constitute a universal community of communication. This means that questions of intercultural understanding and interreligious dialogue can only be rationally settled upon the level of argumentative discourse and those actions which constitute it. It remains to see if this is indeed the case, or if the program of universal argumentation does not run up against insurmountable limitations at precisely the moment it attempts to become a global form of life.

The universalist claim for argumentative discourse has been most clearly and radically formulated under the title of an "ethics of discourse" by Karl-Otto Apel.[11] His thesis is that "the *rational argumentation* that is presupposed not only in every science but also in every discussion of a problem, in itself presupposes the validity of universal, ethical norms."[12] For Apel, the *situation of argumentation* is an *a priori* condition of the possibility of any meaningful human action (including speech acts) and a foundation of universally valid ethical norms. Let us look again at what exactly the "situation of argumentation" is.

It is the situation in which individuals and groups express their needs by means of *assertions*. To make an assertion is a complex matter. It includes, as we have seen, that one makes a claim to truth (Habermas would add the claims to truthfulness and rightness also), not only against the community in which one at any given time and place is involved, but against an unlimited community in which all possible objections and counter arguments are taken into account. To make an assertion means that one is prepared to justify it, to give reasons for it and to accept counter assertions as capable of refuting it. One must be willing to withdraw it and revise it until a consensus has been reached. Furthermore, it implies that one already "has" certain concepts, such as "assertion," "truth," "meaning," "contradiction," and so on as part of a commonly shared horizon of meaning within which argumentation can occur. If all this cannot be presupposed for all parties in a dispute, then there can be no meaningful argumentation and consequently no real dispute, which of course implies that there can occur no rational process of resolving a conflict.

Now if the situation of argumentation is to be a necessary presupposition of *all* rational discourse, then we have the right to assume that it must also ground the possibility of *arguing about argumentation* itself—that is, about what counts as "rational," as an "argument," as an "assertion" and so on. We saw above that the conflict of interpretations on the level of worldviews creates a situation in which a consensus about the meaning of concepts such as "truth," "reality," "assertion" and so on cannot be presupposed.[13] Once it becomes clear that the real problems of communication are located at the level of *disputed criteria* and not on the level of matters of fact, then the rules governing argumentation can no longer be presupposed, for they themselves are in question.[14] Can a conflict about the rules of argumentation be resolved argumentatively?

Argumentative discourse gives reasons. Reasons, however, are recognizable *as such* only in terms of criteria of validity and procedures of verification which relate validity claims to the criteria so that these claims may be seen to agree or disagree with the criteria. Giving reasons, therefore, is a communicative activity which is only possible when all parties to a dispute accept the criteria of validity as unproblematically given. One cannot argue for or against the validity of the criteria themselves. For this either begs the question by appealing to the very criteria which are in need of foundation, or it presupposes another set of criteria to be commonly accepted. That we cannot argue about argumentation itself in no way implies, as Apel asserts, the universality of argumentative discourse. On the contrary, it is precisely here that the limitations of argumentation become apparent.

To limit the scope of communicative action to argumentative discourse in a situation characterized by radical pluralism and dis-continuity on the level of criteria amounts to blinding out the real problem, since criteria of validity would never be called into question but would be reaffirmed in every argumentative attempt to relativize them. This is a refusal to admit the possibility of rationally dealing with conflicts arising from radical differences in worldviews. It also denies the possibility of there being other rules of argumentation, of there being an other-rationality. According to this view, if rules enabling argumentation cannot be presupposed, then there would be no rules governing argumentation at all, and, since argumentation *is* a rule-governed activity, there would be no argumentation, but only non-discursive violence. That this, indeed, is the consequence of the attempt to universalize argumentation may be seen by examining the program of an ethics of discourse.

Wolfgang Kuhlmann, who has devoted an important book to the problem of the communication community as a foundation for ethics, summarizes the ethics of discourse under four norms.[15] First, insofar as we speak at all we are obliged to be rational; that is, we act not arbitrarily and blindly but upon the basis of reasons.[16] This obligation follows from the commitment which a speaker makes to the pragmatic conditions of the possibility of speech itself. To enter into discourse is already to accept as binding the conditions enabling it.[17] Not to do this, for example, by making claims which do not admit of argumentative verification, amounts to what may be called a "pragmatic contradiction"; that is, contradicting what one does (speaking) by what one says.[18] To commit a pragmatic contradiction is tantamount to excluding oneself from the human community which is linguistically constituted.

This implies, secondly, that we ought to enter into argumentative discourse with the community from which alone we can obtain the assurance that the reasons we have are indeed rational, and not merely the mad ravings of a private language.[19] This can only be a universal and unlimited community of communication.

Third, argumentation and attaining a consensus is not merely a theoretical matter among those who principally have the same interests and find themselves in the same social and economic position of equality, but a matter of cooperation among men and women with very different interests and under conditions of inequality. Therefore, we ought to seek not only a theoretical consensus but also a practical consensus about how we are to solve problems external to the situation of argumentation which impinge upon it.[20]

This leads directly to the fourth and most important rule, which says that we ought to do what is practically necessary in order to make argumentation possible. This rule carries with it the recognition that in the actual community at any given time the real situation is such that we are prevented from building a consensus by means of free and undistorted procedures of argumentation. Therefore, we are obliged, in the name of argumentation, *to suspend argumentation and act strategically* so that argumentation becomes possible.[21]

This fourth rule, we claim, reveals a difficulty in the program of the ethics of discourse. It is the view of the ethics of discourse that human community—and thus human existence—is based upon collective actions which are only legitimate when they arise from a consensus about needs and values, and that consensus can only be attained through the mediation of claims of all sorts via argumentation. The thesis is that actions are reasonable and legitimate to the extent that they are arrived at by means of argumentation. For argumentation alone can insure that our proposals for action are meaningful and true. Argumentation alone can guarantee that we do not think and do merely what *we* (as individuals or limited community) *believe* to be right—which would amount to reverting to the ideological position of the private speaker. This presupposes that argumentation is, in fact, possible, and that the social and political conditions enabling it exist.

But if the conditions allowing discourse are not in fact realized because of the conflict of radically different horizons of meaning and value, then we cannot communicate on the level of argumentative discourse at all. Consequently, we cannot reach a consensus about how to realize the conditions of argumentation. This, however, means that at the very moment when argumentation should mediate universal communication, we are forced out of the situation of argumentation altogether and determined to "speak" a discourse which sets boundaries absolutely. At a certain stage in every dispute, therefore, first-level discourse becomes inevitably replaced by a boundary discourse which sets the limits, the criteria of what counts as an argument, as true, real and meaningful. But since the theory of communicative action and the ethics of discourse do not provide for the possibility of any other form of discourse than argumentation, establishing the conditions of argumentation cannot be carried out discursively. Where argumentation stops, strategic action begins.

Stated as a dilemma: According to the ethics of discourse, we can act ethically if the conditions of discourse (as argumentation) are already realized. But if they were already realized, there would be no real ethical problem, for the ideal would have been achieved and all *basic* conflicts overcome. If, however, the ideal, unlimited community of discourse has not been achieved and there is, therefore, a serious threat to meaning and, therefore, also an ethical problem of what we should do to achieve it, then it would seem that the ethics of discourse cannot help us, for no consensus could *argumentatively* be reached about proposed courses of action. Every individual and group would be thrown back upon unilateral decisions to legitimate its policies and programs.[22] But such a decisionism, which plays directly into the hands of the postmodern theorists who quite explicitly base reason upon power, is precisely what the ethics of discourse was designed to avoid.

At the very moment when argumentative discourse is called upon to establish universal communication, it breaks down and transgresses the boundaries of argumentation. Indeed, since the theory of communicative action and the ethics of discourse have absolutized argumentation and not included the possibility of a higher level of discourse within their purview, they must at this point endorse transgressing the bounds of language altogether. A universal discourse, therefore, must be more than argumentation. If we wish, nevertheless, to hold on to the basic insight of the ethics of discourse (namely, that to speak at all is to accept as binding the conditions enabling speech — that is, those communicative actions which are forms of participation in a truly universal community of communication), then the fourth norm must be modified such that it does not allow the suspension of communication while still prescribing "strategic" action.

The question now becomes: What sort of action would be admissible *within* an ethics of discourse which is no longer merely an ethics of argumentation? The mere claim that we are acting in the name of the universal community is as good and as bad as any other claim used to legitimate political or social action. Why is *this* particular claim better than, say, the claim to act in the name of conscience, or of God, or of the superior race or whatever? And if, as it stands, it is not different, what would make it a claim not merely about our subjective view of what the universal community requires of us, but a discursively legitimated claim of the universal community itself? As we shall presently see, this is the question which philosophical hermeneutics proposes to answer.

Before examining the claim to universality which hermeneutics has raised for second-level, boundary discourse, let us summarize the results of our discussion. So long as the ethics of discourse claims the right to transgress the bounds of communication and "go behind" language, it can give us no guidelines for our action, but only take effect after non-discursive, that is, irrational and therefore violent action has established the social and political conditions of its possibility. This in turn means that discourse is not grounded, as both Habermas and Apel assert, in the situation of argumentation free from all constraint, but in irrational and violent force. We can *talk* now because we have *fought* in the past. It is the reason of power which grounds the power of reason.

The attempt to universalize argumentative discourse leaves us with a vision of a rational world based upon irrational force.[23] In this view, there is only rationality and irrationality, but no other-rationality. In terms of the language-game model of linguisticality, this means that one particular interpretation of the rules of discourse is set up as the rules themselves, which plunges us directly into the absurdity of a private language. Logical absurdity is pragmatic violence. For we may understand violence as that which closes off and limits the principally universal horizon of communication; as that which draws in the boundaries of the "hermeneutical circle" so as to exclude "other-rationality."[24]

It is never merely the *alienation* (Marx) or *repression* (Freud) of the "self" which constitutes the primary form of irrationality and violence, as Habermas and Apel would have us believe, but the exclusion and suppression of the "other," who threatens our lifeworld with total transformation. No *theoretical explanation* of the causes of distorted communication based upon Marxist and/or Freudian models, therefore, can solve this problem, for such explanatory theories and the therapeutic or revolutionary strategies derived from them presuppose that the problem is the *alienated self* and not the *excluded other*. These theories allow only the secondary effects upon the self of the primary violence of the exclusion of the other to come into view. Consequently, they can offer no more than treatments of the symptoms of violence and are therefore not protected from their own violence. Recovery of the alienated or repressed self inevitably becomes an attempt to reconstruct and reaffirm the one-sided self-assertion of our own crippled life-world, even if this project is undertaken in the name of reason, or of the human species.

This is what lies behind Gadamer's criticisms of Habermas and Apel. Our hermeneutical circle is not really broadened by a critical social science which absolutizes Western models of suspicion. The theoretical subject who employs a critical social science and who claims the right and the ability to go behind language in order to liberate it finds itself necessarily trapped within the very constraints it sought to escape.[25] Here, the claim to universality remains unfounded.

THE UNIVERSALITY OF HERMENEUTICS

Since Gadamer does not explicitly relate his hermeneutics to Wittgenstein, it is necessary to show how this might be done in order to establish the relevance of philosophical hermeneutics to the diatopical model of communication.

In order to link up Wittgenstein's thought with philosophical hermeneutics, I will argue that the structure of language-games is similar to that of the hermeneutical circle (as conceived by Gadamer). Just as the rules of a language-game make certain speech acts possible, so does the projection of a totality of meaning open up a domain within which interpretation may operate. This basic analogy will provide an opportunity to explicate the pragmatic conditions of that form of discourse which sets the boundaries of language-games and projects horizons of meaning. At the same time, I will claim that just as for Wittgenstein the possibility of a universal language rests upon a specifically "philosophical" language-game which overcomes one-sided attempts to reform language and restrict meaning to one particular set of rules, so also, for Gadamer, the universality claimed for philosophical hermeneutics can only be achieved when hermeneutical discourse becomes able to overcome arbitrary limitations of the *scope* of the hermeneutical circle. This will put us in a position to ask whether Gadamer's program of a philosophical hermeneutics actually fulfills the task of a universal discourse, or whether unlimited communication and intercultural understanding do not call for a still wider conception of discourse than Gadamer has proposed: namely, a discourse of disclosure.

Let us begin by asking: What is the structure of language-games? For Wittgenstein, as we saw, language-games are "games" and can be "played" because they are rule-governed activities necessarily constituted by the fundamental distinction between actually following the rules and merely *believing* that one is following the rules. In other words, it belongs to the logical — and ontological — structure of language-games that the rules actually constitutive of the game are never flatly identical with the current *interpretation* of the rules.

For this very reason language-games are essentially *open* to interpretation and can change; indeed, it is their very nature to be constituted by an "interpretation," that is, a *projection* of possibilities which could be otherwise and never a deterministically fixed behavior pattern. Were this not so, it would be meaningless and impossible to ask and answer the question, What game are we playing? For there could be no other game. That we can — indeed, must — ask this question is based upon the constitutive "other-rationality" or "plurivocity" of every language-game, that is, upon the fact that the game can be played differently. From the point of view of a philosophical hermeneutics, we can say that it is other-rationality which grounds the hermeneutical structure of understanding.[26]

In the classical formulation of the hermeneutical circle, understanding moves from the whole to the part and from the part back to the whole. Just as every word in a sentence is understood in terms of a projection of the meaning of the whole sentence, so the entire sentence is understood from every particular word. Similarly, every sentence in a text can only receive its meaning from a projection of the meaning of the text as a whole, while the meaning of the whole text depends upon the particular sentences it is made up of. And finally, just as every text can itself only be understood within its context — that is, the entire lifeworld, age, or culture within which it arises — so also can a cultural epoch only be understood from its concrete representations in texts and artifacts of all sorts.

Within a given whole, however, the parts are not all equally significant. Not every word in a sentence or every sentence in a text has the same importance. The whole is greater than the sum of the parts precisely because the *order* of the parts among themselves is not a mere result of adding up the parts, but is, as Gadamer emphasizes, a "judgment," or a "projection" of one particular way among other possible ways in which the parts "fit" together. Similarly, the rules of a language-game are never merely reducible to the sum of the speech acts it "contains", but are the criteria which determine speech acts to constitute a promise or a curse, an argument or a proclamation. The projection of the meaning of the whole required by the hermeneutical circle is, therefore, comparable to the interpretation of the rules of a language-game. For in both cases it is only *within* such a pre-understanding of meaning that anything at all becomes possible and knowable.

What the pragmatics of argumentative discourse leaves unthematic and presupposes as the unproblematic acceptance of commonly shared criteria is for hermeneutical boundary discourse the matter at issue. But it is an issue which arises not as a contestable validity claim. Indeed, the issue of lifeworld boundaries arises as a *crisis of meaning* resolvable only by a specific form of communicative action which projects a horizon of totality, unity and closure not, however, as a merely subjective interpretation, but as the self-interpretation of the community, of the tradition as a whole.[27]

The internal tendency of hermeneutics towards formulating a claim to universality received its fulfillment with the advent of Heidegger's "hermeneutical phenomenology."[28] "Understanding" (*Verstehen*) for the early Heidegger is no longer one method of knowing among others which a principally a-historical and interest-free subject has at its disposal, but the very act of human existence itself. Indeed, we can no longer speak of a "subject" at all, but of *Dasein*, that is, of human being as the "place" (*Ort*) where the world constituting difference between being and beings breaks out. Human existence, however, does not for this reason forfeit its finitude. On the contrary, *Dasein* exists as an issue for itself, as the possibility of being other. *Dasein* cannot escape "facticity." *Dasein* is always already being-in-the-world before it comes to the possibility of autonomous rationality and objective knowledge. The understanding of being (*Seinsverständnis*) as which *Dasein* realizes itself as being-in-the-world is always a "thrown project"; that is, it is an interpretation of possibilities for being which are not created from nothing, but creatively taken over from the historical situation in which *Dasein* stands.

For Heidegger an understanding of being has always already been "spoken" before beings may appear to us *as* this or that kind of entities. An understanding of being is not a validity claim which could be argumentatively contested or vindicated. It is a "project" (*Entwurf*) of possibilities for our own being as well as that of entities. This project is inescapably conditioned by the "thrownness" of *Dasein* into its past. Understanding, therefore, is not a method of getting beyond or outside of the historical traditions in which we live, but is the way of being of the tradition itself — that is, insofar as historical temporality occurs through human existence. Hermeneutics is no longer a theme of epistemology; it now becomes "fundamental ontology." As such it is no longer a discourse concerned with matters of fact, but with the meaning of being, with circumscribing the whole within which entities may appear. For this reason we may speak of hermeneutical discourse as a "boundary" discourse.

This development was carried further by Hans-Georg Gadamer. The ontological involvement of the knower of history in the history he or she knows prohibits any claim to scientific objectivity while at the same time founding the claim of hermeneutics to universality. In the Preface to his major work, *Truth and Method*,[29] Gadamer expresses this debt to Heidegger:

> Heidegger's temporal analytics of human existence (Dasein) has, I think, shown convincingly that understanding is not just one of the

various possible behaviours of the subject, but the mode of being of There-being itself. This is the sense in which the term "hermeneutics" has been used here. It denotes the basic being-in-motion of There-being which constitutes its finiteness and historicity, and hence includes the whole of its experience of the world. Not caprice, or even an elaboration of a single aspect, but the nature of the thing itself makes the movement of understanding comprehensive and universal.[30]

Gadamer proposes, therefore, not a *methodological* hermeneutics concerned with elaborating rules and procedures for the valid interpretation of texts, but a "philosophical hermeneutics" whose aim is:

> to discover what is common to all modes of understanding and to show that understanding is never subjective behavior toward a given "object," but towards its effective history—the history of its influence; in other words, understanding belongs to the being of that which is understood.[31]

Thus we arrive at the point where hermeneutics becomes awareness of the effect which history has upon knowledge, or as we might say, *knowledge of history becomes history of knowledge*. In Gadamer's terms, hermeneutics brings us to a "consciousness of effective history" (*wirkungsgeschichtliches Bewusstsein*).[32]

Once raised to the level of effective historical consciousness, knowing can no longer claim to stand autonomously outside tradition and to criticize all authority as "prejudice" as did Western scientific rationalism with its orientation to argumentative discourse.[33] Instead, we must acknowledge our "belongingness" (*Zugehörigkeit*) to tradition and admit that the primary task of thought is not criticism but "preservation" of what has been handed down to us. Thus is hermeneutical boundary discourse constituted by a temporal orientation toward the past and a dynamic which might be termed repetitive insofar as it emphasizes the renewal of given patterns of meaning and action embedded in founding events and texts. For Gadamer, however, this does not imply a conservative and reactionary subservience to the past, for tradition contains within itself the seeds of the new. Time itself continually separates us from ourselves, from the given horizon which immediately conditions our thought and action, letting it fall into the distance of the past. From out of this estrangement, the past comes back to us as a question.

The past places our present horizon into question, just as we seek the answers to our present questions in the past. This is because texts and other "works" coming down to us through tradition carry with them their own horizon of meaning. The "foreign" horizon of the past confronts and challenges our present horizon, making it "problematical" in its totality and causing a *crisis of meaning* which can be resolved only when the two horizons "fuse" into a new, encompassing horizon. "Fusion of horizons" (*Horizont-verschmelzung*) occurs, therefore, whenever meaning emerges and understanding takes place. The fusion of horizons is the way in which tradition itself through human understanding becomes "productive" of ever new and ever different ways of thinking and acting.[34] This transformative effect of tradition Gadamer terms "application." Thus it is not individuals who raise and vindicate validity claims, but a transcendent source which speaks through individuals in such a way as to resolve a crisis of meaning, much like a religious conversion.[35]

The universal scope and the transcendent source of boundary discourse implies that application cannot be seen as a secondary, practical "application" of theoretical knowledge — that is, as something men and women may or may not do once understanding has already been attained via argumentation in a hypothetical attitude of distance from pressures to act and decide. To speak boundary discourse means that one takes a stand on the issue that one is for oneself. There is no neutral ground upon which arguments about the appropriation of one's own existence in history could be coolly discussed. On this level of discourse, to speak is to decide.

It is important for an appreciation of the universality claim of hermeneutics to see that understanding, which occurs as fusion of horizons, application and decision is coterminous with human experience in all its dimensions, the artistic and political as well as the historical and religious. There is, indeed, no aspect of experience which is not fundamentally structured by boundary discourse, that is, by hermeneutical understanding. According to Gadamer, this is a consequence of the "linguisticality" (*Sprachlichkeit*) of experience.[36] Humans are the beings who speak. And as Gadamer puts it, "Being that can be understood is language." The universality of hermeneutics, therefore, is based upon the *ontological* priority of language as that in and through which beings, including human beings, come to appear.

To be is to be interpreted, that is, to be "as" this or that. There is nothing which is not always already in some way or another interpreted in language. Further, this revealing function of language is not, and cannot be, something that men and women might do upon their own initiative, for it is a presupposition and condition of anything that humans do that beings have already come to show themselves within a world horizon. In an expression which summarizes the entire program of an ontological hermeneutics, it is not humans who speak so much as language which "speaks" human existence.

On the basis of this brief discussion of philosophical hermeneutics, we can now summarize the pragmatic conditions of boundary discourse. First of all, communicative action which sets the rules of the game and establishes the criteria of validity is not a meaningful activity because one thereby makes a claim to validity, a claim which may be either true or false; for argumentation, as we have seen, is only possible once the criteria are "given." Boundary discourse, therefore, is not meaningful because it is either true or false; its meaning *is* its truth. In other words, *to understand boundary discourse is to accept its truth*. For boundary discourse opens up a region of being, a "world" of meaning, a field of action into which one can be taken up. Entering into a new world has traditionally been called a "conversion" (*metanoia*). The conversion experience involves a total turning about in one's view of reality and life. One leaves the old world, which has sunk into meaninglessness, and is taken up into the new world.

Second, where the pragmatics of argumentation prescribe the making of validity claims, which can be criticized and vindicated through procedures of verification, the pragmatics of boundary discourse prescribe the *proclamation* of an absolute truth which can only be "verified" in procedures of initiation, socialization and conversion.

This is to say, thirdly, that boundary discourse consists not in constative, normative and expressive speech acts, but in proclamative speech acts undertaken as *mission*. The proclamation of boundaries arises neither out of the autonomous initiative of the subject nor as a subjective response to a contested validity claim, but as a response to a total crisis of meaning which articulates itself as an absolute claim arising from a transcendent source which "calls," "empowers," "sends" and "commissions." Such speech acts demand unrestricted engagement and place one's very existence at stake. Consequently, they cannot be carried out by a pragmatics of hypothetical distance from decision and action. Boundary discourse demands either acceptance or rejection. The yes or no answer does not, however, rest upon insight into the validity of reasons, but expresses a necessarily groundless decision of faith. This is the reason why boundary discourse cannot be "criticized." For the only possible contestation of boundary discourse is by means of another boundary discourse and not argumentation. Revelation can only be criticized by revelation, mission by counter-mission.

Fourth, communicative actions which articulate themselves as conversion, proclamation and mission are *exclusive/inclusive*, for they draw a boundary and make a distinction between those who belong and those who do not belong. The community which boundary discourse establishes pretends also to be a universal community, not however because consensus alone can guarantee truth, but because the crisis of meaning to which second-level discourse responds articulates all of reality between the poles of chaos and order and forces boundary discourse to circumscribe the limits of the "world." Beyond the boundaries there is only meaninglessness and disorder. Thus does boundary discourse constitute a communication community which secures itself against the meaninglessness and chaos of a not yet ordered reality by making a distinction between those who "belong" and those who are "excluded," between the "saved" and the "damned," between the "civilized" and the "barbarians."

Fifth, boundary discourse is *narrative, repetitive and mythical* discourse.

Since belongingness to a group, a culture, a people or a religion cannot be conceived as an autonomous achievement of the individual — belongingness is a presupposition for any subjective achievements — boundary discourse articulates itself as *repetitive* proclamation of a language which has always already been "spoken." Nothing completely new or unheard of is proclaimed. Instead, it is a matter of what was, is now and always will be, since the beginning of time. As proclamation of founding events which took place at the beginning of the world, such discourse is necessarily *narrative*. For the continuity of a common history on the basis of founding events is necessarily a narrative recounting rather than an abstract generalization based upon counting up experiences of reality testing and progressive learning. This gives boundary discourse a *temporal orientation toward the past and a repetitive dynamic* of retrieval or renewal of founding acts and patterns of meaning which are typical of *mythic* speech. For this reason it is appropriate to speak of boundary discourse not as "logical," but rather as "mythological."[37]

Finally, communicative actions which proclaim mythic world-boundaries are only performatively effective when they are carried out as *witnessing* to and as *ritual enactment* of the founding structures of the community. For the community, although not founded by individual initiative, is nonetheless dependent upon individual actions in order to be concretely reproduced. If the code, the entire worldview were not "expressed" in every speech act and thus witnessed, confirmed, sanctioned, endorsed, realized and made effective in concrete communicative actions and decisions of all sorts, then no communication at all would be possible. Only in this way do the criteria of validity achieve the common acceptance which they require in order to function as standards for argumentative claims. When communicative actors set criteria in this way, however, they make no claims, rather, they "give witness" to the validity of the criteria out of which they speak in that they internalize them in their lives and *ritually enact* them in everyday interactions. Communicative action upon the second level of discourse, therefore, aims at establishing the solidarity not of a community of argumentation, but of a community of *confession*.

Above and beyond its argumentative function, every speech act has, therefore, a witnessing and representing function by means of which the code itself is communicated. It is on this level of discourse that the ability of communicative action to mediate cultural reproduction, socialization and group solidarity — that is, those functions which Habermas would have us believe can be fulfilled by argumentative discourse alone — is to be grounded. Boundary discourse, therefore, is that communicative action which *produces socialization, integration into a community and personal as well as cultural identity.* None of these can be produced by argumentation for argumentative discourse presupposes that they are already given.

In summary: Heidegger's existential phenomenology uncovered a level of human existence beneath the subject-object duality which constitutes argumentative discourse. Insofar as *Dasein* exists as "being-in-the-world," it is essentially "being-with" others. The speaker as well as the addressee of second-level boundary discourse is always more than the individual. For Gadamer *Dasein* becomes the community which constitutes itself as a historical tradition through hermeneutical retrieval of founding patterns of meaning and action. Hermeneutical understanding is not the act of an autonomous rational subject. The communicative action through which collective identity emerges and reaffirms itself in history is, therefore, not argumentation, but narrative proclamation, mission, conversion and confession through ritual enactment. These are the pragmatic conditions making that discourse possible which "sets" the criteria of validity, the lifeworld horizon circumscribing a community of communication.

Despite the claims to universality which philosophical hermeneutics makes, the question must now be asked if the pragmatics of convincement constituting boundary discourse are indeed such as to allow truly universal communication. Since every attempt to set boundaries is articulated as narrative proclamation and mission and is "understood" in procedures of conversion, socialization and ritual enactment—all of which institute an *exclusion* of the other in order to define the self—it is questionable that an other-rationality can be acknowledged. Indeed, boundary discourse seems inevitably destined to become what in Chapter 1 was called *apologetic universalism*.

As we saw in the discussion of the development of Christian theology and Secular Humanism in Chapter 1 and as the history of colonialism shows, universalism becomes apologetic the moment it realizes that it does not speak into an empty horizon. Even when it overcomes all resistance and is successful, the "world" in which "the truth" is proclaimed is never neutral, but is itself always already constituted by a boundary discourse of its own. Precisely because it sets boundaries, however, mythic discourse cannot acknowledge the existence of another myth. It must project neutrality, chaos, wilderness, unclaimed territory upon all which is outside it or which is there before it comes upon the scene. For it is always order, cosmos, civilization and meaning which it itself establishes. Consequently, the pragmatics of boundary discourse tend inevitably to articulate communicative action as procedures first of leveling, of disappropriating the other by claiming their truths and values as one's own; and thirdly, by incorporating the other's worldview into one's own by whatever means prove successful.

Furthermore, as we saw, the existence of the group as a cultural identity capable of reproducing itself through historical time depends upon the success with which it can speak its myth. Because second-level discourse sets boundaries, it has no other criterion of validity than the success or failure of the founding act. We know that a proclamation is valid only when we accept it and it knows itself as valid in its success, that is, in the *power* which becomes effective in it. This means that there is no opposition between truth and power possible on the level of boundary discourse, for critique can only arise from another mythic discourse with its own narrative of identity, its own existence and power at issue.[38] Since the individual as well as the collective exist as issues for themselves, as the question of identity (who are we?), there is no answer to this question which is not at the same time an expression of power. Here truth is indeed the "lie" in the service of life, as Nietzsche said it was.[39]

For this reason Habermas and Apel, unlike Gadamer, maintain that understanding and communication cannot be grounded in a consciousness which has conceded its autonomy to tradition. This defeats, they argue, the very purpose of the struggle for knowledge which consists in the critique of institutionalized prejudice and authority.

It is the ideals of the Enlightenment, the goal of freeing humanity from enslavement to the past, which informs the project of a *critical social science* as Habermas and Apel conceive it. The rehabilitation of "prejudice" as a necessary condition of understanding which follows from the attempt to universalize boundary discourse cannot but appear to them a romantic reaction. A truly universal understanding, they argue, cannot give up its right to *go behind* language and uncover those extra-linguistic forces which systematically distort communication even before it begins. Language, according to this view, which is informed by Marx and Freud, is emphatically *not* in order as it is and not to be trusted to "speak" the world and humankind as they truly are.

To give hermeneutics over to the benevolent hand of a transcendent "sending of Being" and abstain from all methodological distanciation, objectivation and subjection of tradition to critique can only amount to limiting the scope of understanding to what the constellation of psychological and social powers at any time allows. Critique and the progress of knowledge become impossible. We may well be able to understand always *differently*, as Gadamer says, but not for that reason to understand *better*.[40]

It is definitely a weakness of Gadamer's position that he fails to acknowledge that the problem of "how to get into the circle in the right way" is a *methodological* problem.[41] Here is where the methodology of intercultural understanding as theology of religions may make a contribution. The problem of *how* to get into a truly universal hermeneutical circle is not solved by merely pointing out *that* we are always already in it. For this only pushes the question back a step further to the problem posed by Apel and Habermas of the right way and the wrong way to be in it. Here the suspicion of ideology raised against philosophical hermeneutics must be taken seriously.[42]

For Gadamer, the problem hermeneutics must deal with is *misunderstanding*. Misunderstanding, however, arises against a presupposed common background of agreement. Thus Gadamer can rhetorically ask:

Is it not, in fact, the case that every misunderstanding presupposes a "deep common accord"?[43]

For Habermas and Apel, on the other hand, hermeneutics cannot presuppose a "common accord" for the very reason that the problem it must deal with is not misunderstanding, but *ideology*. Ideology is what happens to discourse when extra-linguistic forces do *violence* to language. Violence, according to this view, distorts communication in two ways: First violence acts as a "censor" and prohibits free and open discussion which is necessary to form a consensus about future goals and present means. Secondly, it distorts language by "disguising" itself and thus creating the illusion of agreement when in fact there is none. This prevents us from subjecting those factors which condition us to rational control, whether they be social inequalities or psychological repressions.

Ideology is basically different from misunderstanding because it cuts certain sectors of experience off from rationality and consigns them to an uncontrollable sphere of irrationality. Since the causes of the distortion of discourse are no longer within the realm of language, they cannot be approached by hermeneutics, which operates only within the domain of discourse, but solely by the methods of explanatory science which were developed precisely to bring the extra-human realm of nature within the grasp of reason and control.[44] The danger which Habermas and Apel see in Gadamer's philosophical hermeneutics is that by assuming a pre-given accord and claiming that the scope of hermeneutical discourse is universal it in fact merely hypostatizes the past and perpetuates a state of violence.

Consciousness of effective history, according to these thinkers, should not result in a blind loyalty to the past, but make us aware of our responsibility to the *future*. The fundamental direction of hermeneutics must, therefore, be turned around and pointed toward the future consistent with the temporal orientation of argumentative discourse. This means that consensus cannot be presupposed as something *already given*, but must be *anticipated* as the goal of a *methodical* and *practical* program of human self-realization.[45]

The attempt to universalize argumentative discourse, however, cannot itself avoid violence as soon as it tries to legitimate itself and vindicate argumentation by means of strategic action. As we saw, once the level of conflict reaches the shared criteria of meaning which make argumentation possible in the first place, argumentation ceases and it becomes necessary to proclaim boundaries. This is the insight which lies behind Gadamer's criticisms of Habermas and Apel. Our hermeneutical circle is not really broadened by a critical social science which absolutizes argumentative discourse. The theoretical subject who employs a critical social science and who claims the right and the ability to go behind language in order to legitimate strategic action aimed at liberation finds itself necessarily trapped within the very constraints it sought to escape. Here, just as in the case of boundary discourse, the claim to universality remains unfounded and communication is inevitably overcome by violence.

Therefore, against the programs to universalize either argumentative discourse or boundary discourse it is necessary to hold fast to the essential point that the problem which universal communication must face is *neither ideology nor misunderstanding*, which are only the effects of violence on the surface of language, but violence itself, which, like the coils of a snake, constricts both understanding and explanation. This is a problem which can only be dealt with by a "pragmatics of non-violence."

SATYAGRAHA: TOWARDS A GLOBAL FORM OF LIFE

For both argumentative and proclamative discourse, the diatopical space of the encounter between worldviews, cultures and religions can only be a field of battle. The self-legitimation of argumentative discourse, as we saw, leads into the meaninglessness of decisionism and extra-discursive strategic action, whereas the attempt of proclamative boundary discourse to legitimate itself can only occur through a repetition of the proclamation which leads into the violent pragmatics of apologetic universalism. Upon neither of these levels of discourse is one truly able to perceive the space of encounter as an open space in its own right, that is, as a space of disclosure. Just as argumentation can only be placed in "question" upon a higher level of discourse, the level of boundary setting; so can boundary discourse only be placed in "question" upon a still higher level, namely, that of disclosure. For boundary discourse is first seen *as such* and thus able to be placed into question at the moment of encounter with another myth. The pragmatic enactment of the encounter—that is, how we enact our myths—depends upon whether the space of encounter is opened up or from the outset closed down and suppressed. It is the space of encounter which grants and makes possible "worlds" by providing the opening from out of which mythological discourse draws the ability to identify itself, even if at the moment of self-identification a cultural tradition blinds out or represses the *other* which enables it. This is the diatopical space which precedes all identity and may therefore be called a space of difference, of dis-continuity, of dis-closure. What is the discourse peculiar to this meta-level, this diatopical space of encounter? And what pragmatic conditions constitute its meaning and validity?

Boundary discourse, we have seen, projects unity, totality and universality, but cannot criticize this projection or place itself into question. A discourse capable of doing this cannot, therefore, be a discourse of closure. Instead, it must dis-close boundaries. It can accomplish this, however, only if it articulates an opening, a clearing, a horizon not of identity, but of difference. Difference of what? We may speak of this difference in two ways: first, the difference we are here concerned with may be said to be a *discourse of difference*, and secondly, a *difference of discourse*.

Disclosive discourse is a *discourse of difference*, rather than identity, because it lets the difference between what Panikkar has termed transcendent faith and particular beliefs appear as such.[46] On the level of disclosure faith is not identified with belief and belief not mistaken for faith. Onto-logically speaking, disclosive discourse lets the "ontological difference" between Being and beings "be" — i.e., it opens up, grants and articulates this foundational distinction. By holding open the space between Being and beings it does not forget Being, as do all affirmations of identity, unity, oneness, totality and plenitude based upon exclusion of the other.[47] Within a discourse of disclosure identity is not constituted by exclusion. Within a discourse of closure an entity is what it is because it is *not* other than itself, whereas within a discourse of disclosure a thing is what it is because it *can* be other.

Disclosive discourse is also at the same time a *difference of discourse*, or, analogous to the ontological difference, we may speak here of a "discursive difference." The discursive difference consists first in disentangling the three levels of discourse themselves. The very project of Western meta-physics, of ontotheology, which arises from mistaking Being for the most general property of beings and/or the highest entity (God) — together with all the consequences this has had for Western thought — might be traced to the confusion of argumentative discourse with boundary discourse. The myth of logos (logocentrism) and the program of a universal discourse of argumentation in the name of "enlightenment" are only possible once the logos has been elevated to the rank of a boundary discourse and the dif-ference between internal, logical and boundary discourse has been sup-pressed. Furthermore, dis-closing the closures of identity which boundary discourse necessarily establishes pluralizes discourse upon the level of proc-lamation so that other myths may appear as possible co-responses within the space of encounter. Proclamative narration thus becomes capable of enacting a dialogical rather than a polemical and apologetical encounter. There arises a belonging together on the level of ultimate horizons of mean-ing which precludes in-difference to the existence of the other and the consequent violent pragmatics of apologetic universalism.

Only a discourse based upon pragmatic conditions of convincement which do not rely upon power can fulfill the requirements of a discourse of disclosure. For disclosive discourse must ground and insure the mean-ingfulness of both argumentative and proclamative discourse by reaching into and going beyond the dimension of that primal violence which first imposes limits upon communication by excluding the other. It can accom-plish this task only if it succeeds in transforming practices of psychological and social *resistance*, which otherwise are condemned to being either the ineffectual symptoms of a lost oneness or futile attempts to found meaning, into the pragmatic conditions of unlimited communication and a universal community. A *pragmatics of non-violence* opens up a horizon of encounter and thus carries discourse into the realm where power confronts and excludes the other, thereby transforming the violence of exclusion into a solidarity from which speech may arise. It can do this because it opens human existence to the cosmic and the divine, thus grounding a "cosmotheandric" solidarity upon which alone a truly universal community can be based.[48]

It was Mahatma Gandhi who most clearly worked out the pragmatic conditions for this third level of discourse as a pragmatics of non-violence. Gandhi termed the pragmatic conditions of such a universal discourse *satyagraha*. It is a widespread misunderstanding that the techniques of passive resistance such as mass demonstrations, boycotts, strikes, non-cooperation and civil disobedience may, without further ado, be identified with Gandhi's *methodological* conception of non-violence. "*Satyagraha*," claims Gandhi, "is not predominantly civil disobedience, but a quiet and irresistible pursuit of truth."[49] It is this *epistemological* dimension of Gandhi's method of resolving conflicts which gives us the right to speak of a "pragmatics of non-violence" and to seek in Gandhi's thought a solution to the problem of interreligious understanding.

Gandhi's intention was, therefore, not merely to develop new techniques for strategic action which could serve the realization of particular interests, but rather, to develop a method of resolving the "conflict of interpretations" on the level of basic convictions such that a *new truth*, hitherto unknown, could emerge from the struggle. *Satyagraha* literally means "holding on to truth," and Gandhi explicates it in terms of three concepts: *satya* (truth), *ahimsa* (non-violence) and *tapas* (self-suffering). Let us turn now to a brief explanation of these three concepts.

Satya: Truth

Satya is the Sanskrit word for truth, but since it comes from the root "*sat*" which at once means truth and God, Gandhi concludes that truth *is* God.[50] From this *religious* concept of truth, which, according to Gandhi even atheists and skeptics can accept, for both acknowledge some kind of truth, Gandhi derives the following principles of his pragmatics of non-violence. First, truth is imperishable and indestructible. Whatever happens, truth will conquer and falsity will be merely passing. Second, he who acts in truth will succeed even if at first his actions remain ineffective. Even if one man or woman alone acts in truth, he or she will be able to resist the most powerful tyranny, for it is in fact God who is acting through them. Third, only those actions which arise from truth can be politically effective and institute human community. As Gandhi put it:

> Truth binds man to man in association. Without truth there can be no social organization.[51]

Ahimsa: Non-Violence

Of course, one may object that this is an ideal which could only be realized if truth were something which immediately appeared to all men and women as self-evident. In reality this does not occur. Like Pilate, we may ask: What is truth? At this point, Gandhi's second concept, *ahimsa* or non-violence, becomes important. Before the Hunter Committee, which investigated the massacre at Amritsar, Gandhi gave the following testimony:

> Q. However honestly a man may strive in his search for truth his notions of truth may be different from the notions of others. Who then is to determine the truth?
> A. The individual himself would determine that.
> Q. Different individuals would have different views as to truth. Would that not lead to confusion?
> A. I do not think so.
> Q. Honestly striving after truth is different in every case.
> A. That is why the non-violence part was a necessary corollary. Without that there would be confusion and worse.[52]

What separates Gandhi from all utopian fanatics is his thoroughly realistic appraisal of the ability of men and women to know absolute truth. He writes: "we will never all think alike and we shall always see Truth in fragment and from different angles of vision."[53] The absolute truth can, therefore, not be our possession, but must rather be our goal. This is the reason why non-violence must be our method, our means, since it alone can lead to this goal. If we force our view of the truth upon others, we inevitably raise a partial truth to an absolute status and thus prevent the exchange of views which alone could give us the complete truth. Insofar as we prohibit all correction of our position by means of violence we remain bound to our partial truth. Gandhi used to illustrate this point with the following story:

> It appears that the impossibility of full realization of Truth in the mortal body led some ancient seeker after Truth to the appreciation of ahimsa. The question which confronted him was: "Shall I bear with those who create difficulties for me, or shall I destroy them?" The seeker realized that he who went on destroying others did not make any headway but simply stayed where he was, while the man who suffered those who created difficulties marched ahead, and at times even took the other with him. . . .[54]

Although we can never possess the absolute truth, we can approach it by means of non-violence. This is the reason why non-violence is capable of instituting community. It participates in the power of truth. Gandhi expressed this conviction in the "Credo of Non-Violence" which he published in *Harijan* in 1935:

> a. Non-violence implies as complete self-purification as is humanly possible.

b. Man for man the strength of non-violence is in exact proportion to the ability, not the will, of the non-violent person to inflict violence.

c. Non-violence is without exception superior to violence, i.e., the power at the disposal of a non-violent person is always greater than he would have if he was violent.

d. There is no such thing as defeat in non-violence. The end of violence is surest defeat.

e. The ultimate end of non-violence is surest victory—if such a term may be used of non-violence.[55]

Much in this credo will remain obscure until we have examined the third concept with which Gandhi explains *satyagraha*, namely, *tapas*, or self-suffering. For the moment, however, it is enough to point out that such a credo was so important for Gandhi because he could not accept the traditional priority of the end over the means in political theory. The end cannot legitimate the means, he argued, first, because it is simply not so that in everyday life one sharply distinguishes between ends and means. Secondly, no one is so knowledgeable and self-certain that he can afford to take for granted the moral value of the means he employs. Third, it is a fact that it is only the means which we have under our control and not the ends; and it is for what we have under our control that we must be responsible. Fourth, since the means determines the effect, it is much rather the case that they must be legitimated in themselves, for we are in any case obliged to do what is good.

For Gandhi, non-violence is a means which is also the end itself. Ends and means are one and the same:

Without ahimsa it is not possible to seek and find Truth. Ahimsa and Truth are so intertwined that it is practically impossible to disentangle and separate them. Ahimsa is the means; Truth is the end. Means must always be within our reach, and so ahimsa is our supreme duty. If we take care of the means, we are bound to reach the end sooner or later.[56]

The problem, of course, is not solved by this identification of ends and means. For how are we to know that our conception of truth is indeed incomplete? Do not all ideologies and worldviews assume that they do, in fact, possess the whole truth? And if one is convinced that one knows the truth, one is legitimated in employing all possible methods to insure that this truth is realized. This is the problem which we confronted above in our discussion of the ethics of discourse. The impossibility of being able to argue about argumentation itself seems to force the ethics of discourse to give up its own principles the moment truly serious conflicts on the level of worldviews arise. For a consensus about what counts as reasonable, in such a situation, can no longer be presupposed. It is to answer this objection that Gandhi introduces the third concept, *tapas*, into his definition of *satyagraha*.

Tapas: Self-Suffering

After fifty years of experience of ideological conflicts, Gandhi was convinced that the only way that an ideological absolutization of a particular worldview could be broken was by means of *solidarity with the enemy and voluntary self-suffering*. For in every ideological conflict each party takes the resistance of the other to be a confirmation of its previous condemnation of the other's position.[57] This in turn legitimates the suspension of communication and the use of coercion of one sort or another. But if the opponent does not answer violence with the same, and nonetheless continues to resist, then, according to Gandhi, no one can remain secure within his prejudices. Those who use violence will be compelled to ask themselves where the opponent takes the courage and the moral force necessary in order to resist non-violently. They will be forced to acknowledge the solidarity which the opponent continues to uphold and to admit that the opponent does have some truth after all.

At this point they have already placed their own ideology in question and the walls of non-communication have been broken through. For when the one party sees that the other takes the suffering arising from the conflict upon themselves and does not answer with violence, then their own fear and mistrust are overcome and an open and sincere dialogue becomes possible. In this way, non-violence becomes *critique of ideology*.[58]

Of course, this critique does not function if it is only directed towards the other and not at the same time against one's own ideology. Indeed, Gandhi conceived non-violent resistance primarily as a *self-critique*. This is clear from the rules which he established for every non-violent struggle. To these rules belong the following precepts and code of discipline:[59]

1. Reduce demands to a minimum consistent with truth and continually reassess them self-critically.
2. Search constantly for a solution to the conflict which the opponent can fully accept.
3. Refuse to surrender essentials in negotiation. There can be no compromise with truth.
4. Insist upon full agreement on fundamentals before accepting a settlement.
5. Harbor no anger but suffer the anger of the opponent.
6. Protect opponents from injury even at risk of your own life.

According to these rules, the conflict itself must be carried out within the domain of discourse. We achieve no real and lasting advance if we succeed in realizing our goals and establishing our claims, but do not learn more of the truth. The scope of rationality must be extended into the realm of power and the actual conflict must be conceived and carried out *as* a search for truth, as a uniquely praxis-oriented method of inquiry. This is essential for a proper understanding of Gandhi's conception of the non-violent pragmatics of universal discourse.

A universal community of discourse may be realized to the extent that the power of weapons is replaced by the power of the spirit. This spiritual force, which Gandhi called "soul-force," is only attainable by means of *tapas*. Gandhi saw conflicts as unavoidable in the development of society, indeed, in the development of the entire cosmos. The course of history is, therefore, inevitably bound up with suffering. For out of every conflict there arises a certain amount of suffering.[60] In terms familiar to Christian thought, we might say that the task and privilege of humans as co-responsible for the perfection of creation is to accept this suffering, take it voluntarily upon themselves and thus transfigure it into a creative rather than a destructive force:

> If love or non-violence be not the law of our being, the whole of my argument falls to pieces, and there is no escape from a periodical recrudescence of war. ... I know that it cannot be proved by argument. It shall be proved by persons living it in their lives in utter disregard of consequences to themselves. There is no real gain without sacrifice.[61]

Most men and women, however, because they are *ignorant* of this their true nature, react automatically with *fear* in a conflict situation. They attempt to avoid the suffering which the conflict brings with it by pushing it off onto others. It is this "natural" reaction which, according to Gandhi, is the source of violence. In fact, violence *is* nothing other than the attempt to escape the suffering in a situation of conflict by thrusting it onto the other party in the dispute. Non-violence, on the other hand, consists precisely in voluntarily taking as much of this suffering upon oneself as possible. This is what Gandhi means by *tapas*.

The struggle for material security which has been placed at the root of human action in modern theories of society from Hobbes to Habermas is incapable of accounting for community. A one-sided over-valuation of the productive aspect of action, understood, for example, as *labor* and the technical or instrumental rationality accompanying it, has the effect of detaching us from the dimension of the holy and eclipsing a discourse of disclosure. We become closed in upon ourselves in a world open only to the deterministic horizon of the past or an arbitrary will to power directed towards self-realization in an empty future.[62]

The idea of a worldview, or religion, as we saw, implies the enclosure of a whole series of relationships within a systematic totality; first, relationships to the "cosmic," that is, to nature, to the material and the biological levels of being; secondly, relationships which may be termed "anthropolog-ical," that is, psychological and socio-cultural relationships among humans; and finally, relationships to the divine or transcendent dimension of being. The idea of a space of disclosure within which religions are constituted raises the question of "unity" beyond the boundaries set by any closure of possibilities for articulating these cosmo-the-andric relations. If it is so that the "truth" of any worldview is at the same time inevitably an expression of its *power to be*, to be what it is in distinction from and opposition to what it is not, then communication beyond the boundaries of our worldview may be said, paradoxically, to express a certain *power not to be*, that is, an acceptance of *death*. The communication strategy derived from the dis-course of disclosure is, therefore, nothing other than the attempt to estab-lish solidarity with the other beyond the boundaries imposed by our form of life, that is, beyond the at any time given conditions of economic, political and ideological *security*. Not the imposition of our myth, but the solidarity with the other at risk of "death" is what the discourse of disclosure aims at communicating. When communication takes place within the space of the between, therefore, it must express an unlimited cosmotheandric soli-darity.

It is only when the inevitable conflict of worldviews is carried out non-violently that the claim of a discourse to express the myths of all parties involved becomes *convincing*. Neither argument nor rhetoric nor power can make a discourse of disclosure convincing. Its validity arises only from a pragmatics of non-violence, for only non-violence can establish a solidarity with the opponent which extends beyond the limits of "life." And it is only because non-violence carries discourse beyond these boundaries that non-discursive power and violence are not the "last word." Non-violence opens a truly global horizon for communication, for the openness to transcen-dence, to the dimension of the holy which grants humans a universal soli-darity with the divine, the cosmos and all other men and women frees us from self-interest sufficiently to stave off the reaction of fear which tends to come when our personal and cultural identity, our lifeworld, is threat-ened in an ideological conflict. We have at least the chance to experience ourselves as capable of transforming a conflict through self-suffering into a creative opportunity for advancement of the entire community.

In summary, *satyagraha* is a self-suffering (*tapas*), non-violent (*ahimsa*) search for truth (*satya*). It unites religion and politics, private and public spheres of action, thus overcoming the gap between theory and praxis which has troubled our culture in one way or another for centuries. It binds the progressive orientation of argumentative discourse to the regressive ori-entation of hermeneutics in a discourse of disclosure and shows thereby that the search for enlightenment and liberation does not take place apart from the spiritual dimension wherein natural, human and divine possibili-ties intertwine. It is politically effective because it frees us from fear of authority and power, thus giving us the strength to act for the good (regardless of what we perceive it to be!). In *satyagraha*, the means is the end. For this reason it is truly universal. No matter how different and apparently exclusive of each other worldviews are, they can be taken up into a universal discourse only when the conflict of interpretations is fought out on the basis of a pragmatics which creates "cosmotheandric" solidarity.[63]

Gandhi consciously developed *satyagraha* as an alternative to the currently dominant theory of conflict resolution by means of a balance of power or war. He tested it and refined it for fifty years in many different situations and under the most varied conditions. He presents it to us as a result of "scientific" research, and as a method for extending the realm of freedom and rationality into the domain of power and violence and of realizing here and now, in the present, the ideal of an unlimited community of discourse. *Satyagraha* is not a political strategy, but a way of incorporating strategic action into an ethics of discourse which is not merely an ethics of argumentation. It is an epistemological method designed to overcome irrationality and criticize ideology at its roots. It is, therefore, only reasonable when he states:

> Just as for conducting scientific experiments there is an indispensable scientific course of instruction, in the same way strict preliminary discipline is necessary to qualify a person to make experiments in the spiritual realm.[64]

Confronted with such a claim we find ourselves in a similar position to those learned men and princes of the Church at the time of Galileo. With his newly discovered telescope, Galileo could see things which no man or woman before him had perceived and thus could verify theories which until then had been dismissed as wild speculations. When Galileo presented his instrument to the learned men of his time and challenged them to look and see for themselves that the heavens really were as he had said, there were those who refused because—and here is the parallel to Gandhi's teaching—as they claimed, no one could possibly learn anything new and useful from such a thing.[65]

Surely one reason why Gandhi has not been taken seriously has to do with the above mentioned confusion of *satyagraha* with what is often called "passive resistance." Many objections have been raised against passive resistance which do not affect *satyagraha*. For example, it has been claimed that non-violent resistance actually causes conflicts and suffering. Further, that it is, despite its claims, violent especially when it takes the form of mass demonstrations. That it leads to anarchy and functions merely to excuse criminality. And finally, its epistemological significance has been fully overlooked.

Gandhi himself rejected the concept of "passive resistance." He found it insufficient and misleading. He claimed that *satyagraha* differed from passive resistance on at least five essential points. First, he considered passive resistance a weapon of the weak, of those who could not use weapons, while *satyagraha* was a weapon of the strong, of those who could but chose not to use violence. Second, for him passive resistance allowed injury and hatred of the opponent, while *satyagraha* strictly prescribed solidarity with the opponent and a genuine interest to help. Third, self-suffering, which for *satyagraha* is essential, is for passive resistance merely accidental and considered something one should avoid if possible.

Fourth, passive resistance is not universally applicable; since it is potentially violent, one cannot use it in all situations, for example, within the family or the near community. Fifth, Gandhi considered passive resistance to be something negative, something which fights primarily *against* something else and not *for* it. And sixth, passive resistance is a political strategy, while *satyagraha* is a unique pragmatic method for the pursuit of truth. *Satyagraha* is always directed to discovering the truth, toward working out a solution which is really the best for all parties concerned and not merely a compromise based upon a strategic balance of power.

Furthermore, *satyagraha* cannot be said to produce anarchy because it can only be practiced by men and women who are committed to the realization of a universal community of discourse and coordinating common actions on the basis of consensus. And finally, since no one today can escape the consequences of cultural and religious pluralism, or begin from any other presupposition, *satyagraha* is not only a method for the resolution of conflicts on the social and political levels, but primarily on the level of fundamental beliefs.

Thus Gandhi could speak of *satyagraha* as "a process of conversion."[66] To enter into and bear a conflict as a search for truth implies the readiness to revise one's previous beliefs. On the level of boundary discourse, of fundamental convictions or "religious" truths, this revision, as we saw, can only occur as a conversion experience. For Gandhi, however, the pragmatics of conversion need not imply exclusion. Indeed, from the point of view of a discourse of disclosure, power and exclusion are the opposite of conversion not only politically, but also ideologically. For an exclusive, confessional conversion results in a change which, in fact, is no change at all, but a mere repetition. Here the temporal orientation of boundary discourse toward the past and the dynamic of proclamative repetition are "turned" around. In terms of the debate between a theory of argumentation and a philosophical hermeneutics, experiencing conversion as the ideological reflection of constantly shifting constellations of power can only result in understanding *differently*, but not in understanding *better*. Just as argumentation first becomes meaningful within the proclamation of boundaries, so does boundary discourse first become meaningful within a pragmatics of non-violence. This means that in the global situation the proclamation of one's faith becomes *convincing* only on the level of a pragmatics of non-violence. The aim of *satyagraha*, if we can speak of it having an end beyond itself at all, is a *mutual conversion* of all parties involved in a conflict.

Satyagraha, therefore, is a procedure for what may be called *methodological conversion*.

Methodological conversion, we recall, stood at the center of the method for a theology of religions which we reconstructed from the pioneering work of Raimundo Panikkar. Panikkar clearly saw that if the encounter of religions and worldviews does not give rise to a conversion to the truth on all sides, then the outcome can only be coercion of one sort or another. The history of colonialism as well as the problems confronting us today under the titles of the North–South and East–West conflicts testify amply to this fact. The problem, however, was how we could make sense of the possibility of a radical transformation of our system of thought such that it would remain within the domain of discourse. It was in order to solve this problem that Panikkar proposed a diatopical model of communication.

Peter Winch raised this same problem in regard to the social sciences. In the later philosophy of Ludwig Wittgenstein, Winch saw a possibility of avoiding the objectivism of the "scientific worldview" while at the same time escaping from the pitfalls of relativism. Wittgenstein's pragmatic semantics shows that understanding is not to be achieved by reducing all that is "other" to the self-certainty of a principally monological consciousness by means of a methodological solipsism, but instead, by giving up the apologetic projection of one's own interpretation of the rules and *participating* in what the other is doing. This changes the fundamental direction of knowledge in modern Western thought from a movement in which knowledge arises by taking the other into the self into a movement of understanding by means of going out to the other. *Not methodological solipsism, but methodological conversion is the beginning of knowledge.*

It is clear, however, that participation cannot lead to understanding if it merely means breaking off all relations with one's previous beliefs. This would amount to what we have termed "jumping over" into another culture. He who "jumps over" neither avoids the conflict, for he merely exchanges roles, nor really achieves understanding, for his mode of thinking remains apologetic and polemic. No higher truth has emerged from the encounter. How then do we participate without jumping over? *Satyagraha* gives an answer. The pragmatics of non-violence allow us to remain faithful to our own beliefs while at the same time realizing that they are not the absolute truth, but only an interpretation — an interpretation which can profit from the knowledge which our opponent has of the truth.

It remains, nonetheless true, that we cannot help believing what we believe. As Wittgenstein might put it, we "play the game" as we must. On the level of disclosive discourse this does not imply that we cannot be open to other interpretations of reality. All parties to the dispute about a universal discourse agree that such openness is a necessary condition of the meaning and truth of whatever we may believe. The problem which divides the parties to the discussion is *how* we can be open, that is, under what pragmatic conditions of convincement universality may be achieved. For philosophical hermeneutics it is by trusting in the productivity of tradition, and for the ethics of argumentation it is by means of a theoretically informed critical praxis. But both of these programs, as we saw, cannot avoid the primal violence of exclusion of the other if they are not taken up into a discourse of disclosure which is able to preserve their universalist intentions upon the basis of a pragmatics of non-violence.

My thesis is that Gandhi can help us solve this problem. For *satyagraha* shows us how we can create that "deep common accord" which, as Gadamer quite rightly claims, is the necessary presupposition of all understanding and which Habermas and Apel also cannot avoid without doing violence to discourse. Out of the cosmotheandric solidarity which *satyagraha* makes possible, there comes forth a disclosure of a new horizon of meaning, or as Panikkar puts it, a "new myth" encompassing all parties in the dispute.[67] This is what makes non-violence the pragmatic condition for a universal discourse. For it reaches into the realm of violence and broken communication and performs there a gesture which binds this realm back (*re-ligare!*) to a truly universal community and thus opens up the possibility of transforming violence into discourse, meaninglessness and irrationality into meaning and truth. We come to see the world anew and through the language of this vision the world itself becomes a "new creation."

The attempt to demonstrate the necessity of a theology of religions as a way out of the crises of Christian and secular universalism led to the question of whether or not a universal language in which not only theology and secular thought, but all worldviews could mutually appropriate each other was possible. This question turned out to be the question of the possibility of a critique of ideologies, for in a pluralistic situation in which thinking has always already taken sides, an ideologizing of thought seems unavoidable. That our present situation is indeed one of "radical pluralism" was the outcome of the discussion in Chapter 1.

The question of the foundations for a theology of religions, thus became the epistemological question of a possible *global thinking*. With the help of Winch and Wittgenstein, and the discussion concerning the pragmatic conditions of a universal discourse, we saw that this is really the question of a *global form of life*, that is, that it could not be settled in abstraction from a method for resolving those conflicts which are not merely theoretical, but which arise beyond the normal bounds of discourse and argumentation in the realm of irrational force.

We argued, further, that criteria of meaning, truth and reality are not valid merely within a certain culture, which would lead to indifferentism and relativism, but first become meaningful via openness to correction from without, that is, in serious and open dialogue. Thinking is meaningful and rational to the extent that it is prepared to acknowledge other forms of rationality and to change its interpretation of the rules of thought and of the very meaning of "reality," "truth" and "meaning" through such a dialogue. But, since human life is always in some way meaningful life, such totalistic transformations of the lifeworld are not mere theoretical matters which could be discussed coolly in a hypothetical attitude; they are transformations of our very being and identity. In this sense, the encounter with the other is always an encounter with "death," a threat to our "life." Consequently, acknowledgment of the other is acceptance of suffering, of the risk of loosing our "selves." Only the openness to transcendence, the holy, roots us in a solidarity with the other beyond whatever of ourselves we may give up in the encounter. The requirement of methodological conversion, which must be placed at the center of any interreligious understanding, receives here its epistemological justification. And this in turn is made *practically* possible through Gandhi's method of non-violent resolution of conflicts, which allows for participation without compromising truth. Our search for a global form of life, that is, the pragmatic conditions which make universal claims convincing, has ended in *satyagraha*.

Philosophy, whose status in the present global situation is a matter of controversy, therefore, becomes intercultural hermeneutics. It can neither be the self-declared servant of secular universalism, nor the hidden instrument of a Christian apologetics. Its task is simply to understand the other. Since intercultural understanding, for its part, is only realizable upon the basis of a pragmatics of non-violence, or in other words as a discourse of disclosure which is essentially related to transcendence, the universal language it speaks may be termed "religious." Intercultural hermeneutics becomes theology and together they make up the *theology of religions*.

This of course changes the current meaning of the concepts of "philosophy," "theology" and "religion," a change which represents a re-structuring of the disciplinary boundaries of the Western "episteme." But since the present understanding of these concepts, as well as the present structure of Western thought, is largely determined by the ideological and therefore meaningless apologetics of Christian and secular universalisms, a renewal of their meaning within a *new universalism* would seem called for and legitimate.

The two basic decisions which Tillich posited as necessary presuppositions for a theology of religions—namely, the decision to overcome orthodox-exclusivism and the decision to overcome secular rejectionism—have been demonstrated to be both possible and necessary. Therewith is the method which we won from the work of Raimundo Panikkar, and which flows from Tillich's presuppositions, also grounded. The theology of religions can no longer remain a merely accidental occupation on the periphery of the business of theology, but must take its place in the center of all serious theological endeavor; that is, if a non-apologetic universalism is to be realized. That a *new universalism* must take the place of the old apologetics is not the pious wish of a few special disciplines, but the inner need of thought itself.

Notes

The figures in brackets refer to the chapter [1, 2, 3 or 4] and the note where a text is first mentioned. Chapter and note numbers are separated by a slash. Numbers not separated by a slash refer to the note above in the same chapter.

INTRODUCTION

1. Cited in Christian Humphreys, *Buddhism* (Hammondsworth: Penguin, 1951), p. 11.

2. Each description is legitimated as a description of *the elephant* only *through* the others.

1. OPENING UP THE HORIZON FOR A GLOBAL THEOLOGY

1. See the rich bibliography in Horst Bürkle, *Einführung in die Theologie der Religionen* (Darmstadt: Wissenschaftliche Buchgesellschaft, 1977), and Paul F. Knitter, *No Other Name? A Critical Survey of Christian Attitudes Toward the World Religions* (Maryknoll, N.Y.: Orbis, 1985). For Bürkle, it is a matter of giving "examples and models" of the interreligious dialogue, instead of "systematic theological expositions" (p. 3). Bürkle sees that the interreligious dialogue demands that the theologian be prepared "to place in question and—where necessary—correct his ways of thinking and the ideas and concepts which are current in the context of his own tradition in their application to other religious traditions" (p. 4). But the question remains unanswered of *how* the theologian is to do this. Certainly, "the deeper and more encompassing gain for one's own tradition occurs in the encounter with the foreign tradition," but it is precisely such a gain that one misses in the concrete dialogues which Bürkle conducts with Hinduism, Buddhism and the religions of Africa. What is gained, for example, in the dialogue with Hinduism when concepts such as "myth" and "history" (p. 44) are employed in their Western Christian meaning instead of being thought through anew? But how can they be thought through anew, when they are simply presupposed as the common ground upon which the dialogue should take place? How can we conduct the dialogue when perhaps no such common ground can be presupposed? The reader searches in vain for answers to these important methodological questions. Perhaps the reason why Bürkle does not get beyond traditional Western Christian self-understanding lies in the fact that none of the theological models which he finds "in present theological tendencies"— among which are Benz, Ratschow, Pannenberg, Rosenkranz, Rahner, Ratzinger, Schlette—accomplish this. Bürkle would like to see Tillich in this line, but overlooks thereby the possibility of understanding Tillich more radically. In this respect Knitter's book represents a real advance. Knitter begins with the

problem of cultural and religious pluralism and proceeds to examine secular and Christian models for dealing with this problem, among them W. C. Smith and John Hick. His major concern is dogmatic rather than methodological. He focuses on christological problems as a key to the relation between Christianity and other religions.

2. Printed in Paul Tillich, *The Future of Religions*, ed. Jerald C. Brauer (New York: Harper & Row, 1966), pp. 80–94.

3. Ibid., p. 80.

4. Ibid., p. 83.

5. Cited in J. H. Randall, *The Making of the Modern Mind* (Cambridge, Mass.: Houghton Mifflin, 1940), p. 96.

6. See René Descartes, *Meditations on First Philosophy* in *The Philosophical Works of Descartes*, 2 vols., trans. and ed. by E. S. Haldane and G. R. T. Ross (Cambridge: Cambridge University Press, 1967), vol. I, p. 144.

7. It would be interesting to read Descartes from the point of view of the search for certainty of existence, i.e., certainty of salvation. This view would place Descartes into the context of the crumbling certainty based upon the Bible manifested in the religious controversies of the 16th and 17th centuries and the emerging promise of securing existence through science and technology. It would also make apparent the difference between the Augustinian "cogito" and Descartes' version.

8. See Immanuel Kant, "What is Enlightenment?" in *The Philosophy of Kant*, ed. C. J. Friedrich (New York: The Modern Library, 1949), p. 132.

9. This remains so even after Kant's abstract conception of autonomy has gone through the criticisms of Hegel, Marx, Nietzsche, Freud and now lately structuralism, systems theory and post modernism. For at the bottom of these criticisms there remains as motivating force, the presupposition that men and women are by nature free and self-determining, even though—indeed because!—the concrete struggle for liberation continues to discover ever more factors which condition and determine this freedom.

10. See the discussion of these approaches in the chapter entitled "Five Basic Models in Contemporary Theology" in David Tracy, *Blessed Rage for Order: The New Pluralism in Theology* (New York: Seabury, 1979), pp. 22–42.

11. In Paul Tillich, *What is Religion*, trans. and ed. by James L. Adams (New York: Harper & Row, 1969), pp. 27–121.

12. Ibid., pp. 27–28.

13. Ibid., p. 28.

14. See Descartes' grounding of the independence and autonomy of reason precisely upon the ability of reason to know what it cannot know, *Meditations of First Philosophy* [6], p. 149: "I shall proceed by setting aside all that in which the least doubt could be supposed to exist, just as if I had discovered that it was absolutely false; and I shall ever follow in this road until I have met with something which is certain, or at least, if I can do nothing else, until I have learned for certain that there is nothing in the world that is certain." See also the epistemological application of this principle in Kant's *Critique of Pure Reason*, trans. by N. K. Smith (New York: St. Martin's, 1965), p. B xxxv; where the autonomy of thought is grounded upon *"previous criticism of its own powers."*

15. See P. Tillich, *What is Religion* [11], pp. 28–29.

16. Wolfhart Pannenberg has also emphasized the universalistic structure of revelation. See especially "Toward a Theology of the History of Religions" in *Basic*

Questions in Theology, trans. by J. H. Kehm (Philadelphia: Westminster Press, 1971), vol. II, pp. 65–118.

17. See P. Tillich, *What is Religion* [11], pp. 29–30.

18. Within Western culture the trends and events which led to the fragmentation of reality and the "event" of radical pluralism are first, *colonialism* (which will be discussed later); second, the rise of two *conflicting universalisms* within Western culture in the form of Christianity and Secularism (which is the subject of the present discussion); third, the discovery made by *comparative linguistics* (Humboldt, Whorf, Sapir) and *linguistic philosophy* (Wittgenstein), that our view of the world is determined by the structure of our language and that different languages disclose different worlds; fourth, *historicism*, the discovery of historical relativity which showed that the philosophy of history had run aground with its project of constructing a single human history, either developmentally or cyclically; and finally, the outcome of the discovery of historical relativity in the *sociology of knowledge*, namely, the awareness that all thinking is socially conditioned; see Karl Mannheim, *Ideology and Utopia*, trans. by L. Worth and E. Shils (New York: Harcourt, Brace & World, 1936), and P. L. Berger and T. Luckmann, *The Social Construction of Reality* (New York: Anchor, 1967). See also the discussion of the sociology of knowledge below.

19. For a vigorous restatement of this 19th-century thesis see Jürgen Habermas, *Theory of Communicative Action*, trans. T. McCarthy (Boston: Beacon Press, 1984).

20. This is still the hope of those who have not yet realized the implications of the *global situation*. In this situation Western-scientific rationality cannot claim universal validity. Even the promising program of an ideology critique proposed by K.-O. Apel (see above all *Towards a Transformation of Philosophy*, trans. G. Adey and D. Frisby [London: Routledge & Kegan Paul, 1980]), and Jürgen Habermas (see *Knowledge and Human Interests*, trans. J. J. Shapiro [Boston: Beacon Press, 1971]; and *Theory of Communicative Action* [19]), have remained committed to the "autonomous rationality" of the European Enlightenment, which, from the global point of view, is itself thoroughly *ideological*. See the discussion below in Chapters 3 and 4.

21. Precisely this right is still something which Christian theology presupposes as self-evident, rather than feeling the need to support it with arguments.

22. See P. Tillich, *What is Religion* [11], p. 30.

23. Ibid.

24. It may seem unjustified to assimilate a problematic which Tillich specifically assigns to the philosophy of religion to Christian theology. Considering Tillich's understanding of the close connection between philosophy of religion and theology, however, this is legitimate. Even if one were to object that Tillich himself explicitly distinguishes the two, one would have to explain how the "Unconditioned," which is the object of the philosophy of religion, according to Tillich, is really different from the "God" of Judeo-Christian revelation, as Tillich understands this revelation. Furthermore, one would have to show how the task which Tillich here assigns to the philosophy of religion differs from the task he assigns to theology as a "correlation" of revelation (here religion) with the situation (here philosophy).

25. See Paul Tillich, *Systematic Theology*, 3 vols. (Chicago: University of Chicago Press, 1967). In the following we will argue that the method of correlation is essentially an apologetical method. Here we follow not only Tillich's own statements to this effect, but the matter itself. Nonetheless, there is more involved in the attempt

to reflect theologically upon Secularism than mere apologetics as the work of L. Gilkey (see *Reaping the Whirlwind* [New York: Seabury, 1976]) and David Tracy (see *Blessed Rage for Order* [10]; and *The Analogical Imagination: Christian Theology and the Culture of Pluralism* [New York: Crossroad, 1981]), for example, bear witness to.

26. Ibid., p. 8.

27. Ibid.

28. Ibid., p. 10.

29. See Tillich's definition of apologetics (ibid., p. 6): "Apologetic theology is 'answering theology.' It answers the questions implied in the 'situation' in the power of the eternal message and with the means provided by the situation whose questions it answers." To the extent that the method of correlation forces the partner into the role of the questioner, it may be seen as apologetic in the imperialist sense of the term which we are here emphasizing.

30. "Pragmatics" refers to what we *do* with language and thought. It is a broader term than "logic," which refers only to the structure of language/thought apart from its actual use. Since use determines meaning, however, it is impossible to understand a form of thought apart from the practices or forms of life bound up with it. Therefore, we will be concerned in the following with the *pragmatics* of apologetic universalism, that is, with what sort of language-game theology and Secularism are playing.

31. See Jaroslav Pelikan, *The Emergence of the Catholic Tradition (100–600), The Christian Tradition: A History of the Development of Doctrine*, 5 vols. (Chicago: University of Chicago Press, 1971), vol. I, p. 12.

32. See the discussion of the relation of the New Testament kerygma and the *regula fidei* to tradition and dogma in *Kerygma and Dogma* (New York: Herder and Herder, 1969). It would be mistaken to attribute the development of doctrine merely to external pressures. Karlmann Beyschlag (*Grundriss der Dogmengeschichte, Gott und Welt* [Darmstadt: Wissenschaftliche Buchgesellschaft, 1982]) refuses "to explain the emergence of the apologists merely as a reaction to the anti-Christian agitation and persecution of the church from without," for it was just as much a concern "internal to the church" to answer the question of "what spiritual relevance Christianity could claim in reference to the non-Christian world," vol. I, (pp. 99–100). [Translation mine.]

33. It would be a mistake to think that the universalistic motive in Christian theology can be attributed to a process of "Hellenization" alone. K. Beyschlag (*Gott und Welt* [32], p. 118), holds up the positive achievements of the apologists against the "Hellenization" thesis of the critical school of the history of dogma (Harnack et al.). To the extent that they made use of the late antique philosophical theology, they "prevented the assimilation of Christ into the lower world of gods and demons." Secondly, they "secured the claim of Christianity to an eternal truth and uniqueness." And finally, they prevented "Christianity from becoming an affair for sectarian religious enthusiasts." Jaroslav Pelikan (*Catholic Tradition* [31]), also finds " 'hellenization' too simplistic and unqualified a term for the process that issued in orthodox Christian doctrine" (p. 45). For "in some ways, it is more accurate to speak of dogma as the 'dehellenization' of the theology that had preceded it and to argue that 'by its dogma the church threw up a wall against an alien metaphysic' " (p. 55). And he concludes that "the chief place to look for hellenization is in the

speculations and heresies against which the dogma of the creeds and councils was directed" (p. 55).

34. See J. Pelikan, *Catholic Tradition* [31], p. 19.

35. Ibid., p. 58.

36. Ibid., p. 15.

37. See Paul Tillich, *A History of Christian Thought*, ed. C. Braaten (New York: Harper & Row, 1968), p. 24.

38. Ibid., p. 26. Although he explicitly warns against its dangers, Tillich can still go on to say: "This is the apologetic form of theology which I use in my own systematic theology, that is, the correlation between question and answer" (pp. 26–27). Since it will be our thesis that this three-step method is typical for theology even today, let it be noted here that this is also the basic procedure of the theology of Karl Rahner. For Rahner also (see *Foundations of Christian Faith*, trans. W. Dych [New York: Seabury, 1978], p. 11), "philosophy" and "theology" are correlated as question to answer: "in the foundational course we must reflect *first of all* upon man as the universal question which he is for himself, and hence we must philosophize in the most proper sense. This question, which man *is* and not only *has*, must be regarded as the condition which makes hearing the Christian answer possible. *Secondly*, the transcendental and the historical conditions which make revelation possible must be reflected upon ... so that the point of mediation between question and answer, between philosophy and theology, will be seen. *Thirdly* and finally, we must reflect upon the fundamental assertion of Christianity as the answer to the question which man is, and hence we must do theology."

39. See J. Pelikan, *Catholic Tradition* [31], p. 18.

40. Ibid., p. 21. It should be clear that our intention is not to berate past theologians from the superior standpoint which historical hindsight might grant us. Rather, we are concerned with a structure or a specific 'pragmatics' peculiar to universalistic thinking as it has emerged in the Western tradition—both Christian *and* secular. See in this regard the discussion of the nature and function of apologetics from the point of view of sociology in P. Berger and T. Luckmann, *The Social Construction of Reality* [18]. According to Berger and Luckmann, "theology" arises from the biological and psychological need of men and women to "legitimate" and thus stabilize existing forms of interaction (roles and institutions). For a society can "function" only when the actions of its individual members can be coordinated into common actions, or when certain patterns of behavior are mutually accepted and mutually expected. These shared definitions of roles and institutions must be integrated into a totality, a "symbolic universe" of meaning which gives an individual an answer to the question of who he/she is and what he/she has to do, not only in relation to another person but also in relation to nature and the gods and other groups. As Berger and Luckmann put it: "the symbolic universe provides a comprehensive integration of *all* discrete institutional processes. The entire society now makes sense. Particular institutions and roles are legitimated by locating them in a comprehensively meaningful world" (p. 103). But they add, "it is important to realize that the institutional order, like the order of individual biography, is continually threatened by the presence of realities that are meaningless in *its* terms" (p. 103). Deviations from the norms defining accepted social roles are a threat to the existence of the society. In order to secure its own survival, therefore, a society must find ways of incorporating all that is "new" and "strange" into its own structure. "Theology" in this view is a "conceptual tool" of "universe-maintenance" (see

pp. 104–116). In order to accomplish its task, theology has at its disposal techniques of inclusion and exclusion. Depending upon whether the threat comes from within or without, these techniques may be termed "therapy" or "nihilation" (p. 112): "Therapy entails the application of conceptual machinery to ensure that actual or potential deviants stay within the institutionalized definitions of reality, or, in other words, to prevent the 'inhabitants' of a given universe from 'emigrating' " (pp. 112–13). "Nihilation, in its turn, uses a similar machinery to liquidate conceptually everything *outside* the same universe" (p. 114). Apologetic is a technique of nihilation since it is concerned with the threat from without: "nihilation involves the more ambitious attempt to account for all deviant definitions of reality *in terms of* concepts belonging to one's own universe. In a theological frame of reference, this entails the transition from heresiology to apologetics. The deviant conceptions are not merely assigned a negative status, they are grappled with theoretically in detail. The final goal of this procedure is to *incorporate* the deviant conceptions within one's own universe, and thereby to liquidate them ultimately. The deviant conceptions must, therefore, be *translated* into concepts derived from one's own universe. In this manner, the negation of one's universe is subtly changed into an affirmation of it. The presupposition is always that the negator does not really know what he is saying. His statements become meaningful only as they are translated into more 'correct' terms, that is terms deriving from the universe he negates" (p. 115). Whether theology can realize itself as universalism *without* making use of the techniques of "therapy" and "nihilation" which come from the psychological and sociological dimensions of reality, is precisely what is at issue in the question of a theology of religions.

41. Ibid., p. 32.

42. Ibid., p. 62.

43. Ibid., p. 32.

44. Ibid., p. 33.

45. Ibid.

46. Ibid., p. 34.

47. Cited in Owen C. Thomas, ed., *Attitudes Toward Other Religions: Some Christian Interpretations* (London: SCM Press, 1969), p. 16.

48. See J. Pelikan, *Catholic Tradition* [31], p. 46. According to Beyschlag (*Gott und Welt* [32], p. 111), "For the apologists, it was not scientific reason which certified revelation, but rather, revelation certified, indeed, excelled the (dominating) scientific reason, in that it saw reason's means of expression and knowledge, as its own and incorporated them into Christian thinking. It is precisely for this reason that the Christian ethic is higher than the pagan (practical proof), therefore also is 'Moses' (i.e., the Old Testament as source of truth) older than Plato (proof from antiquity); therefore Christ must be acknowledged as the earthly appearance of the world-logos (speculative proof), of whose essence the great wise men of the past had had a presentiment, but not yet fully seen." [Translation mine.]

49. Beyschlag, *Gott und Welt* [32], p. 156, emphasizes that the decisive motive behind the development of the "three norms" — the *regula veritatis*, the canon and church office and succession — came from the need to preserve Christian truth "in its entirety."

50. Cited in J. Pelikan, *Catholic Tradition* [31], pp. 66-67.

51. Hegel, of course, is only one example of a general tendency.

52. See *Die Aufklärung im Rahmen des neuzeitlichen Rationalismus* (Stuttgart: Klett-Cotta, 1981).

53. Ibid., p. 111ff. [Translation mine.]

54. Ibid., p. 45. [Translation mine.]

55. See Gotthold Lessing, "The Education of the Human Race," paragraphs 70, 72, 73, 76 in *Lessing's Theological Writings*, ed. and trans. by Henry Chadwick (Stanford: Stanford University Press, 1956), pp. 94-95. Beyschlag ([32], p. 177), points out that the concept of the "education of the human race" is foreshadowed in Irenaeus' concept of the "economy of salvation," or *praeparatio evangelica* and thus is a thoroughly apologetic conception.

56. See G. W. F. Hegel, *The Philosophy of History* (New York: Dover, 1956). p. 78.

57. Ibid., p. 73.

58. See F. Schleiermacher, *Dialektik*, ed. by R. Odebrecht (Darmstadt: Wissenschaftliche Buchgesellschaft, 1976), p. 270: "the transcendent ground of being cannot be something thought, but instead, . . . 'intuited' in 'the religious consciousness'."

59. See Friedrich Schleiermacher, *On Religion: Speeches to Its Cultured Despisers*, trans. by J. Oman (New York: Harper & Row, 1958).

60. Ibid., p. 36.

61. See F. Schleiermacher, *The Christian Faith*, 2 vols., ed. by Mackintosh and Stewart (New York: Harper & Row, 1963), for Schleiermacher's attempt to base traditional dogmatics upon the "consciousness of being absolutely dependent."

62. See F. Schleiermacher, *On Religion* [59], p. 141.

63. Ibid., p. 245.

64. See Paul Tillich, *Perspectives on 19th and 20th Century Protestant Theology*, ed. by C. E. Braaten (New York: Harper & Row, 1967), p. 106.

65. See F. Schleiermacher, *On Religion* [59], p. 249: "all intuitions and feelings of the indwelling of the Divine Being in finite nature have within Christianity been brought to perfection."

66. Ibid., p. 216: "Is there not in all religions more or less of the true nature of religion . . . ?"

67. See Paul Tillich, *Perspectives on 19th and 20th Century Protestant Theology* [64], p. 108.

68. A good example of how liberal apologetics ends in a loss of the substance of Christianity and of religion as well is the program of Peter L. Berger; see *A Rumor of Angels: Modern Society and the Rediscovery of the Supernatural* (New York: Anchor, 1970); and *The Heretical Imperative: Contemporary Possibilities of Religious Affirmation* (New York: Anchor, 1980). Berger wants to separate the method of liberal theology—which he understands as "induction", or "taking human experience as the starting point of religious reflection, and using the methods of the historian to uncover those human experiences that have become embodied in the various religious traditions" (*Heretical Imperative*, p. 115)—from its problematic results (the implicit or explicit assertion of the absoluteness of Christianity, and the complete loss of the uniqueness of the sacred), in order to create a theology adequate to the problems of a modern, pluralistic society. He overlooks the fact, however, that the method cannot be separated from its unacceptable results. It is the method itself which must be changed! For how can an impartial historical science discover the real meaning of the "sacred"? Further, *whose* experience of the sacred

are we going to settle upon as the standard according to which a "reasoned" choice between religions, and not merely a decisionistic assertion of the absoluteness of one's own, be based?

69. It is Barth which Tillich has in mind when he speaks of the dangers of "orthodox-exclusivism." See *Systematic Theology* [25], p. 3ff; and Barth's famous remarks about "religion" in "The Revelation of God as the Abolition of Religion," in *Church Dogmatics*, 1/2 (Edinburgh: Clark, 1956), pp. 280–361. In terms which would have shocked Schleiermacher, Barth writes: "Religion is unbelief. It is a concern, indeed, we must say that it is the one great concern, of godless man. . . . From the standpoint of revelation religion is clearly seen to be a human attempt to anticipate what God in His revelation wills to do and does do. It is the attempted replacement of the divine work by a human manufacture. The divine reality offered and manifested to us in revelation is replaced by a concept of God arbitrarily and willfully evolved by man" (pp. 299–300). See also the discussion of Barth in "The Conservative Evangelical Model: One True Religion," in P. Knitter, *No Other Name* [1], pp. 75–96. It should be noted here that Barth also upheld a universal will of God to save all men in Christ.

70. See Ernst Troeltsch, *The Absoluteness of Christianity and the History of Religions* (Richmond: John Knox, 1971); and "The Place of Christianity among the World Religions," in *Christian Thought: Its History and Application*, ed. by Baron F. von Hügel (London: University of London Press, 1923). For a good discussion see again P. Knitter, *No Other Name?* [1], pp. 23–36. The following is a good statement of Troeltsch's radical historicism, which, just as Barth's orthodoxy, tears apart what Schleiermacher's apologetic program intended to weld together: "Nowhere is Christianity the absolute religion, an utterly unique species free of the historical conditions that comprise its environment at any given time. Nowhere is it the changeless, exhaustive, and unconditioned realization of that which is conceived as the universal principle of religion. The Christian religion is in every moment of its history a purely historical phenomenon, subject to all the limitation to which any individual historical phenomenon is exposed, just like the other great religions." Cited by Knitter from *The Absoluteness of Christianity*, pp. 71, 85.

71. See P. Tillich, *Christianity and the Encounter of the World Religions* (New York: Columbia University Press, 1963).

72. See Bitterli, *Die "Wilden" und die "Zivilisierten"* (Munich: dtv, 1982).

73. Ibid., p. 81. All citations from Bitterli are my translations.

74. Ibid., p. 95.

75. Ibid., p. 85.

76. Ibid., p. 87.

77. Ibid., p. 176.

78. Ibid., p. 115. Bitterli formulates the dilemma of the mission so: "one neither could nor wanted to give up the substance of one's own culture, shrank back, however, from taking radical action in order to integrate the natives into this culture."

79. Ibid., p. 161.

80. See for this entire problem Christian Jäggi, "Zur Methodologie des interreligiösen bzw. interkulturellen Gesprächs aus der Sicht der Ethnologie," in *Indische Religionen und das Christentum im Dialog*, ed. by Hans-Jürg Braun and D. J. Krieger (Zürich: Theologischer Verlag Zürich, 1986), pp. 19–46. Also, Richard Friedli, *Fremdheit als Heimat* (Freiburg, 1974).

81. See Clifford Geertz, *The Interpretation of Cultures* (New York: Basic Books, 1973), for a discussion of how religion and ideology function not only to inform people's actions but are in turn confirmed by these actions.

82. See Wolfhart Pannenberg's essay "Toward a Theology of the History of Religions" (in *Basic Questions in Theology: Collected Essays*, vol. II [16]), for the idea that the religious history of humankind is "a competition between the religions concerning the nature of reality, a competition grounded in the fact that the religions have to do with total views of reality. Only in this way can they provide a basis for the orders of human existence or, in another way, mediate salvation to man" (p. 88). Further: "religious experiences do not possess such self-evidence as isolated events, but by their reference to the whole current experience of existence. The gods of religion confront men as realities distinct from themselves because they are experienced as powers over the whole of man's existence including the world" (p. 104).

83. Raimundo Panikkar speaks of "schizophrenia" as a danger of the interreligious encounter (see *Philosophers on Their Own Work* [Bern: Peter Lang, 1978], p. 201), and Georges Devereux (see *Normal und Anormal: Aufsätze zur allgemeinen Ethnopsychiatrie* [Frankfurt a. M.: Suhrkamp, 1974]) defines schizophrenia, from the socio-cultural point of view, as the misguided attempt to regain a lost or damaged orientation in a society which, due to internal change or external acculturation pressures, can no longer offer its members a stable and coherent orientation. According to Devereux, the schizophrenic attempts to deal with the stress of socio-cultural disorientation by means of *extrapolating* from an *outdated* or *partial* social "map" to the whole socio-cultural world, as if one were to try to orient oneself in present day Europe by means of a map of one particular quarter of the city of Vienna as it was in 1920!

84. See R. Friedli, *Fremdheit als Heimat* [80], p. 45: "The uneasiness and anxiety caused by the encounter with ... unfamiliar political and religious ways of life is not the experience of the new as such, but the fact that the acculturation process which thus begins brings with it personal and social anomie, instability of values and disorientation. These symptoms of a society in the process of change ... give rise to conflicts of conscience between ... the patterns of action which are no longer acceptable and the new alternatives which are not yet verified. The socio-psychological patterns of behavior in the process of cultural change or in the encounter of religions are not objectively analyzed and carried out, but because of haste, nervousness and helplessness [objectivity] is rejected or declared heretical. This is why the encounter of *cultures* is charged with tension and the defense mechanisms tear open discrepancies. The aggression which is thus set free is to be expected insofar as it often serves the purpose of self-defense." [Translation mine.]

85. Friedli (ibid., p. 47), confirms this opinion: "The ruthless communication and the possibilities of comparison which thereby arise have shattered the network of 'taken-for-granted' contexts, but the consequences of these relations and the task of disentangling them must be borne by the different sciences. ... Insofar as Christianity is concerned it is the *theology of religions* which works out the fundamental grounding for this. By means of this Christianity and the religions should get beyond this culture shock which hinders all development." [Translation mine.]

86. What this concretely implies will be seen below. For the moment it is sufficient to note that a methodologically adequate theology of religions cannot be merely the attempt to determine the meaning of other religions according to the

traditional self-understanding of Christianity. An example of a methodologically inadequate attempt to do precisely this is Carl H. Ratschow, *Die Religionen* (Gütersloh: Mohn, 1979): "Under a theology of religions we understand the assessment which Christian faith makes of the pressing plurality of religions" (p. 120). But the methodological question is: *How* "Christian faith" can reach a reliable judgment concerning other religions and cultures when it remains within the boundaries of Western Christianity? Although Ratschow characterizes the mission as "the entrance of the gospel of the Kingdom into participation in the possibilities of expression of those, for whom the gospel is being preached" (p. 128), he is not prepared to expose himself to the "experience of God in other religions" (p. 123). There remains as the authoritative model for theology, "that which happened in the first three centuries" (p. 128), namely, apologetics! The same question, of course, can be asked of any religion. The problem is a general one. This will become clearer in the discussion in Chapters 2 and 3.

87. See Tillich, *Future of Religions* [2].

88. Ibid., p. 91.

89. See Mircea Eliade, "Paul Tillich and the History of Religions," in Tillich, *Future of Religions* [2], pp. 31–36. This citation is taken from p. 31.

90. See P. Tillich, *Future of Religions* [2], p. 80.

91. Ibid., p. 83.

92. Ibid.

93. Ibid., p. 81.

94. Ibid.

95. Ibid.

96. Ibid.

97. There is an interpretation which argues that Tillich thought of this central event as the revelation of New Being in Jesus Christ and not as an event of the future and that he therefore never really got beyond a kind of Christian inclusivism of the sort Schleiermacher had proposed.

98. Ibid., pp. 81–82.

99. Ibid., p. 82.

100. Ibid.

101. Ibid., p. 91.

102. See Karl Marx, "Contribution to the Critique of Hegel's Philosophy of Right," in *Karl Marx and Friedrich Engels On Religion* (New York: Schocken, 1964), p. 41. The phrase "critique of religion" must be understood as subjective *and* objective genitive. Failure to see this is the reason why the Marxist oriented "critical theory" of the Frankfurt School (Adorno, Horkheimer, Habermas) cannot fulfill the task of critique in the 20th century which can only be carried out on *religious* ground, that is, as we will argue below (see Chapters 3 and 4), as a theology of religions.

2. METHOD

1. See Raimundo Panikkar, *Philosophers on Their Own Work* [1/83], p. 200. Contains bibliography.

2. Ibid., p. 201.

3. Ibid., p. 205.

4. Karl Rahner bases his dogmatic theology of the non-Christian religions in

"Christianity and the Non-Christian Religions" (see *Theological Investigations* [Baltimore: Helicon, 1966], vol. V, pp. 115–34), on precisely this fact. The following sentences do not appear in the English translation and are therefore offered here in my translation. They are found on page 137 of the German text. "Earlier another religion was practically also the religion of another cultural circle, a history with which one communicated only on the edge of one's own history. Today it is different. There is no Western culture enclosed within itself any more, no Western culture at all, which could consider itself simply as the center of world history. . . . Today everyone is everyone else's neighbor, and therefore determined by the global communication of life-situations: Every religion which exists in the world "is, as all cultural possibilities and realities of other men, a question and a possibility offered for all." In order to get an idea of the magnitude and significance of the historical shift which occurred in the first half of the 20th century with regard to opening up a global horizon, one need only compare the above statements to the cultural isolationism in which Ernst Troeltsch ended forty years earlier (see "The Place of Christianity Among the World-Religions" in *Christian Thought: Its History and Application* [1/70]). For Troeltsch, "the only religion that we can endure is Christianity, for Christianity has grown up with us and has become a part of our very being" (p. 25). "But this does not preclude," he continues, "the possibility that other racial groups, living under entirely different conditions, may experience their contact with the Divine Life in quite a different way, and may themselves also possess a religion which has grown up with them, and from which they cannot sever themselves so long as they remain what they are" (p. 26). Religious truth is bound to its particular historical and cultural setting and there can be no real encounter or dialogue between such mutually inaccessible realms. "The various racial groups can only seek to purify and enrich their experience, each within its own province and according to its own standards . . ." (pp. 27–28). "There can be no conversion or transformation of one into the other . . ." (p. 30).

5. See Raimundo Panikkar, *The Unknown Christ of Hinduism*, revised and enlarged edition (Maryknoll, N.Y.: Orbis Books, 1981), p. 32.

6. Ibid., p. 34.

7. Ibid., p. 35.

8. Ibid., p. 67f.

9. See R. Panikkar, *Myth, Faith and Hermeneutics* (New York: Paulist Press, 1979), p. 8f.

10. See ibid., p. 9. Panikkar's relation to dialectics is ambiguous. On the one hand, he seems to limit its usefulness to the reconstruction of meaning in history, that is, within the history of one particular culture — this is history as seen from the point of view of this culture; it is "their" history. Nevertheless, he himself employs dialectical constructions without restricting their scope; see for example, "Colligite Fragmenta: For an Integration of Reality" in *From Alienation to At-Oneness*, Proceedings of the Theology Institute of Villanova University, ed. F. A. Eigo (Villanova University Press, 1977), pp. 19–91. Here Panikkar speaks of "three kairological moments" in the "unfolding of consciousness" (p. 35ff.). But since dialectical reconstructions of this sort necessarily presuppose an evolutionist or developmental scheme, it is difficult to apply them in the intercultural encounter, wherein each culture sees itself as the peak of historical evolution. Eric Voegelin (see *The Ecumenical Age*, vol. IV of *Order in History* [Baton Rouge: Louisiana State University Press, 1956 ff.]), admits that his original project of conceiving history as "a process

of increasingly differentiated insight into the order of being in which man participates by his existence" (p. 1) could not be carried out because of "the impossibility
of aligning the empirical types in any time sequence at all that would permit the
structures actually found to emerge from a history conceived as a 'course' " (p. 2).
This would also seem to preclude the possibility of any scheme of dialectical development the moment the one-sided perspective of a given culture is abandoned.

11. See Panikkar, *Myth, Faith and Hermeneutics* [9], p. 9.

12. See Panikkar's essay, "Epoché in the Religious Encounter" in *The Intra-
Religious Dialogue* (New York: Paulist Press, 1978), pp. 39–52, for a discussion of
the limitations of phenomenology in the interreligious dialogue. Panikkar understands *epoché* to mean "putting aside one's personal religious convictions, suspend-
ing judgment on the validity of one's own religious tenets; in a word, bracketing
the concrete beliefs of individual allegiance to a particular confession" (p. 42).
Although he admits that such a methodological device has its place "in the intro-
ductory stage" of "getting to know a particular religiousness by means of unbiased
description of its manifestations," he nonetheless finds it "psychologically impracticable, phenomenologically inappropriate, philosophically defective, theologically
weak and religiously barren" when applied to the interreligious dialogue (p. 43). It
is *psychologically impracticable* because "I cannot act . . . *as if* I did not believe in
these tenets" (p. 45); *phenomenologically inappropriate* because "it is a methodological error to leave outside the dialogue an essential part of its subject matter" (p.
47); *philosophically defective* first, because the bracketing of ultimate convictions
would imply that "there is no *doer* left to perform such a maneuver," and secondly,
because philosophical encounter "requires a sincere and unconditional search for
truth and there can be no such search if my truth is removed from the sight of my
partner . . ." (p. 48); *theologically weak* because it would imply that faith is "a kind
of luxury" (p. 48) of "no fundamental relevance for my humanity" (p. 49); and
finally, the *epoché* is *religiously barren* because it would "delete at a stroke the very
subject matter of the dialogue" (p. 49), namely, religion. Panikkar concludes: "The
peculiar difficulty in the phenomenology of religion is that the religious *pistema* is
different from and not reducible to the Husserlian *noema*. The *pistema* is that core
of religion which is open or intelligible only to a *religious* phenomenology. In other
words, the belief of the believer belongs essentially to the religious phenomenon.
. . . This being the case, the *noema* of a religiously skeptical phenomenologist does
not correspond to the *pistema* of the believer. The religious phenomenon appears
only as *pistema* and not as mere *noema*" (p. 51).

13. See "The Category of Growth in Comparative Religion: A Critical Self-
Examination" in Panikkar, ibid., pp. 53–75, especially p. 67, where Panikkar again
emphasizes that: "To elaborate a Philosophy of Religion we need to take religions
seriously and, further, to experience them from within, to believe, in one way or
another, in what these religions say. . . . Religions are not purely objectifiable data;
they are also essentially personal, subjective. . . . Without that belief no philosophy
of religions is possible."

14. For a forceful and convincing presentation of this view of understanding
other religions see the methodological studies of M. Eliade in *The Quest: History
and Meaning in Religion* (Chicago: University of Chicago Press, 1969).

15. See R. Panikkar, "Verstehen als Überzeugtsein," in *Neue Anthropologie*,
edited by H.-G. Gadamer and P. Vogler as vol. 7 in the series *Philosophische Anthropologie* (Stuttgart: Thieme, 1975), pp. 132–167. This citation is taken from p. 134

and is, as are all other citations from this essay, translated by me. Here we are not concerned with the philosophical foundations of the interdependence of truth and meaning which Panikkar postulates. This will be taken up in Chapters 3 and 4 below.

16. Ibid., p. 136.

17. Ibid., p. 135.

18. Ibid., p. 137.

19. Ibid., p. 143.

20. See Panikkar, "Verstehen als Überzuegtsein" [15], p. 145. The hermeneutical requirement that the one to be understood must be able to "find himself" in the interpretation was already decisively formulated by W. B. Kristensen: "Let us not forget that there is no other religious reality than the faith of the believers. If we want to make the acquaintance with true religion, we are exclusively thrown on the pronouncements of the believers. What we think, from our standpoint, about the essence and value of foreign religions, surely testifies to our own faith or to our conception of religious belief, but if our opinion of a foreign religion differs from the meaning and the evaluation of the believers themselves, then we have no longer to do with their religion. Not only our own religion, but every religion is, according to the faith of the believers an absolute entity and can only be understood under this aspect." Cited in C. J. Bleeker, "The Phenomenological Method," *Numen*, 6 (1959), pp. 106–7. This statement has haunted the methodology of the science of religions until today. As we will argue below, the "ghost" will only be exorcised when the possibility of "methodological conversion" is explicitly acknowledged.

21. See Panikkar, *Unknown Christ* [5], p. 43.

22. It is my purpose to correct this situation and show that the idea of a "methodological" conversion must replace the "confessional" understanding of the event of conversion, and then to show its importance also for a general theory of understanding. I shall argue below (see Chapter 4) that the universality of hermeneutics as well as an adequate theory of communication in a global situation is only conceivable on the basis of *methodological conversion*. This is so because no lifeworld, no universal horizon of meaning—which is the necessary condition of knowledge of innerworldly matters—is simply "given"; rather, it must be appropriated, internalized and made one's own through an "event" both personal, social and transcendent which is most adequately conceived as a conversion; though, of course, not as a confessionally biased, polemical and apologetic conversion, as this term is normally understood. In this sense, conversion lies at the beginning of all knowledge, or in other words, knowledge is always grounded in a conversion. What sort of conversion this is, whether methodological or confessional/apologetic is decisive for the question of whether the knowledge therein grounded will be truly universal.

23. These moments of the biblical idea of *metanoia* are taken from Rudolf Schnackenburg's article *"metanoia"* in *Herders Theologisches Taschenlexikon* (Freiburg: Herder, 1973), vol. 5, pp. 60–63.

24. See the article "Conversion" by Lewis Rambo in the *Encyclopedia of Religion*, Vol. 4, pp. 73–79.

25. According to Carl-Heinz Ratschow (*Die Religionen* [1/86]), we can employ the concept of faith: "only in relation to God the Father of Jesus, because the relation to God in other religions is only accessible to us from the outside." For "he who has an insight into the devotional relationship to a God, worships this God

and becomes His devotee." Therefore, as Christians, we must reject this insight; and this constitutes the "unbridgeable hiatus" and the "insurmountable difficulty" which accompanies every "theological comparison of religions" (pp. 123–24). [Translation mine.]

26. This is a constant theme of Panikkar's work. See especially, "Faith as a Constitutive Human Dimension" in Panikkar, *Myth, Faith and Hermeneutics* [9], pp. 188–229; and "Faith and Belief: A Multi-religious Experience" in Panikkar, *Intra-Religious Dialogue* [12], pp. 1–23.

27. See Panikkar, *Myth, Faith and Hermeneutics* [9], p. 190.

28. That this statement does not amount to an attempt to ground cross-cultural universals theologically, will be seen in Chapter 3 and 4 below where it is justified in terms of a pragmatic semantics.

29. See Panikkar, *Unknown Christ* [5], p. 52.

30. See Panikkar, *Myth, Faith and Hermeneutics* [9], p. 6.

31. See Panikkar, *Unknown Christ* [5], p. 59. "Mysticism" here should not be understood as the mere negation of all differences, the "night in which all cows are black" (Hegel), but, as we will see later on, a pragmatic condition of universal validity.

32. See Panikkar, *Myth, Faith and Hermeneutics* [9], p. 205.

33. Ibid., pp. 207–8.

34. Ibid., p. 207.

35. Ibid., p. 202. See also Panikkar, *Unknown Christ* [5], p. 60: "Faith is not a matter of reifying the living expression of a mystical or 'supernatural' act into a belief in some crystallized and disconnected formulations. The act of faith is a gift of God, through which I participate in the divine knowledge that God has of himself and, in himself, of everything else; it is a simple, vital act which needs only a minimum of intellectual explicitness."

36. This becomes clear when we consider that *as* formulations of faith all religious doctrines are *functionally similar*. See Panikkar, *Intra-Religious Dialogue* [12], p. 22: "I am not suggesting that all beliefs are equal and interchangeable; I am saying that in a certain respect they exhibit the same nature, which makes dialogue, and even dialectics, possible. Moreover, I assert they are generally equivalent in that every belief has a similar function: to express Man's faith, that faith which is the anthropological dimension through which Man reaches his goal—in Christian language, his salvation."

37. Thus is the "insurmountable difficulty" of all "theological comparison of religions" which, according to Ratschow, *Die Religionen* [1/86], has condemned all interreligious dialogue to failure, in principle overcome.

38. See Panikkar, *Myth, Faith and Hermeneutics* [9], p. 191.

39. See Panikkar, *Intra-Religious Dialogue* [12], p. 18. This qualifies what was said above about mysticism.

40. See for example the remarks in *The Trinity and the Religious Experience of Man* (Maryknoll, N.Y.: Orbis, 1973), p. 43: "I am convinced that the meeting of religions cannot take place on neutral territory, in a 'no man's land'—which would be a reversion to unsatisfactory individualism and subjectivism. ... it is scarcely possible to speak of these subjects from outside one or another tradition, for it is these very traditions that have determined the terminology."

41. See Panikkar, *Unknown Christ* [5], p. 32.

42. See Panikkar, *Intra-Religious Dialogue* [12], pp. xviii–xix, where Panikkar

argues against indifferentism under the title of *parallelism.* "Religions would," in this view, "be parallel paths and our most urgent duty would be not to interfere with others, not to convert them or even to borrow from them, but to deepen our own respective traditions so that we may meet at the end, and in the depths of our own traditions." But this view is "not free of difficulties. . . . First of all, it seems to go against the historical experience that the different religious and human traditions of the world have usually emerged from mutual interferences, influences and fertilizations. It too hastily assumes, furthermore, that every human tradition has in itself all the elements for future growth and development; in a word, it assumes the self-sufficiency of every tradition and seems to deny the need or convenience of mutual learning, or the need to walk outside the walls of one particular human tradition — as if in every one of them the entire human experience were crystallized or condensed."

43. See Panikkar, *Unknown Christ* [5], pp. 33–34. Panikkar continues in the same place: "Coexistence, furthermore, will not satisfy the traditional Christian understanding, which is that Christianity embodies the *Mystery* that God has revealed for the whole World. . . . Either Christianity gives up its claim to universality, catholicity, and then coexists peacefully with other religions, or it has to explain its claim with a theory . . . that shows the reasonableness and righteousness of such a claim. Otherwise it will bear the burden of being a fanatical and exclusive religion seeking to destroy everything that is not to its particular taste. . . . Similarly, Hinduism cannot be satisfied with merely coexisting with a militant Christianity such as claims that it has a 'right and duty' (jurisdiction) over the whole world. . . . In other words, either Hinduism gives up its conviction that it is the 'everlasting religion,' at least for the Indian people, or it has to explain how another *dharma* can satisfy the exigencies of its own self-understanding. If it were to coexist with a merely passive Christianity, respecting the actual *status quo* — being based on the fundamental principle of modern Hinduism, i.e. the relative equality of all religions — this would imply the transformation of Christianity into yet another of the various branches of Hinduism."

44. See Panikkar, *Intra-Religious Dialogue* [12], p. 5.

45. See R. Panikkar, *Kultmysterium in Hinduismus und Christentum* (Freiburg: Alber, 1964), pp. 62ff.; and "Colligite Fragmenta" [10], p. 35f.; and Eric Voegelin, *Order in History* [10], vols. I and II for a discussion of such totalistic transformations. It was this which Karl Jaspers had in mind when he spoke of an "axial period" in human history.

46. See Panikkar, *Unknown Christ* [5], p. 15.

47. Ibid., p. 40.

48. Ibid., p. 29.

49. See Panikkar, *Myth, Faith and Hermeneutics* [9], p. 4.

50. For a full discussion of the pragmatic conditions of validity of second-level discourse see Chapter 4 below.

51. Ibid., p. 21.

52. See the discussion below in Chapter 4.

53. Ibid., p. 6.

54. See the discussions of symbol in Panikkar, *Intra-Religious Dialogue* [12], p. xxv.; and also in *Kultmysterium* [45], pp. 126–51.

55. See Panikkar, "Man and Religion: Dialogue with Panikkar" *Jeevadhara* (Jan.–Feb., 1981), p. 13.

56. See Panikkar, *Intra-Religious Dialogue* [12], p. 7: "I believe in God who made the universe, in a Christ who redeemed mankind, in a Spirit who is our pledge of everlasting life and so forth. For me all these phrases are just translations into a given language understandable in a given tradition, of something that outsoars all utterance. I refer to those dogmas (as they are called) which make sense of my life and convey what truth is for me. I cannot dispense with these phrases because they make up my belief; but neither must I forget that they are phrases, neither more nor less."

57. See Panikkar, *Myth, Faith and Hermeneutics* [9], p. 7.

58. The basic "cosmotheandric vision" which informs Panikkar's thought is perhaps nowhere so clearly expressed as in "Colligite Fragmenta" [10], pp. 68ff. Panikkar writes: "The cosmotheandric principle could be stated by saying that the divine, the human and the earthly—however we may prefer to call them—are the three irreducible dimensions which constitute the real. ... They are constitutive dimensions of the whole, which permeates everything that is and is not reducible to any of its constituents. ... Everything that exists, any real being, presents this triune constitution expressed in three dimensions" (p. 74). These dimensions are: first, "every being has an abyssal dimension, both transcendent and immanent" (p. 75); second, every being "is within the range of consciousness; it is thinkable and, by this very fact, connected with man's awareness" (p. 76); and third, every being "stands in the world and shares its secularity" (p. 78). As we shall see in Chapter 4, a one-sided reduction of reality to either cosmic, divine or human dimensions cannot ground meaning. We shall see that only a "hermeneutics of non-violence" can realize the *cosmotheandric solidarity* which alone preserves the openness of the symbol to transcendence.

59. See in this context Panikkar's remarks on "comparative theology" in "Rta-tattva: A Preface to a Hindu-Christian Theology," in *Jeevadhara* (Jan.–Feb., 1979), p. 22: "strictly speaking 'comparative theology' is not possible if by this we under-stand an independent theological comparison of theologies. From which (neutral) theology do we start? And further, to which theology would belong the theological comparison? If only to one of the two compared or to a third one, in both cases comparative theology would have no authority for the theology which is not carrying out the theological comparison. And this is my point: 'comparative theology' has to belong equally to both of the two theologies being compared: it is at the intersection of them; it is a theology that criticizes previous theological positions from a point of view accepted by the positions concerned. A Hindu-Christian theology is not a Christian theology alone, exclusively accepting or rejecting Hindu tenets. Nor is it a Hindu theology performing a similar function. Nor can it be a third independent type of theology, a theological reflection of the nature of these two religions from the point of view of say Islamic theology, or pure Reason. A Hindu-Christian the-ology has to be equally Hindu and Christian, a valid theological enterprise for these two."

60. See for this entire problem the discussion in "Man and Religion: A Dialogue with Panikkar" [55], pp. 5–32. Instead of speaking in terms of "myth," "symbol" and "logos," Panikkar here distinguishes between religions 1, 2 and 3: "So when I speak of religion, of Christianity to make it very clear, I speak of religion 1, religion 2, and religion 3 (r^1, r^2, r^3) or Christianity 1, Christianity 2, and Christianity 3. It is this: Christianity 1 is Christendom, is Christian culture, is Canon Law, Christianity lived in an incarnated, and thus limited but effective way. It is the whole socio-

cultural setup in which a religion is alive. This is Christianity 1, r^1 in general. Christianity 2 or r^2 is, to speak in Christian vocabulary, the sacramental level, the ecclesial level, the *sacramentum mundi*, the *ecclesia extra quam nulla salus*, if you want. This is not identical with the Processions, with the Canon Law, with Pius XII or Bonifacius VIII; it is deeper and yet is always visible, material; it is the tantric aspect, the sacramental dimension, the psycho-spiritual-material fact into which you enter through religion 1. The moment you become mature in any religion you discover that it is very good to go, say, to the *Meenakshi* temple, but that the important thing is not just *Meenakshi*, but something beyond, behind and yet not totally severed from its symbol. The religions, i.e. religions 1, are all on the same level. Christianity 1 is not better off than any other religion. It could even be worse. It is for the historians to decide. Religions here are all equivalent, are historical facts. However on the sacramental level (r^2), all these religions are complementary to each other. They complement and often supplement each other. These are living symbols through which I enter into that which religions stand for: the fulfillment of my being. And then there is religion 3 which Christians call the Mystery, the centre, and that cannot be complementary because there cannot be many centres. My approach to religion 3 is always limited depending on r^1 and r^2. So that I cannot say regarding religion 3 that it is one or many; there is neither one nor many. I see it in and through r^1 and r^2 reaching as far as I can r^3. But I do not exhaust r^3 at all" (p. 16).

61. See Panikkar, *Myth, Faith and Hermeneutics* [9] p. 9f.

62. See Panikkar, *Unknown Christ* [5], p. 12.

63. See Panikkar, *Intra-Religious Dialogue* [12], p. 10. Also interesting in this connection is Panikkar's answer to the question of whether the interreligious dialogue does not carry with it a certain risk in "Dialogue with Panikkar" [66], p. 22: "A total risk, of dying, and you believe that you may rise again, but you really don't know it. The resurrection is not a trick. There is real religious risk in religious dialogue, if you take the faith or beliefs of all your fellow beings seriously."

64. See Panikkar, *Intra-Religious Dialogue* [12], p. 14.

65. See Panikkar, *Myth, Faith and Hermeneutics* [9], pp. 242–43.

66. Ibid., p. 381.

67. It will be the task of Chapters 3 and 4 of this study to take up these questions on the level of a philosophical foundation of the interreligious dialogue as intercultural hermeneutics and demonstrate the possibility of a universal language as discourse of dis-closure.

68. That a faithful and critical understanding of one's own revelation can only be attained through understanding all other revelations is a consequence of the methodological concept of "conversion."

69. See Panikkar, *Intra-Religious Dialogue* [12], p. 33.

70. Ibid., p. xxii.

71. See Panikkar, *Unknown Christ* [5].

72. For a thorough discussion of the analogy problem, see L. Bruno Puntel, *Analogie und Geschichtlichkeit I* (Freiburg: Herder, 1969). Although the functional equivalence between Christ and Ishvara looks like a classical *similitudo proportionum*, that is, a relation of relations according to the schema: $a/b = c/d$, it is not this, for this would degrade both symbols to the level of interchangeable elements in a formal structure. On the other hand, the similarity between Christ and Ishvara is also not a typical analogy *unius ad alterum*, for then, Christ and Ishvara would

be subjugated to a third, higher moment. See also David Tracy, *Analogical Imagination* [1/25].

73. See Panikkar, *Intra-Religious Dialogue* [12], p. 33.

74. See the essay "Growth in Comparative Religion" [12], pp. 69–70. Panikkar develops this idea against the background of his "cosmotheandric vision": "I submit that the one category able to carry the main burden in the religious encounter and in the further development of religion (and religions) is *growth* . . . religious consciousness is something more than an external development of a knowing organ that at a certain moment discovers something of which it was not previously aware. And, since religious consciousness is an essential part of religion itself, the development of this consciousness means the development of religion itself. Secondly, it amounts to more than just a development in personal consciousness; at the very least human consciousness is set in evolution. What develops, in fact, is the entire cosmos, all creation, reality. The whole universe expands. In a word, there is real growth in Man, in the World and, I would also add, in God, at least inasmuch as neither immutability nor change are categories of the divine."

75. Ibid., p. 10.

76. Ibid., p. 61.

77. See Panikkar, *Unknown Christ* [5], p. 163.

78. See Panikkar, *Intra-Religious Dialogue* [12], p. 19; and also the important programmatic essay "Metatheology as Fundamental Theology" in Panikkar, *Myth, Faith and Hermeneutics* [9], pp. 322–34.

79. See Panikkar, *Intra-Religious Dialogue* [12], p. 17. Here Panikkar finds himself in basic agreement with Heidegger's notion of truth as disclosure and Hans-Georg Gadamer's understanding of hermeneutics as not reducible to objective methods. We will return to this point below in Chapter 4.

80. The question of which persons, groups or institutions may be considered "representative" of a particular religion is, of course, a matter for itself. Most probably this question would have to be answered differently within each different tradition. Representative status is also, as we shall see below, not independent of preparedness for interreligious dialogue.

81. Ibid., p. 14.

82. Ibid., p. 30.

83. Ibid.

84. Ibid., p. 64.

85. Ibid., p. 36.

86. Ibid., p. 15.

87. See the discussion of hermeneutics below, Chapter 4.

88. It is for this reason that neither the "regressive hermeneutics" of a psychoanalytic model, nor the "progressive hermeneutics" of a model based upon Hegelian dialectics can really claim universality and thus the right to criticize ideology as Habermas, for example, asserts. Furthermore, no hermeneutics which limits itself to the historical retrieval of founding texts, as does Gadamer's philosophical hermeneutics, can fulfill this requirement. See the discussion in Chapter 4.

89. See Panikkar, *Unknown Christ* [5], p. 7.

90. Ibid., p. x.

3. FOUNDATIONS

1. See Richard J. Bernstein, *Beyond Objectivism and Relativism* (Philadelphia: University of Pennsylvania Press, 1983).

2. Ibid., p. 8.

3. Ibid.

4. Following M. Foucault (see *The Archeology of Knowledge* [New York: Pantheon Books, 1972]), who defines "episteme" as "the total set of relations that unite, at a given period, the discursive practices that give rise to epistemological figures, sciences, and possible formalized systems . . .," I use this term to denote the peculiar character of Western thought as a whole, its structural uniqueness and identity.

5. For the following discussion concerning ideology, see Hans-Joachim Lieber, *Ideologie: Eine historische-systematische Einführung* (Paderborn: Schoeningh, 1985); and Kurt Lenk, ed., *Ideologie* (Frankfurt a. M.: Campus, 1984); Karl Mannheim, *Ideology and Utopia* [1/18]; Max Horkheimer and Theodore W. Adorno, *Dialectic of Enlightenment*, trans. J. Cumming (New York: Seabury Press, 1972); and Th. W. Adorno, ed., *The Positivist Dispute in German Sociology*, trans. G. Adey and D. Frisby (London: Heinemann, 1976); Peter L. Berger and Thomas Luckmann, *The Social Construction of Reality* [1/18]; R. Panikkar, "Tolerance, Ideology and Myth" in *Myth, Faith and Hermeneutics* [2/9]; Hans Barth, *Truth and Ideology*, trans. F. Lilge (Berkeley: University of California Press, 1976); Jürgen Habermas, ed., *Hermeneutic und Ideologiekritik* (Frankfurt a. M.: Suhrkamp, 1971). I am not concerned so much with the history of a concept, as with the contours of an entire problematic which has come to be identified by the term "ideology."

6. The *American Heritage Dictionary* defines "ideology" as "the body of ideas reflecting the social needs and aspirations of an individual, group, class, or culture." Historically, the concept of "ideology" goes back to the French Enlightenment, specifically, to the *Eléments d'idéologie* of Antoine L. C. Destutt de Tracy (1754–1836) and is already there understood as a "science of ideas" conceived with the intention of criticizing and replacing inherited prejudices. See the historical discussion in H.-J. Lieber, *Ideologie* [4], p. 19ff.

7. Some see Freudian psychoanalysis, because it recognizes unconscious motivations and thought processes, also as a critique of ideology in this sense. There is indeed a striking parallel between dreams and false consciousness. For a dream also has a hidden "truth" disguised by its manifest form. And this disguising of the truth can also be discovered to stand in the service of "interests." Psychoanalysis does indeed become ideology-critique the moment cultural creations—such as religion, myth, art and politics—become assimilated to dreams, that is, analyzed upon the analogy of neurotic symptoms as products of sublimated unconscious desires. For the significance of Freud for the problem of ideology, see P. Ricoeur, *Freud and Philosophy: An Essay on Interpretation*, trans. D. Savage (New Haven: Yale University Press, 1970); and J. Habermas, *Knowledge and Human Interests* [1/20].

8. See Karl Marx, "Preface to a Contribution to the Critique of Political Economy" in *Karl Marx and Frederick Engels: Selected Works* (New York: International Publishers, 1969), p. 182.

9. See Karl Mannheim, *Ideology and Utopia* [1/18], p. 3.

10. Ibid., p. 9.

11. Ibid., p. 41.

12. See Ernst Topitsch, "Über Leerformeln" in *Probleme der Wissenschaftstheorie*, Festschrift für Victor Kraft, edited by Ernst Topitsch (Vienna: Springer, 1960); and "Begriff und Funktion der Ideologie" in *Sozialphilosophie zwischen Ideologie und Wissenschaft* (Neuwied: Luchterhand, 1961); and Hans Albert, *Treatise on*

Critical Reason, trans. M. V. Rorty (Princeton, N. J.: Princeton Univ. Press, 1985); and Karl Popper, *The Open Society and its Enemies*, 2 vols. (London: Routledge & Kegan Paul, 1945).

13. See above all Th. W. Adorno, ed., *The Positivist Dispute in German Sociology* [5]. And also see Jürgen Habermas, "Technology and Science as 'Ideology'," in *Toward a Rational Society*, trans. by J. J. Shapiro (Boston: Beacon Press, 1970), pp. 81–122.

14. Kenneth Baynes, James Bohman, and Thomas McCarthy, who have edited an important book concerned with this aspect of contemporary philosophy (see *After Philosophy: End or Transformation?* [Cambridge, Mass.: MIT Press, 1987]), define "postmodernism" as "a critique of the modern ideas of reason and the rational subject." For the postmodern thinkers, including Jean-François Lyotard, Jacques Derrida, Richard Rorty and Michel Foucault, "it is above all the 'project of the Enlightenment' that has to be deconstructed, the autonomous epistemological and moral subject that has to be decentered; the nostalgia for unity, totality, and foundations that has to be overcome; and the tyranny of representational thought and universal truth that has to be defeated" (p. 68).

15. See Richard Rorty, *Consequences of Pragmatism* (Sussex: Harvester Press, 1982), p. xiv. See also *Philosophy and the Mirror of Nature* (Princeton: Princeton University Press, 1979).

16. R. Rorty, *Consequences of Pragmatism* [15], p. xxxvii.

17. Ibid., p. xix.

18. Ibid., p. xxx.

19. Ibid., p. xvii.

20. Ibid., p. xli.

21. Ibid., p. xlii.

22. Richard Bernstein also has doubts about Rorty's program. See *Philosophical Profiles: Essays in a Pragmatic Mode* (Cambridge: Polity Press, 1986), pp. 53–54: "To tell us, as Rorty does over and over again, that 'to say the True and Right are matters of social practice' or that 'justification is a matter of social practice' or that 'objectivity should be seen as conformity to norms of justification we find about us', will not do. We want to know how we are to understand 'social practices', how they are generated, sustained, and pass away. But even more important we want to know how they are to be *criticized*. For in any historical period we are confronted not only with a tangle of social practices, but with practices that make competing and conflicting demands upon us."

23. Rorty explicitly appeals to Nietzsche when he identifies (see *Consequences of Pragmatism* [15], p. xlii) with "the sense that there is nothing deep down inside us except what we have put there ourselves, no criterion that we have not created in the course of creating a practice, no standard of rationality that is not an appeal to such a criterion, no rigorous argumentation that is not obedience to our own conventions." And with secular pathos he goes on to describe a post-philosophical culture as one "in which men and women feel themselves alone, merely finite, with no links to something Beyond." Obviously we are dealing here with a postmodern version of secular universalism.

24. See Friedrich Nietzsche, *The Will to Power*, trans. W. Kaufmann and R. J. Hollingdale (New York: Vintage, 1967), Nrs. 493, 616.

25. Jean-François Lyotard (see *The Postmodern Condition* [Minneapolis: University of Minnesota Press, 1984]), speaks of "agonistics" to characterize the prin-

cipally polemical nature of language games. See also M. Foucault's thesis (*Discipline and Punish: The Birth of the Prison*, trans. A. Sheridan [New York: Vintage, 1979]), that there is no contradiction between "truth" and power (pp. 27–28): "We should admit ... that power and knowledge directly imply one another: that there is no power relation without the correlative constitution of a field of knowledge, nor any knowledge that does not presuppose and constitute at the same time power relations. ... In short, it is not the activity of the subject of knowledge that produces a corpus of knowledge, useful or resistant to power, but power/knowledge, the processes and struggles that traverse it and of which it is made up, that determines the forms and possible domains of knowledge."

26. It should be clear that the problem of the *other* has been with us since the very beginning. In Chapter 1 we saw how Christian theology formed itself into an apologetic universalism precisely in order to deal with the problem of the other, namely, the problem of the other *without*, which the Jewish and Hellenic worlds represented, and the problem of the other *within*, represented by the danger of heresy. In reaction to these two forms of the other, apologetic universalism articulated itself into "apologetics" properly speaking, which was directed toward the external opponent, and "dogmatics," which was directed toward the other within. These structures repeat themselves in modern Secularism in that complex of problems subsumed under the term "ideology." False consciousness, or ideology, is seen as *alienated* consciousness. The other without and the other within are taken to be forms in which consciousness has become estranged to itself and can therefore be "apologetically" exposed and criticized and "dogmatically" appropriated. Whether or not ideology-critique can move away from "apologetics" and "dogmatics" and their underlying assumptions depends, I contend, upon the possibility of founding an intercultural hermeneutics as theology of religions.

27. See Peter Winch, *The Idea of a Social Science and Its Relation to Philosophy* (London: Routledge & Kegan Paul, 1961); and "Understanding a Primitive Society," *American Philosophical Quarterly*, 1, no. 4 (Oct., 1964), pp. 307–24. For the discussion surrounding Winch, as well as a reprint of the above mentioned essay, see Bryan R. Wilson, ed., *Rationality* (Oxford: Blackwell, 1970); and also M. Hollis and S. Lukes, eds., *Rationality and Relativism* (Cambridge, Mass.: M.I.T. Press, 1982). Michael Theunissen (*Der Andere: Studien zur Sozialontologie der Gegenwart* [Berlin: de Gruyter, 1977]), examines the attempts to ground a theory of intersubjectivity as well as an ontology of the social in the traditions of transcendental idealism (phenomenology included) on the one hand, and the "dialogical" school of M. Buber on the other. His conclusion is that transcendental phenomenology cannot escape *solipsism* while dialogism ends in *mysticism*: "Either the immediate encounter with the Thou will be sought for in its peculiar medium, the existential praxis of dialogical self-realization, but then not actually analyzed, but rather merely proclaimed. Theory gives itself over to praxis and loses itself in edification. Or the immediate encounter with the Thou is pushed aside into the sphere of intentionality and then indeed analyzed, but with inadequate concepts and insufficient models" (p. 495). [Translation mine.] In view of this result we feel justified in turning toward linguistic philosophy for a solution. Such a solution would unite the praxis orientation of dialogical personalism with the theoretical/semantic orientation of phenomenology. This is precisely what I propose under the title of a pragmatics of convincement; see Chapter 4.

28. Cited by Winch in "Understanding a Primitive Society" [27], p. 308.

29. Ibid., p. 307.

30. (Oxford: Oxford University Press, 1937).

31. See P. Winch, "Understanding a Primitive Society" [27], p. 308.

32. Ibid., p. 309.

33. Ibid.

34. Ibid.

35. Ibid.

36. Ibid.

37. Ibid., p. 312.

38. Ibid.

39. Ibid., p. 314.

40. Ibid.

41. Ibid., p. 312.

42. This is Jürgen Habermas' argument against Winch's relativism. See the Introduction to *Theory of Communicative Action* [1/19].

43. See Winch, "Understanding a Primitive Society" [27], pp. 312–13.

44. See P. Winch, *The Idea of a Social Science* [26], p. 100–101. This, of course, does not excuse thought from the obligation to be internally consistent. The point of the argument is rather to transpose the problem of rational coherence from the formal-logical level, where it cannot be relevantly applied to worldviews to the *transcendental-pragmatic* level, that is, to the level where worldviews are actually located. It is here that Karl-Otto Apel has taken up Winch's argument and carried it further. See *Towards a Transformation of Philosophy* [1/20]; and also J. Habermas' discussion of Winch in *Zur Logik der Sozialwissenschaften* (Frankfurt a.M.: Suhrkamp, 1982).

45. See Ludwig Wittgenstein, *Philosophical Investigations*, trans. G. E. M. Anscombe (New York: Macmillan, 1953), p. 194.

46. Cited in Gibson Winter, *Liberating Creation: Foundations of Religious Social Ethics* (New York: Crossroad, 1981), p. 98.

47. Ibid., pp. 100–101.

48. Ibid., p. 98.

49. This formulation of the problem of conflicting worldviews connects post-modern theories of power (see the discussion of Rorty and Nietzsche above) with Wittgenstein's critique of a private language.

50. See "Understanding a Primitive Society" [27], p. 317.

51. Ibid., p. 318. See also the discussion of the problem of rationality and relativism in Bryan Wilson, *Rationality* [27]; and Martin Hollis and Steven Lukes, eds., *Rationality and Relativism* [27]; and Wendy D. O'Flaherty, *Dreams, Illusions and other Realities* (Chicago: University of Chicago Press, 1984).

52. See Ludwig Wittgenstein, *Tractatus Logico-Philosophicus*, trans. D. Pears and P. McGuinness (London: Routledge & Kegan Paul, 1961). Winch (see ibid., p. 313) compares "the disagreement between [himself] and Evans-Pritchard to that between the Wittgenstein of the *Philosophical Investigations* and his earlier *alter ego* of the *Tractatus Logico-Philosophicus*." All citations from Wittgenstein's *Tractatus* will be accompanied in the text by the paragraph numbers. Out of the vast literature on Wittgenstein, here are some recent overviews: J. O. Urmson, *Philosophical Analysis* (Oxford: Oxford Univ. Press, 1967); K. T. Fann, *Wittgenstein's Conception of Philosophy* (Berkeley: Univ. of Calif. Press, 1971); P. M. S. Hacker, *Insight and*

Illusion (London: Oxford Univ. Press, 1972); A. Kenny, *Wittgenstein* (Cambridge, Mass.: Harvard Univ. Press, 1973).

53. "Semantics" is the *theory of meaning*, that is, the theory of how words and sentences receive meaning. On the distinction between realist and pragmatic semantics see Franz von Kutschera, *Philosophy of Language*, trans. B. Terrel (Dordrecht: Reidel, 1975); and Karl-Otto Apel, *C. S. Peirce: From Pragmatism to Pragmaticism* (Amherst, Mass.: University of Mass. Press, 1981); and "From Kant to Peirce: the Semiotical Transformation of Transcendental Logic" in *Towards a Transformation of Philosophy* [1/20]; and *Sprachpragmatik und Philosophie*, ed. by K.-O. Apel (Frankfurt a.M.: Suhrkamp, 1976). According to Apel (*Towards a Transformation of Philosophy*, p. 101): "The discovery of the pragmatic dimension of the sign function and consequently of sign-mediated knowledge can be traced back to Peirce's semeiotics, his doctrine of categories and relational logic. Its crucial point lies in the recognition that *cognition, as a sign-mediated function, is a triadic relationship that cannot be reduced to a dyadic relationship . . . .*" Following Peirce, Charles Morris (see "Foundations of the Theory of Signs," in *Encyclopedia of Unified Science*, I, no. 2 [Chicago: University of Chicago Press, 1938]) expressed this triadic structure in the simple statement that "a sign refers to something for someone" (p. 3), from which he abstracted three dimensions of the process by which something functions as a sign (semiosis), namely, the *syntactical* relation of signs among themselves, the *semantical* relation of signs to things they denote, and the *pragmatical* relation of signs to those who use them. But Morris fell behind Peirce when he assigned the study of the use of signs (pragmatics) to the behavioral sciences and separated pragmatics from semantics. Wittgenstein demonstrated that reference and logical coherence alone cannot account for *meaning*. The basic insight of the *pragmatic semantics* which Wittgenstein proposed is that the actual *use* of language determines its meaning. As Kutschera puts it (see *Philosophy of Language*, p. 79), pragmatic semantics claims that "language is a human way of acting, which is integrated into the context of the entire human life-situation. Therefore, its function is always to be analyzed against the background of this context. The realistic approach according to which the semantic function, the meaning of a linguistic expression may be determined independently of the context of use is thus false." Apel concludes (*Transformation*, p. 101): "Amongst other things, this means that cognition can be reduced neither to the relation-free givenness of mere sense data (classical positivism, especially that of Ernst Mach), nor to a dyadic subject–object relationship (which merely elucidates the resistance experienced when the self clashes with a non-self), nor to dyadic relationship between theories and facts in the sense of semantics (logical positivism). . . . Nor can cognition be understood as the bare mediation through concepts as in *Kant's transcendental synthesis of apperception.*" Apel will combine the insights of Peirce with J. Royce's idea of an unlimited community of interpreters and the later Wittgenstein's philosophy of language-games in order to construct a "transcendental hermeneutics" or "universal pragmatics" as an alternative to what he calls "scientism." Despite important differences, which will become clear later, my own argument is heavily indebted to Apel as well as Habermas.

54. See Erik Stenius (*Wittgenstein's Tractatus* [Oxford: Basil Blackwell, 1960]) for a thorough discussion of the Kantian implications of Wittgenstein's early thought.

55. The sentence: "The broom stands in the corner" might be taken as an

example of an elementary proposition, since it is composed of two names of objects, the broom and the corner, and of a simple relation between them, namely, that the broom is standing in the corner. This most simple combination of objects constitutes a "fact." We can compare the *sentence*, "The broom stands in the corner," with the *fact*, whether the broom actually is standing in the corner. Now this sentence may be combined with other sentences of the same sort by means of the logical connectors "and," "or," "if-then," as for example: "The broom stands in the corner *and* the chair stands against the wall." The truth or falsity of *this* complex sentence depends upon whether the elementary propositions of which it is composed are true or false. If, for example, the broom actually stands in the corner, but the chair does *not* stand against the wall, but is in the middle of the room, then the *entire* sentence is false. The sentence is true, if both elementary propositions are true. Out of the possible combinations of true and false values for each of the elementary propositions the following truth-functional table is generated:

(p) The broom . . .	*(q) The chair . . .*	*p and q*
T	T	T
T	F	F
F	T	F
F	F	F

For Wittgenstein's self-critique of truth-functional logic and its metaphysical foundations in the theory of simple objects and elementary propositions, see *Philosophical Investigations* [45], nrs. 46 ff.

56. For good discussions of the significance of Wittgenstein's biography for an understanding of his philosophy, see Allen Janik and Stephen Toulmin, *Wittgenstein's Vienna* (New York: Simon and Schuster, 1973); and Kurt Wuchterl and Adolf Huebner, *Wittgenstein* (Reinbeck bei Hamburg: Rowohlt, 1979).

57. Wuchterl and Heubner (see *Wittgenstein* [56], p. 16) write: "Actually all the known sources lead to the conclusion that his [Wittgenstein's] philosophy was always *ethically* determined and only superficially had to do with positivism." [Translation mine.]

58. This is not to say that there is no mutual dependence between truth and meaning. Indeed, the upshot of the entire discussion of a "verification principle" (see Oswald Hanfling, *Logical Positivism* [Oxford: Basil Blackwell, 1981]) has been to show that pragmatic criteria of validity do in fact determine meaning. I know what a statement means when I know its pragmatic conditions of validity. What the rise and fall of logical positivism has shown, however, is that the interdependence of validity and meaning cannot be adequately grasped upon the metaphysical and epistemological basis which the logical *empiricists* presupposed. So long as truth is supposed to consist in *empirical verification/falsification*, it cannot function as a criteria of meaning; not even for first-level argumentative discourse. As soon as we dispense with this scientistic prejudice, however, it can be shown that conditions of validity determine meaning on all levels of discourse, though in different ways.

59. See K. T. Fann (see *Wittgenstein's Conception of Philosophy* [52]) for a discussion of this distinction. Fann writes: "We can say things with *sense* only *within*

the limits of language. Attempts to say anything *about the limit* of language result in senseless propositions, and attempts to say anything about *what lies on the other side of the limit* end in *nonsense*. . . . The failure to understand Wittgenstein's distinctions results in misinterpreting the *Tractatus* as an anti-metaphysical treatise" (p. 25).

60. This leads directly to the aporias of a totalizing critique of reason by reason as has been pointed out by Habermas in *The Philosophical Discourse of Modernity* (Cambridge, Mass.: M.I.T. Press, 1987). Habermas argues that every radical critique of "modernity," that is, of "rationality," inevitably leads to the performative contradiction of implicitly presupposing the very reason one wishes to deconstruct.

61. See K.-O. Apel, *Towards a Transformation of Philosophy* [1/20], p. 153: "If the transcendental ego or subject in the sense of formal logic is identical with the world-limiting form of language, in such a way that for each ego the same ideal form of description of the world is *a priori* valid, then it requires no inter-subjective communication (in the sense of a pre-understanding) of the world. In short, a *transcendental pragmatics* or *hermeneutics* of the world as the practically significant 'lifeworld' or situational world is neither necessary nor possible. Indeed, in the transcendental dimension, there exist only 'solitary' natural scientists. Each of them functions completely self-sufficiently as the transcendental subject of the description of the world in the objective thing-fact-language that, by means of a guarantee — one might even say, a mystical, transcendental or metaphysical guarantee — is the language of all other subjects."

62. K.-O. Apel (ibid., p. 154) sees here an important connection between the methodological solipsism of modern philosophy and the dichotomy between explanation and understanding in the human sciences: "In my opinion, Wittgenstein's statement formulates precisely the (modern) *significance of methodological solipsism in the analytical philosophy of language* inasmuch as it is presupposed by logical empiricism. It does not deny the *existence* of other subjects but rather the transcendental pragmatic or transcendental hermeneutic *presupposition* of communication with other subjects for my world and self-understanding. In accordance with the presupposition of *methodological solipsism* found in the *Tractatus*, it must, in principle, be possible for a scientist to reduce all other scientists — not to mention the remaining existent human beings — to objects of his 'description' and 'explanation' of their behavior. My thesis is indeed that precisely this position becomes the ultimate, no longer reflected upon presupposition of the neopositivist notion of an objectified unified science (in the 'thing-language' of description and explanation according to laws)."

63. Apel (ibid., p. 150) makes it clear that although a logically formalized language may serve well to express propositions of fact, and even logical relations, it cannot express different interpretations, or disagreement about the conventions which define it. To absolutize such a language, which is the project of the "unified science" movement, can only mean the elimination of an entire dimension of rationality, namely, the *pragmatic* dimension: "Speech-acts — such as assertions, questions, requests, protestations, etc. — that testify to the linguistic 'communicative competence' of human beings, in so far as they activate the propositional content of statements in discourse, can find no place in formal language since they do not belong to the objective syntactic-semantic dimension but to the subjective, pragmatic dimension of language. This pragmatic dimension of communicative utterance or speech-acts must, in a physicalist scientific language, itself be made the object

of semantic reference, and that means the object of a behavioristic science." This is indeed what Wittgenstein intends, when he maintains that the subject is not in the world. For whatever of the subject *is* in the world becomes automatically an object of scientific *explanation*. The existential encounter with others and with oneself remains outside of rational knowledge. There can be no place in this strict dichotomy between *a priori* and *a posteriori* for a "human" science which has for its "object" the subject itself. Only from the point of view of a "transcendental pragmatics" do existential individuals, as subjects of irrational value decisions become existential interpreters, as participants in a rational struggle for meaning. This will become clear in the discussion below of a "global form of life."

64. This is literally the "last word" of the new German edition of Karl Popper's famous *Logik der Forschung* (Tübingen: Mohr, 1984). He writes (p. 452): "All knowledge is suppositional knowledge. The various suppositions (*Vermutungen*) or hypotheses are our intuitive inventions (and thus according to their origin, *a priori*). They are eliminated by experience, bitter experience and so their replacement by better suppositions is encouraged. Therein, and therein alone, lies the contribution of experience to science." [Translation mine.]

65. Karl Popper (see *The Open Society and its Enemies* [12]) is an eloquent witness to this. He writes (p. 265): "Facts as such have no meaning, they gain it only through our decisions." And further (p. 217f.): "The rationalist attitude is characterized by the importance it attaches to argument and experience. But neither logical argument nor experience can establish the rationalist attitude; for only those who are ready to consider argument or experience, and who have therefore adopted this attitude already, will be impressed by them. That is to say, a rationalist attitude must be first adopted if any argument or experience is to be effective, and it cannot therefore be based upon argument or experience. . . . But this means that whoever adopts the rationalist attitude does so because without reasoning he has adopted some decisions, or belief, or habit, or behavior, which therefore, in its turn must be called irrational. Whatever it may be, we can describe it as an irrational *faith in reason*. . . . critical rationalism . . . recognizes that the fundamental rationalist attitude is based upon an irrational decision, or upon faith in reason." In *The Logic of Scientific Discovery* (New York: Basic Books, 1959), p. 108, Popper admits that it is not only at the level of basic attitudes toward reality, but also at the level of empirical testing of hypotheses that science ends in decisionism: "From a logical point of view, the testing of a theory depends upon basic statements whose acceptance or rejection, in its turn, depends upon our *decisions*. Thus it is *decisions* which settle the fate of theories. To this extent my answer to the question, 'How do we select a theory?' resembles that given by the conventionalist; and like him I say that this choice is in part determined by considerations of utility."

66. See Hans Albert, *Treatise on Critical Reason* [12], pp. 75–76: "Whereas existentialism stresses decision with its free and undetermined nature, emphasizes its irrationality, and declares scientific knowledge essentially uninteresting precisely because of its objectivity, positivism places the emphasis upon knowledge and objectivity, stressing its foundability and rational character, while dismissing decision and commitment to the realm of subjectivity and arbitrariness as philosophically uninteresting. One side seeks to eradicate objective knowledge because it allegedly fails to make contact with existence; the other seeks to avoid subjective decision because it appears to be outside the sphere of rationality. However little they may have to say to one another, it is nevertheless clear that both movements start to some extent

from common presuppositions." Albert goes on to speak of three common presuppositions of positivism and existentialism: First, the sharp distinction between rationality and existence; second, the instrumental conception of science, that is, defining science as purposive rationality directed toward technology; and third, decisionism with regard to the goals which one sets for one's knowing and acting. Contrary to Albert's intention, however, the discovery that decisionism *also* lies at the basis of science does not solve the real problem. For it is precisely the common source and mutual interdependence of positivism and existentialism (a relationship which K.-O. Apel has termed the "Western system of complementarity") which prevents an adequate critique of Secularism. The ideological function of this system is to channel critical impulses into one camp or the other, thus forcing them to exhaust themselves in mere shadow boxing. It is K.-O. Apel who has seen this most clearly. In *Towards a Transformation of Philosophy* [1/20], p. 233, Apel writes: "From our perspective, however, it immediately becomes clear that analytical philosophy and existentialism by no means contradict each other in their ideological function, but rather they complement one another. They corroborate each other through a kind of division of labour by mutually assigning to one another the domain of objective scientific knowledge, on the one hand, and the domain of subjective ethical decisions on the other." And he concludes (p. 235): "The complementarity between the value-free objectivism of science, on the one hand, and the existential subjectivism of religious acts of faith and ethical decisions, on the other, proves to be the modern philosophical-ideological expression of the liberal separation of the public and private spheres of life which has developed in the context of the separation of church and state. For in the name of this separation, and that means with the aid of secularized state power, Western liberalism first of all made religious belief less binding and then, correspondingly, increasingly restricted the binding character of moral norms to the sphere of private decisions of conscience."

67. Ludwig Wittgenstein, *On Certainty* (New York: Harper & Row, 1972), ed. G. E. M. Anscombe and G. H. von Wright, trans. D. Paul and G. E. M. Anscombe.

68. This is the tendency of K.-O. Apel's reception of Wittgenstein. See "Wittgenstein and the Problem of Hermeneutic Understanding" in *Towards a Transformation of Philosophy* [1/20], pp. 1–45; and "Wittgenstein und Heidegger" in the German edition, *Transformation der Philosophie* (Frankfurt a.M.: Suhrkamp, 1973), vol. I, pp. 225–75. J. Habermas follows Apel's interpretation in *Zur Logik der Sozialwissenschaften* [44].

69. On Wittgenstein's later thought see, apart from the general works listed in note [52] above, G. P. Baker and P. M. S. Hacker, *Wittgenstein: Understanding and Meaning—An Analytical Commentary on the Philosophical Investigations* (Chicago: Univ. of Chicago Press, 1980); and David Bloor, *Wittgenstein: A Social Theory of Knowledge* (New York: Columbia Univ. Press, 1983); and Nicholas F. Gier, *Wittgenstein and Phenomenology* (Albany: State Univ. of New York Press, 1981). Citations from the *Philosophical Investigations* will be noted in the text by means of the paragraph numbers.

70. In the *Tractatus* Wittgenstein had said: "The meanings of simple signs (words) must be explained to us if we are to understand them" (4.026).

71. In the *Tractatus* Wittgenstein had given clear answers to these questions. The criteria of meaning were the *a priori* logical form of picturing on the one hand, and the simple objects of the world, to which names immediately refer, on the other. Now, however, Wittgenstein refuses to bind himself to one fixed answer.

When the attempt is made to reduce the meaning of language to fixed criteria, Wittgenstein points out that there are always other relevant criteria. If, for example, as in *realism*, the meaning of words is reduced to their reference relation to an external reality, Wittgenstein shows, as in the above discussion of ostensive definition, that with a definition of this sort we never actually reach the things themselves but remain ever within language. If, as in *idealism*, meaning is reduced to an *a priori* logical form, or to mental processes, or Platonic ideas, Wittgenstein shows, as we shall presently see in the following discussion of the famous "private language argument," that language is only meaningful within a historically and socially determined praxis. Against *behaviorism*, which would reduce language to such a praxis, understood as stimulus–response behavior, Wittgenstein demonstrates that language is only understandable through participation and never by means of mere observation and description.

72. This expression is taken from K.-O. Apel. See "The Communication Community as the Transcendental Presupposition for the Social Sciences" in *Towards a Transformation of Philosophy* [1/20]. Apel offers as a second title of this essay (p. 136): "The transcendental language-game of the unlimited communication community as the precondition for the possibility of the social sciences." We will discuss Apel's attempt to found an ethically oriented social science on the basis of Wittgenstein's thought in Chapter 4 below.

73. See especially the Wittgenstein reception of the "German school," that is, K.-O. Apel and J. Habermas. See also Jörg Zimmermann, *Wittgensteins sprachphilosophische Hermeneutik* (Frankfurt a.M.: Klostermann, 1975).

74. Saul A. Kripke (see *Wittgenstein: On Rules and Private Language* [Cambridge, Mass.: Harvard Univ. Press, 1982], p. 101) concludes his discussion of the private language argument with the comment: "The solution turns on the idea that each person who claims to be following a rule can be checked by others. Others in the community can check whether the putative rule follower is or is not giving particular responses that they endorse, that agree with their own. The way they check this is, in general, a primitive part of the language game . . . ."

75. On the for us important problem of "cultural solipsism," see Kripke [ibid.], p. 146: "Many things that can be said about one individual on the 'private' model of language have analogues regarding the whole community in Wittgenstein's own model. In particular, if the community all agrees on an answer and persists in its view, no one can correct it. There can be no corrector *in* the community, since by hypothesis, all the community agrees. If the corrector were outside the community, on Wittgenstein's view he has no 'right' to make any correction. Does it make any sense to *doubt* whether a response we all agree upon is 'correct'?" This seems to speak for a perfect analogy between the private speaker and the "closed" community which, as Kripke says, is incorrigible *if* it does not allow for radically other — we are tempted to say *heretical* — views. The language of such a community, we would conclude, is nothing other than a private language, that is, no language at all. But far from accepting a perfect analogy between private speakers and a closed community, which would lead to the necessity of recognizing other forms of life, that is, other communities, Kripke tends to see an irreconcilable disjunction between *understanding* and *explanation* here. It is clear that we can understand what our community agrees in. This agreement is *our* form of life. *Other* forms of life, Kripke now argues, can, by definition, not be understood; instead, if they are conceivable at all, then they can only be *explained* by objective, behavioristic methods.

The logical problem at the basis of this disjunction arises in the following way: it seems that *if* we *can* be corrected, then only by someone who is *in* "our" community, for to learn by correction *is* to become integrated into a community. Understanding is participation! Again, if meaning is a function of community agreement, radical disagreement within the community becomes inconceivable (= meaningless). Therefore, there can be no corrector either within the community or without. It is easy to see where this reasoning ends: in cultural solipsism! Whatever the community says is right is right. In order to avoid this difficulty we must distinguish between the "community" as we know it at any given time and the *universal community of discourse* which functions as the transcendental condition of the possibility of corrigibility. To accept inter- and intra-communal corrigibility implies that *other* forms of life must be seen to be *internally related* to our own, and that *the* community in which conflicts of forms of life are acknowledged and worked through is necessarily a *global* or *universal communication community* whose constitutive *agreement* consists not in a fixed set of roles/rules, but in the dynamic, historical *struggle for meaning* wherein only the openness for correction counts as the basis of *our* form of life.

76. K.-O. Apel, for one (see "Wittgenstein und Heidegger" in *Transformation der Philosophie* [68], vol. I, pp. 268–69), sees in this statement the expression of a basic tendency toward *conservatism* in Wittgenstein's thought, which robs it of its critical potential. Apel writes: "In the *Philosophical Investigations* there is no other answer to the question, why Wittgenstein's philosophy, which, as descriptive phenomenology of the uses of language, 'leaves everything as it is,' does not also leave the language-game of speculative metaphysics also as it is. The suspicion of meaninglessness is pragmatically turned toward those language-games which in the context of living praxis no longer function—language-games by which the machine of language idles.

"The practical test of the validity of a 'use of language' cannot, according to Wittgenstein, lie in the fact that a sudden understanding of a linguistic expression which had perhaps long been held not to be understandable might lead to a historical foundation of new forms of life—as is explicitly provided for by theological and philosophical interpretation of texts. . . . His analysis of language-games is ahistorical and—what almost goes without saying—is without any further goal (for example, that of a progressive correction of language and form of life in the direction of a deepening of our understanding of the world and of ourselves, and in the elimination of all hindrances to human understanding." [My translation.] This interpretation overlooks, it seems to me, the significance of the fact that Wittgenstein purposely leaves the question open as to *what* and *how* language really *is*. This, by the way, gives Apel occasion to criticize Wittgenstein for not being sufficiently "self-reflective." In fact, according to Wittgenstein, the *practical functioning* of language is *always disrupted*, that is, so long as certain "pictures" of language are being imposed upon its free and varied way of being. Meaning is not merely given, as Apel would have Wittgenstein suppose. On the contrary, for Wittgenstein it is a task. Meaning arises out of the philosophical critique of distorted and meaningless language-games. Far from supposing that presently existing language is fully in order, Wittgenstein actually presupposes the practical non-functioning of this language and its ever present meaninglessness. That is why there is a need for philosophy. *How* language really *is* could only be understood on the basis of a global form of life or a universal community of non-distorted communication. To "leave language as it is" means, therefore, not at all a conservative, uncritical conformism, but much rather the liberation of language from those ideological distortions which precisely *do not leave it as it is*. One could hardly be more critical!

77. Perhaps the reason why Apel and Habermas cannot appreciate the critical potential of Wittgenstein's thought is that they are still caught in the modern secular "picture" of the autonomous, rational subject who can only understand itself and only seeks understanding for the purpose of self-affirmation. See K.-O. Apel, *Towards a Transformation of Philosophy* [1/20], p. 29: "The description of a language-game in which opinions are both expressed and understood — either in words or in the form of subsequent behavior — is indeed nothing more than a relative estrangement of one's own meaning and understanding. . . . What is revealed in every aspect of this objectivistic, quasi-behavioristic tendency in modern science and analytical philosophy is ultimately only that circuitousness of human self-understanding which was recognized by Hegel: its 'mediation' through 'exteriorization' (*Entäusserung*)." It is precisely this, it seems to me, which is *not* to be found in Wittgenstein's thought. For the dialectical self-mediation of the absolute subject through self-exteriorization is grounded in the methodological solipsism of modern metaphysics. It was against this that Wittgenstein directed his private language argument. For such a self-mediating subject the *other* can only be considered as exteriorized self. *Other*, in the authentic sense, it is not and cannot be. It is for this reason that the Hegelian dialectic cannot free itself from the program of absolute knowledge, as many commentators would like it.

78. These distinctions are *logical* and should not be confused with the psychological and sociological distinction between the normal and the abnormal. Abnormal, or deviant behavior may be very *meaningful*. Indeed, as Georges Devereux (see *Normal und Anormal* [1/83]) has pointed out, most cultures actually prescribe the ways in which one may acceptably go mad. Such culturally specific typical patterns of "irrationality" are what makes diagnosis possible. In opposition to Devereux and his rejection of cultural relativism, however, I maintain that diagnosis of psychological or sociological pathology is a task of a *second order* which should not be confused with the primary *hermeneutical* task of understanding reality. If one does this, one automatically introduces an unexamined criterion of what is normal and abnormal and thus claims for oneself a *neutral position* independent of all cultural determinateness. Ethnopsychiatry, as Devereux understands it, does in fact claim cultural neutrality analogous to the affective neutrality of the psychoanalyst. It can do this, however, only on the basis of an uncritical commitment to Freudian determinism. The distinction made here between rationality, irrationality and other-rationality has only secondarily to do with mental or social "health," and primarily with the conditions of "mind" as such. This does not, however, prevent us from seeing the struggle for understanding as, from the beginning, a struggle against "schizophrenia" in Devereux's sense of a defensive *blinding out of large portions of reality*. Meaning is never merely given, but rather is always a task. And meaninglessness is never factually "healthy" or without "guilt."

79. The possibility of "other-rationality" is completely unknown both to structuralism and systems theory, for both are based upon the attempt to explain "apparent" otherness in terms of a "depth" structure wherein the other is an "opposite" within a closed, a-historical system consisting of a finite number of parts. Structural-functional systems theory cannot understand a meaning radically different from the structure of a given communication system. There simply is no positive meaning beyond the system, which could open it up to new possibilities. See the discussion

by Paul Ricoeur in "Structure and Hermeneutics" in *The Conflict of Interpretations* (Evanston, Ill.: Northwestern Univ. Press, 1974), where he compares and opposes structuralism to hermeneutics. Ricoeur writes (p. 55): "The structuralist explanation bears (1) on an unconscious system which (2) is constituted by differences and oppositions (by signifying variations) (3) independently of the observer. The interpretation of a transmitted sense, consists in (1) the conscious recovery of (2) an overdetermined symbolic substratum by (3) an interpreter who places himself in the same semantic field as the one he is understanding and thus enters the 'hermeneutic circle'." This amounts to a primacy of hermeneutics over structural analysis, for as Ricoeur says (p. 60): there is "no structural analysis ... without a hermeneutic comprehension of the transfer of sense (without 'metaphor,' without *translatio*), without that indirect giving of meaning which founds the semantic field, which in turn provides the ground upon which structural homologies can be discerned." See also the critique of Luhman's systems theory in Habermas, *The Philosophical Discourse of Modernity* [60] p. 368ff.

80. It is this fact which allows Winch (see "Understanding a Primitive Society" [27], p. 318), to base intercultural understanding upon the assumption of "formal analogies between their behavior and that behavior in our society which we refer to in distinguishing between rationality and irrationality."

4. THE NEW UNIVERSALISM

1. See E. Goffman, *Frame Analysis* (Cambridge, Mass.: Harvard University Press, 1974), for a classical discussion of lifeworld frames of action and meaning.

2. See in this connection Heidegger's analysis of anxiety in *Being and Time* (trans. J. Macquarrie and E. Robinson [New York: Harper & Row, 1962]) as awareness of the limits of the "world," that is, of being in the face of nothingness.

3. See Jürgen Habermas, *Theory of Communicative Action* [1/19], vol. 1, p. 165: "The symbolically pre-structured reality constitutes a universe which must remain hermetically closed and not understandable to the view of an observer incapable of communicating. The lifeworld opens itself only to a subject who makes use of his competence to speak and act. He creates accessibility for himself to the extent that he at least virtually participates in the communications of the members of that universe and thus himself becomes at least potentially such a member." For this reason, methods of "objective," value-free knowledge employed in the *explanation* of natural processes or animal behavior cannot be used to *understand* human *action*, which is essentially linguistic. Understanding another person, another language-game, another form of life, another culture or religion requires *communication* with the other and communication cannot be replaced methodologically by *observation*. See P. Winch, *The Idea of a Social Science* [3/27], p. 89: "understanding must necessarily presuppose, if it is to count as genuine understanding at all, the participant's unreflective understanding. And this in itself makes it misleading to compare it with the natural scientist's understanding of his scientific data." Habermas has based his distinction between "communicative action" and "strategic or instrumental action" upon this insight. The attitude of an actor seeking to causally bring about some effect in nature or in a similar way to influence another person's behavior is fundamentally different from the attitude of a speaker who is saying something to someone. This latter, as we shall see, attempts to bring about consensus and coordinated action by means of speech acts which make disputable validity claims.

4. See R. Panikkar, "Verstehen als Überzeugtsein" [2/15]. Panikkar here defends the thesis that to understand is to be convinced for discourse in general. I will argue, however, that this thesis is only applicable for what I call second-level boundary discourse, but not for argumentative discourse.

5. Let us recall what Wittgenstein had to say about a similar situation: "Is it wrong for me to be guided in my actions by the propositions of physics? Am I to say I have no good ground for doing so? Isn't precisely this what we call a 'good ground'? Supposing we met people who did not regard that as a telling reason. Now, how do we imagine this? Instead of the physicist, they consult an oracle. (And for that we consider them primitive.) Is it wrong for them to consult an oracle and be guided by it? — If we call this 'wrong' aren't we using our language-game as a base from which to *combat* theirs? And are we right or wrong to combat it? Of course there are all sorts of slogans which will be used to support our proceedings. Where two principles really do meet which cannot be reconciled with one another, then each man declares the other a fool and heretic. I said I would 'combat' the other man, — but wouldn't I give him *reasons*? Certainly; but how far do they go? At the end of reasons comes *persuasion*. (Think what happens when missionaries convert natives.)" *On Certainty* [3/67] (608–12).

6. See Jürgen Habermas, *The Theory of Communicative Action*, Vol 1 [1/19] p. 18.

7. See J. Habermas, *The Philosophical Discourse of Modernity* [3/60] p. 358–59.

8. Ibid., p. 296 and 298.

9. Formal, deductive arguments and empirical, inductive arguments may be seen to be anchored in informal argumentation the moment one asks where first premises themselves are grounded or how empirical facts are to be interpreted. To ask these questions is to step out of a merely semantic analysis into the realm of pragmatics and to investigate the "uses" of argument. See S. Toulmin, *The Uses of Argument* (Cambridge, 1958), and the critique by Habermas in *The Theory of Communicative Action* [1/19]. Despite broadening the scope of what counts as "logic," Habermas is not prepared to broaden the scope of what counts as "logical" insofar as the traditional association of logic with argumentation leads him to identify rationality with argumentation.

10. Here I follow the analysis of validity claims made by Habermas in *The Theory of Communicative Action*, Vol 1 [1/19] pp. 8-43 and 273-339.

11. See K.-O. Apel, "The *a priori* of the Communication Community and the Foundations of Ethics: the Problem of a Rational Foundation of Ethics in the Scientific Age," in *Towards a Transformation of Philosophy* [1/20]. As opposed to Habermas, who proposes his theory of communicative action as empirically falsifiable, Apel argues by means of a strict transcendental deduction from the givenness of communicative action to the normative, pragmatic conditions of its possibility.

12. Ibid. p. 257.

13. Neither Apel nor Habermas would accept this formulation of the problem, since they would insist that the reason why there is no consensus is due to ideology conceived as *systematically distorted* communication, that is, *alienated* meaning and not because there really are *other* forms of thought. As we shall see below, the problem of argumentation about argumentation returns even within this understanding of ideology, for there is no way to assert, on the one hand, that the situation of argumentation is a condition of knowledge which we cannot go behind, while, on the other hand, to claim one can go behind it and discover those factors con-

ditioning it. This in fact is what Apel and Habermas do when they appeal to Freudian psychoanalysis as a model for a *critical* social science. As Ricoeur and Gadamer have pointed out, however, the therapeutic "explanation" is really one *interpretation* among others which can claim no privilege in the conflict of interpretations. See P. Ricoeur, "Hermeneutics and Critique of Ideology," in *Hermeneutics and the Human Sciences* (ed. and trans. J. B. Thompson [Cambridge: Cambridge University Press, 1981]); and H.-G. Gadamer, "Replik," in *Hermeneutik und Ideologiekritik* [3/5].

14. Following Wittgenstein, Lyotard (see *The Postmodern Condition* [3/25]) has convincingly shown that all non-trivial communicative interactions have an "agonistic" character. Every move in a language-game, if it is not a merely automatic reaction, is free and potentially innovative. Every move, therefore, is a possible reinterpretation of the rules of the game. From this point of view, Habermas' theory of communicative action, insofar as it presupposes that argumentation is only possible *within* a common horizon, or lifeworld, runs the risk of trivialization, for it blinds out the important problems and conflicts of our time which are all conflicts on the level of basic convictions and thus may be construed as questions about just what "game" we are and should be "playing."

15. See *Reflexive Letztbegründung: Untersuchungen zur Transzendentalpragmatik* (Munich: Alber, 1985), p. 184ff. The following citations from Kuhlmann are all translated by me.

16. Ibid., p. 185: "If we really and sincerely wish to know something, if we are sincerely interested in the solution of a problem, then we are obliged to attempt to find the solution by means of rational argumentation."

17. Apel (*Transformation of Philosophy* [1/20], p. 269) writes: "I believe that — within the framework of a transcendental-philosophical radicalization of the later Wittgenstein's work — one must point out that everyone, even if he merely *acts* in a *meaningful* manner — e.g. takes a decision in the face of an alternative and claims to understand himself — already implicitly presupposes the logical and moral preconditions for critical communication."

18. Kuhlmann speaks of the "principle of practical non-contradiction" (*Reflexive Letztbegründung* [15], p. 191ff.), and Dietrich Böhler ("Transzendentalpragmatik und kritische Moral," in *Kommunikation und Reflexion*, ed. by W. Kuhlmann und D. Böhler [Frankfurt: Suhrkamp, 1982], pp. 90–91) defines "pragmatic inconsistency" as that form of meaninglessness which "has to do with a contradiction within an activity of argumentation, which as such is situated within a relationship of communication and acknowledgment among persons (as participants in argumentation). Therefore this contradiction destroys the expectations of other persons and can be compared to breaking a promise. For with the act of assertion the one arguing raises a claim to validity against (himself and) others. He thereby awakens the *expectation* that he himself is willing and able to vindicate this claim in mutual discussion. Further, he *recognizes* the others as representatives of the community in which claims may be tested, the community into which he himself has entered by virtue of making the assertion. This means: He acknowledges the right of the other to criticize and judge and he *obliges* himself to produce propositions which are credible and worthy of discussion and to participate seriously in a critical discussion of them. The dialogical relationship of a community of argumentation thus sketched out is a reciprocal relationship of acknowledgment and obligation. This social relationship is destroyed when the one making assertions, in what he says, takes back the claim to validity of the performative act (and thus the recognition

of the others as well as his own obligation)." [My translation.]

19. W. Kuhlmann, *Reflexive Letztbegründung* [15], p. 189: "If we are sincerely interested in the solution of a problem, then we must attempt to find a solution which everyone could accept, that is, we must attempt to attain a rational consensus."

20. Ibid., p. 208: "Attempt to come in all cases in which your interests could collide with the interests of others to a rational practical consensus with them."

21. Ibid., p. 214: "Always attempt to contribute to the (long run) realization of those conditions which further the realization of the ideal community of communication, and be always concerned that the already existing conditions enabling the realization of the ideal community of communication are preserved." As Kuhlmann then explains: "This implies that practical discourse can, under certain conditions, be suspended until, by means of strategic action, the conditions are realized which would first allow it to appear at all meaningful and responsible to enter into a practical discussion with participants and those affected by the issue in question."

22. This becomes embarrassingly clear in the admission with which K.-O. Apel concludes his programmatic essay on "The *a priori* of the Communication Community and the Foundations of Ethics" [1/20], p. 285: "In connection with this outlined strategy of emancipation there arises, however, an extremely delicate moral problem. This is the following question: In what situation and by virtue of what criteria may one participant in a communicative exchange claim for himself an emancipated consciousness and consider himself, therefore, to be authorized to act as a social therapist?" After arguing for a rational foundation of ethics against the irrational decisionism of the private ethics of liberalism, Apel is compelled to concede his entire program with the remark: "At this point . . . everyone must take upon himself a non-groundable . . . 'moral' decision of faith."

23. Rene Girard (see *Violence and the Sacred*, trans. P. Gregory [Baltimore: Johns Hopkins University Press, 1977]), sees violence as constitutive of social order and thus "discourse." Violence limits discourse and, according to Girard, that is right and good. In a kind of reverse Hobbesianism, Girard argues that order arises from a war of all against all not in that the group submits equally to the violence of one (the absolute monarch), but in that the one (the scapegoat) suffers equally the violence of all. In that we are all violent not *against* each other, but *with* each other against a surrogate victim, unanimity, peace and order come into being. Myth, ritual, religion and almost all social institutions which have arisen from them rest upon a foundation of violence, which they covertly commemorate and whose beneficial effects they strive to preserve. Apart from the reductionism characteristic of Durkheim and Freud in this thesis, it rests upon that fundamental confusion of being and power which Nietzsche thought through to its end. There can be no universal order and no universal discourse, for order is itself an act of violence distinguishing self from the other and consigning the other to the role of surrogate victim. The other is not one who can correct my view of reality, but one who contributes to upholding my world in that he suffers the violence my world cannot contain.

24. It is "other-rationality" which grounds Lyotard's "agonistics." For it is only the essential openness of language-games to new interpretations of their rules which makes the innovative use of language that Lyotard emphasizes possible. Of course, he does not see that it is precisely this openness which grounds the universality and

continuity of reason and thus falls back into a Nietzschian relativism typical of the postmodern vision.

25. See note 22 above.

26. See Gadamer's version of "other-rationality" (*Truth and Method* [New York: Seabury, 1975], p. 405): "it is always, in whatever tradition we consider it, a human, i.e. a linguistically constituted world that presents itself to us. Every such world, as linguistically constituted, is always open, of itself, to every possible insight and hence for every expansion of its own world-picture, and accordingly available to others."

27. It is from this that the well-known "contradictions" of the hermeneutical circle are derived; namely, how can one know the whole before the parts and the parts before the whole, and how can one stand inside the circle in order to understand, if one must already have understood in order to stand inside the circle. The purely logical objections to the hermeneutical circle are only overcome when the circumference of the circle is extended to its uttermost limit, that is, when it becomes "universal." For only then does the vicious circle become a "vital" circle. Gadamer writes (ibid., p. 261): "The circle, then, is not formal in nature, it is neither subjective nor objective, but describes understanding as the interplay of the movement of tradition and the movement of the interpreter. The anticipation of meaning that governs our understanding of a text is not an act of subjectivity, but proceeds from the communality that binds us to the tradition. But this is contained in our relation to tradition, in the constant process of education. Tradition is not simply a precondition into which we come, but we produce it ourselves inasmuch as we understand, participate in the evolution of tradition and hence further determine it ourselves. Thus the circle of understanding is not a 'methodological' circle, but describes an ontological structural element in understanding."

28. See Martin Heidegger, *Being and Time* [2]. Paul Ricoeur (see "The Task of Hermeneutics" in *Hermeneutics and the Human Sciences* [12], pp. 43–44) speaks of a *deregionalisation* of hermeneutics: "I see the recent history of hermeneutics dominated by two preoccupations. The first tends progressively to enlarge the aim of hermeneutics, in such a way that all *regional* hermeneutics are incorporated into one *general* hermeneutics. But this movement of *deregionalisation* cannot be pressed to the end unless at the same time the properly *epistemological* concerns of hermeneutics — its efforts to achieve a scientific status — are subordinated to *ontological* preoccupations, whereby *understanding* ceases to appear as a simple *mode of knowing* in order to become a *way of being* and a way of relating to beings and to being. The movement of *deregionalisation* is thus accompanied by a movement of *radicalization*, by which hermeneutics becomes not only *general* but also *fundamental*." It is admittedly misleading to place Heidegger within the program of philosophical hermeneutics. This applies only to the early Heidegger and only from a particular point of view. The later Heidegger should be read from the point of view of a discourse of disclosure.

29. H.-G. Gadamer, *Truth and Method* [26].

30. Ibid., p. xviii.

31. Ibid., p. xix.

32. In *Kleine Schriften* I (Tübingen: Mohr, 1970), Gadamer defines the consciousness of historical effectiveness so: "By that I mean, first, that we cannot extricate ourselves from the historical process, so distance ourselves from it that the past becomes an object for us. . . . We are always situated in history. . . . I mean that our consciousness is determined by a real historical process, in such a way that

we are not free to juxtapose ourselves to the past. I mean moreover that we must always become conscious afresh of the action which is thereby exercised over us, in such a way that everything past which we come to experience compels us to take hold of it completely, to assume in some way its truth." These lines are cited by Paul Ricoeur in "Hermeneutics and Critique of Ideology," in *Hermeneutics and the Human Sciences* [12], pp. 73–74.

33. See *Truth and Method* [26], p. 244: "The overcoming of all prejudices, this global demand of the enlightenment, will prove to be itself a prejudice, the removal of which opens the way to an appropriate understanding of our finitude, which dominates not only our humanity, but also our historical consciousness." As Gadamer puts it (p. 245): "the prejudices of the individual, far more than his judgments, constitute the historical reality of his being."

34. See Ibid., p. 264: "Time is no longer primarily a gulf to be bridged, because it separates, but is actually the supportive ground of process in which the present is rooted. Hence temporal distance is not something that must be overcome. This was, rather, the naive assumption of historicism, namely that we must set ourselves within the spirit of the age, and think with its ideas and its thoughts, not with our own, and thus advance towards historical objectivity. In fact the important thing is to recognize the distance in time as a positive and productive possibility of understanding. It is not a yawning abyss, but is filled with the continuity of custom and tradition, in the light of which all that is handed down presents itself to us. Here it is not too much to speak of a genuine productivity of process."

35. It is significant that Gadamer (ibid., p. 277) proposes to "redefine the hermeneutics of the human sciences in terms of legal and theological hermeneutics." He writes (p. 275): "In both legal and theological hermeneutics there is the essential tension between the text set down . . . on the one hand and, on the other, the sense arrived at by its application in the particular moment of interpretation, either in judgment or in preaching. A law is not there to be understood historically, but to be made concretely valid through being interpreted. Similarly, a religious proclamation is not there to be understood as a merely historical document, but to be taken in a way in which it exercises its saving effect. This includes the fact that the text, whether law or gospel, if it is to be understood properly, i.e. according to the claim it makes, must be understood at every moment, in every particular situation, in a new and different way. Understanding here is always application." Understanding is *service* of the meaning of the text. It is *event* which inevitably changes us much as does a religious conversion or processes of socialization. Indeed, processes of conversion, initiation and socialization may be seen to constitute the very pragmatic conditions enabling hermeneutical boundary discourse.

36. See ibid., p. 350: "All understanding is interpretation, and all interpretation takes place in the medium of a language. . . ." And he continues (p. 401): "Language is not just one of man's possessions in the world, but on it depends the fact that man has a world at all. . . . Not only is the world 'world' only insofar as it comes into language, but language, too, has its real being only in the fact that the world is re-presented within it. Thus the original humanity of language means at the same time the fundamental linguistic quality of man's being-in-the-world." The linguisticality of experience is *universal* because (p. 411): "there is in every language a direct relationship to the infinite extent of what exists." Were this not so, language would not disclose "world" but merely "habitat." "Every word," Gadamer writes (pp. 415–16), "breaks forth as if from a centre and is related to a whole, through

which alone it is word. Every word causes the whole of language to which it belongs to resonate and the whole of the view of the world which lies behind it to appear. Thus every word, in its momentariness, carries with it the unsaid, to which it is related by responding and indicating. . . . All human speaking is finite in such a way that there is within it an infinity of meaning to be elaborated and interpreted." For Wittgenstein, as well as for Gadamer, we cannot "go behind" language. In Wittgenstein's pragmatic semantics entities are inseparably bound up with knowledge and action. Human possibilities and possibilities of nature are together "projected" in the various uses of language. Further, language-games are never mere conventions, but are the condition of whatever conventions men may make. Language, as Wittgenstein says, is "in order as it is." The linguisticality of experience, therefore, is a function of human forms of life, which, as Wittgenstein says, are "the given" behind which we cannot go. It is significant that Gadamer, just as Wittgenstein, describes the basic movement of language and of experience as "play."

37. For the ontological significance of mythic-religious experience, see Mircea Eliade, *Myths, Dreams and Mysteries*, trans. P. Mairet (New York: Harper & Row, 1960), pp. 17–18: "religious experience engages the whole of a man, and therefore stirs the depths of his being. Religious experience is an experience of existence in its totality, which reveals to a man his own mode of being in the World. . . . Every religion, even the most elementary, is an ontology: it reveals the *being* of the sacred things and the divine Figures, it shows forth *that which really is*, and in doing so establishes a World which is no longer evanescent and incomprehensible, as it is in nightmares, and as it again becomes whenever existence is in danger of foundering in the 'Chaos' of total relativity, where no 'Centre' emerges to ensure orientation. . . . Religion 'begins' when and where there is a total revelation of reality, . . . the religious experience is at once a total crisis of existence and the exemplary solution of that crisis." See also the discussion of "metanarratives" in J.-F. Lyotard, *The Postmodern Condition*.

38. See Eric Voegelin's definition of historical narrative as "historiogenesis" (*The Ecumenical Age* [2/10], p. 59). Voegelin's investigations show that a people constitutes itself in a narrative of conquest in that they "let governance spring into existence at an absolute point of origin, as part of the cosmic order itself, and from that point down they let the history of their society descend to the present in which they live."

39. It is upon this level of discourse that the postmodern theorists are correct in linking knowledge to power. See note 25, Chapter 3 above.

40. See K.-O. Apel, *Towards a Transformation of Philosophy* [1/20], p. 116: "For Gadamer, therefore, the truth of interpretation is not one of progressive, methodical approximation to the ideal of objectivity, but rather one of the revelation of meaning which results from the 'fusion of horizons' of past and present in the historical situation. . . . But this truth must also correspond to a finite situational understanding and self-understanding and can, therefore, never definitively overcome the past. To this extent, the present can never understand the past 'better than it understood itself', but rather it can only understand the past differently."

41. In the words of Heidegger: "What is decisive is not to get out of the circle but to come into it in the right way." See *Being and Time* [2], p. 195.

42. See the discussion in *Hermeneutik und Ideologiekritik* [3/5].

43. See Hans-Georg Gadamer, *Philosophical Hermeneutics*, trans. and ed. D. E. Linge (Berkeley: University of California Press, 1976), p. 7.

44. Thus Apel can say (see *Towards a Transformation of Philosophy* [1/20], p. 125): "the goal of unlimited communication—and this means that of the abolition of all obstacles to communication—also includes the legitimation to temporarily suspend *hermeneutic communications* with the *interpretandum* in order to turn instead to *causal* or *functional* 'explanations' of the empirical-analytical social sciences."

45. Thus Apel may ask: "Is it sufficient to analyze the elucidation of meaning *qua* mediation of tradition as a situationally bounded manifestation of the 'fusion of horizons' which, as a 'game' that has been entrusted to the 'productivity of the age', will always produce different results of practical 'application'? To put it more precisely: the interpreter, who becomes aware of his own function in the interpretative process in the sense of 'consciousness of historical reception', knows that he cannot avoid the 'application' of his understanding to historical praxis. Is he not forced, therefore, to relate his activity to possible communication in a community of action, i.e. to historical praxis? Does he not require in this situation a methodologically relevant principle so that his interpretative activity is related to unlimited potential progress; and this ultimately means the ideal limiting value of an absolute truth of interpretation?" See K.-O. Apel, *Towards a Transformation of Philosophy* [1/20], p. 122–23.

46. See the discussion in Chapter 2.

47. See the various works of J. Derrida for a discussion of the foundational significance of difference (*différence*).

48. The "cosmotheandric vision" is R. Panikkar's answer to those reductionist theories which are either one-sidedly cosmocentric, or anthropocentric, or theocentric. Solidarity with humanity, for example, is futile and destructive if it is not at the same time solidarity with nature and with the divine. Such one-sidedness inevitably does violence to the universality of discourse. See "Colligite Fragmenta" [2/10].

49. See Joan V. Bondurant, *Conquest of Violence: The Gandhian Philosophy of Conflict* (Berkeley: University of California Press, 1967), p. v.

50. Gandhi writes (ibid., p. 17): "The word 'satya' (Truth) is derived from 'sat', which means being. And nothing is or exists in reality except Truth. That is why 'sat' or Truth is perhaps the most important name of God. In fact it is more correct to say that Truth is God, than to say that God is Truth."

51. Cited in Raghavan N. Iyer, *The Moral and Political Thought of Mahatma Gandhi* (Oxford: Oxford University Press, 1973), p. 168.

52. See M. K. Gandhi, *Non-Violent Resistance* (New York: Schocken, 1961), p. 29.

53. Cited in Iyer, *Moral and Political Thought* [51], p. 246.

54. Ibid., p. 231.

55. Ibid., pp. 193–94.

56. Cited in Joan Bondurant, *Conquest of Violence* [49], p. 24.

57. Cases in point are the "resistance" of the patient in psychoanalysis as well as political and social resistance in Marxism.

58. This is the reason why Gandhi had no use for Marxist theories of violent revolution. He writes (see Iyer [51]), p. 247: "Violence interrupts the process and prolongs the real revolution of the whole social structure."

59. See for a complete list Joan Bondurant, *Conquest of Violence* [49], p. 38ff.

60. Suffering is not a mere feeling or a misfortune which overcomes us, but a

metaphysical force which must be dealt with constructively.

61. Cited in R. Iyer, *The Moral and Political Thought of Mahatma Gandhi* [51], p. 194.

62. In Hegel's dialectic of the Master and Slave, labor arises as a reaction to the violence of oppression. "Need" becomes a symbol of past violence, while "labor" is said to mediate mutual recognition and intersubjectivity, thus becoming a symbol of self-consciousness' activity of expressing and reappropriating itself. For Freud, necessity and labor arise from the internalized violence of instinctual denial and the attempt to create substitute satisfactions through art, religion and the products of civilization. In both cases, human existence is projected upon the drama of the self-assertion of the subject against objective forces. Upon this basis alone, however, no authentic *intersubjectivity* can arise. It is not in overcoming the other through labor that mutual recognition becomes possible, but by *self-giving*, which is only possible when participation in a transcendent unity "guarantees" the "reception" rather than the "loss" of self.

63. For this reason cosmotheandric solidarity must be seen as a necessary pragmatic condition of every communicative action in addition to the pragmatics of argumentation and proclamation.

64. Cited in R. Iyer, *The Moral and Political Thought of Mahatma Gandhi* [51], p. 159.

65. Whether this story is historically accurate or not, it has become one of the great myths of "enlightenment" of modern Western culture.

66. See J. Bondurant, *Conquest of Violence* [49], p. 51.

67. It would be a mistake to assume that the third level of discourse I am describing here is some neutral, universal language. For the attempt to speak such a language could only end in setting up the boundaries of another, perhaps a super-myth. This is the fate of Western secularism with its claim to objectivity and the universality of "reason." Third-level discourse is not a language in the obvious sense that logos and mythos are languages. Nonetheless, it is "linguistic" in that it articulates a dynamic and structures a space which determines the pragmatics of boundary discourse in a specific way. The third-level discourse which articulates the space of encounter between religions as a space of *dis-closure* structures the pragmatics of boundary discourse such that narrative, proclamation and experiences of initiation, conversion and socialization constitutive of a religion occur *non-violently*. With regard to mythic self-representation in narrative and proclamation, this implies that a boundary discourse spoken out of the space between religions does not constitute itself by excluding the other. Consequently, it is a discourse in which the different traditions which are at any time involved in the encounter may find themselves truly expressed. For this reason it can be neither a syncretistic composite nor a dialectical synthesis nor even a fusion of horizons. The communication strategy which the diatopical model implies does not aim at the creation of a new and unheard of universal religion by means of one or another of these forms of synthesis. Instead, it is the attempt to speak a language faithful to two or more traditions at once.

Bibliography

Adams, J. L. *Paul Tillich's Philosophy of Culture, Science and Religion*. New York: Schocken Books, 1970.

Adorno, Theodor W. *Negative Dialectics*. Translated by E. B. Ashton. New York: Seabury Press, 1973.

————., and Horkheimer, Max. *Dialectic of Enlightenment*. Translated by J. Cumming. New York: Seabury Press, 1972.

————. et al. *The Positivist Dispute in German Sociology*. Translated by G. Adey and D. Frisby. London: Heinemann, 1976.

Albert, Hans. *Plädoyer für kritischen Rationalismus*. Munich: Piper, 1971.

————. *Treatise on Critical Reason*. Translated by M. V. Rorty. Princeton, N.J.: Princeton University Press, 1985.

————., and Topitsch, E., eds. *Werturteilstreit*. Darmstadt: Wissenschaftliche Buchgesellschaft, 1971.

Andresen, C., ed. *Handbuch der Dogmen- und Theologiegeschichte*. 3 Vols. Göttingen: Vandenhöck & Ruprecht, 1982.

Apel, K.-O. *Der Denkweg von Charles S. Peirce*. Frankfurt a.M.: Suhrkamp, 1970; English translation, *C. S. Peirce: From Pragmatism to Pragmaticism*. Amherst, Massachusetts: University of Massachusetts Press, 1981.

————., ed. *Sprachpragmatik und Philosophie*. Frankfurt a.M.: Suhrkamp, 1976.

————. *Transformation der Philosophie*. 2 Vols. Frankfurt a.M.: Suhrkamp, 1973; English translation, *Towards a Transformation of Philosophy*. London: Routledge & Kegan Paul, 1980.

————., ed. *Praktische Philosophie/Ethik: Dialogue*. 2 Vols. Frankfurt a.M.: Fischer, 1984.

van Baaren, Th. P., and Drijvers, H. J. W., eds. *Religion, Culture and Methodology*. The Hague: Mouton, 1973.

Baker, G. P., and Hacker, P. M. S. *Wittgenstein: Understanding and Meaning*. Vol. I. Chicago: University of Chicago Press, 1980.

Barth, Hans. *Truth and Ideology*. Translated by F. Lilge. Berkeley: University of Calif. Press, 1976.

Barth, Karl. *Church Dogmatics*. Vol. I/II. New York: Scribner's Sons, 1936ff.

————. *Der Römerbrief*. Zürich: Theologischer Verlag, 1940.

Baynes, Kenneth., Bohman, James., and McCarthy, Thomas., eds. *After Philosophy: End or Transformation*. Cambridge, Mass.: M.I.T. Press, 1987.

Benz, Ernst. *Ideen zu einer Theologie der Religionsgeschichte*. Abhandlungen der geistes- und sozialwissenschaftliche Klasse. Mainz: Akademie der Wissenschaften und der Literatur, 1960.

Berger, Peter L. *The Heretical Imperative: Contemporary Possibilities of Religious Affirmation*. New York: Anchor, 1979.

————. *A Rumor of Angels: Modern Society and the Rediscovery of the Supernatural*. New York: Anchor, 1970.

————., and Luckmann, Thomas. *The Social Construction of Reality*. New York: Anchor, 1967.

Bernstein, Richard J. *Beyond Objectivism and Relativism*. Philadelphia: University of Pennsylvania Press, 1983.

————. *Philosophical Profiles: Essays in a Pragmatic Mode*. Cambridge, Mass.: Polity Press, 1986.

————., ed. *Habermas and Modernity*. Cambridge, Mass.: Polity Press, 1985.

Betti, Emilio. *Die Hermeneutik als allgemeine Methodik der Geisteswissenschaften*. Tübingen: Mohr, 1972.

Beyschlag, Karlmann. *Grundriss der Dogmengeschichte*. 2 Vols. Darmstadt: Wissenschaftliche Buchgesellschaft, 1982ff.

Bianchi, U., Bleeker, D. J., and Bausani, A., eds. *Problems and Methods of the History of Religions*. Leiden: Brill, 1972.

Bitterli, Urs. *Die "Wilden" und die "Zivilisierten."* Munich: Deutsche Taschenbuch Verlag, 1982.

Bleeker, C. J. "Die phänomenologische Methode." In Lanczkowski, G., ed., *Selbstverständnis und Wesen der Religionswissenschaft*. Darmstadt: Wissenschaftliche Buchgesellschaft, 1974.

————. "Comparing the Religio-historical and the Theological Method." In *The Rainbow: A Collection of Studies in the Science of Religion*. Supplements to Numen 30. Leiden: Brill, 1975, pp. 12-29.

Block, Irving, ed. *Perspectives on the Philosophy of Wittgenstein*. Cambridge, Mass.: The M.I.T. Press, 1981.

Bloor, David. *Wittgenstein: A Social Theory of Knowledge*. New York: Columbia University Press, 1983.

Böhler, D., and Kuhlmann, W., eds. *Kommunikation und Reflexion*. Frankfurt a.M.: Suhrkamp, 1982.

Braun, Hans-Jürg, and Krieger, David J., eds. *Indische Religionen und das Christentum im Dialog*. Zürich: Theologischer Verlag Zürich, 1986.

Bultmann, Rudolf. *History and Eschatology*. New York: Harper & Brothers, 1957.

————. *Jesus Christ and Mythology*. New York: Scribner's Sons, 1958.

————. *Kerygma and Myth*. Edited by H. W. Bartsch. New York: Harper & Brothers, 1961.

————. *Primitive Christianity*. Translated by R. H. Fuller. New York: Meridian Books, 1956.

Bürkle, Horst. *Einführung in die Theologie der Religionen*. Darmstadt: Wissenschaftliche Buchgesellschaft, 1977.

Comte, Auguste. *Auguste Comte and Positivism: The Essential Writings*. Edited by G. Lenzer. New York: Harper & Row, 1975.

Congar, Yves M.-J. *A History of Theology*. Translated and edited by H. Guthrie. New York: Doubleday, 1968.

Culler, Jonathan. *On Deconstruction: Theory and Criticism after Structuralism*. Ithaca, New York: Cornell University Press, 1982.

Denzinger, H., and Schönmetzer, A., eds. *Enchiridion Symbolorum: Definitionum et Declarationum de Rebus Fidei et Morum*. Freiburg: Herder, 1967.

Derrida, Jacques. *Of Grammatology*. Baltimore: Johns Hopkins University Press, 1974.

————. *Writing and Difference*. Chicago: University of Chicago Press, 1978.

————. *Dissemination*. Translated by Barbara Johnson. Chicago: University of Chicago Press, 1981.

————. *Margins of Philosophy*. Translated by Alan Bass. Chicago: University of Chicago Press, 1982.

Descartes, R. *The Philosophical Works of Descartes*. 2 Vols. Translated and edited by E. S. Haldane and G. R. T. Ross. Cambridge: Cambridge University Press, 1967.

Devereux, Georges. *Normal und Anormal: Aufsätze zur allgemeinen Ethnopsychiatrie*. Frankfurt a.M.: Suhrkamp, 1974.

Dilthey, W. *Der Aufbau der geschichtlichen Welt in den Geisteswissenschaften*. Frankfurt a.M.: Suhrkamp, 1983.

Durkheim, Emile. *The Elementary Forms of the Religious Life*. Translated by J. W. Swain. New York: Free Press, 1965.

————. *The Rules of Sociological Method*. Translated by S. A. Solovay and J. H. Müller and edited by G. Catlin. New York: Free Press, 1964.

————. *Sociology and Philosophy*. Translated by D. R. Pocock. New York: Free Press, 1974.

Eister, A. W., ed. *Changing Perspectives in the Scientific Study of Religion*. New York: John Wiley & Sons, 1974.

Eliade, Mircea. *Cosmos and History: The Myth of the Eternal Return*. Translated by W. R. Trask. New York: Harper & Row, 1959.

————. *Patterns in Comparative Religion*. Translated by R. Sheed. New York: Meridian Books, 1963.

————. "Paul Tillich and the History of Religions." In *The Future of Religions*. Edited by J. C. Brauer. New York: Harper & Row, 1966, pp. 31-36.

————. *The Quest: History and Meaning in Religion*. Chicago: University of Chicago Press, 1969.

————., and J. M. Kitagawa, eds. *The History of Religions: Essays in Methodology*. Chicago: University of Chicago Press, 1959.

Engelmann, Paul. *Letters from Ludwig Wittgenstein*. New York: Horizon Press, 1968.

Evans-Pritchard, E. E. *Theories of Primitive Religion*. Oxford: Clarendon Press, 1965.

Fann, K. T. *Wittgenstein's Conception of Philosophy*. Berkeley: University of California Press, 1971.

Foucault, Michael. *The Order of Things*. New York: Vintage, 1973.

————. *The Archaeology of Knowledge*. Translated by A. M. Sheridan Smith. New York: Pantheon Books, 1972.

————. *Discipline and Punish: The Birth of the Prison*. Translated by A. Sheridan. New York: Vintage, 1979.

Freud, Sigmund. *Totem and Taboo*. Translated by J. Strachey. New York: Norton, 1950.

————. *The Future of an Illusion*. Translated by. J. Strachey. New York: Anchor, 1961.

————. *Civilization and its Discontents*. Translated by J. Strachey. New York: Norton, 1961.

————. *Moses and Monotheism*. Translated by K. Jones. New York: Vintage, 1955.

Friedli, Richard. *Fremdheit als Heimat*. Zürich: Theologischer Verlag Zürich, 1974.

Gadamer, Hans-Georg. *Philosophical Hermeneutics*. Translated and edited by D. E. Linge. Berkeley: University of California Press, 1976.

―――. *Truth and Method*. New York: Seabury Press, 1975.

―――. *Kleine Schriften*. Tübingen: Mohr, 1970.

―――., and Vogler, P., eds. *Philosophische Anthropologie*. Stuttgart: Thieme, 1975.

Geertz, Clifford. *The Interpretation of Cultures*. New York: Basic Books, 1973.

Gier, Nicholas F. *Wittgenstein and Phenomenology*. Albany, New York: State University of New York Press, 1981.

Gilkey, Langdon. *Reaping the Whirlwind: A Christian Interpretation of History*. New York: Seabury Press, 1976.

Girard, René. *Violence and the Sacred*. Translated by P. Gregory. Baltimore: Johns Hopkins University Press, 1977.

Grillmeier, Aloys. *Christ in Christian Tradition*. Vol. I. Translated by J. Bowden. Atlanta: John Knox Press, 1975.

Habermas, Jürgen. *Legitimation Crisis*. Translated by Thomas McCarthy. Boston: Beacon Press, 1975.

―――. *Knowledge and Human Interests*. Translated by J. Shapiro. Boston: Beacon Press, 1971.

―――. *Zur Logik der Sozialwissenschaften*. Frankfurt a.M.: Suhrkamp, 1973.

―――. *Zur Rekonstruktion des historischen Materialismus*. Frankfurt a.M.: Suhrkamp, 1976.

―――. *Theory and Practice*. Translated by John Viertel. Boston: Beacon Press, 1973.

―――. *Toward a Rational Society*. Translated by J. Shapiro. Boston: Beacon Press, 1970.

―――. *Theory of Communicative Action*. Translated by Thomas McCarthy. Boston: Beacon Press, 1984.

―――. *Vorstudien und Ergänzungen zur Theorie des kommunikativen Handelns*. Frankfurt a.M.: Suhrkamp, 1986.

―――. *Der philosophische Diskurs der Moderne*. Frankfurt a.M.: Suhrkamp, 1986.

―――., Henrich, D., and Taubes, J., eds. *Hermeneutik und Ideologiekritik*. Frankfurt a.M.: Suhrkamp, 1971.

Hacker, P. M. S. *Insight and Illusion*. London: Oxford University Press, 1972.

Hanfling, Oswald, ed. *Essential Readings in Logical Positivism*. Oxford: Basil Blackwell, 1981.

―――. *Logical Positivism*. Oxford: Basil Blackwell, 1981.

Hegel, G. W. F. *Theorie Werkausgabe*. 20 Vols. Edited by E. Moldenhauer and K. M. Michael. Frankfurt a.M.: Suhrkamp, 1970.

Heidegger, Martin. *Being and Time*. New York: Harper & Row, 1962.

Heislbetz, Josef. *Theologische Gründe der nichtchristlichen Religionen*. Freiburg: Herder, 1967.

Hempel, Carl G. *Aspects of Scientific Explanation and Other Essays in the Philosophy of Science*. New York: The Free Press, 1965.

―――. *Philosophy of Natural Science*. Engelwood Cliffs, N.J.: Prentice-Hall, 1966.

Hesse, Mary. *Revolutions and Reconstructions in the Philosophy of Science*. Sussex: The Harvester Press, 1980.

Hirsch, E. D. *Validity in Interpretation*. New Haven: Yale University Press, 1967.

Hollis, Martin, and Lukes, Steven, eds. *Rationality and Relativism*. Cambridge, Mass.: M.I.T. Press, 1982.

Horkheimer, Max. *Eclipse of Reason*. New York: Seabury Press, 1974.

―――. *Traditionelle und kritische Theorie*. Frankfurt a.M.: Fischer, 1968.

————., and Adorno, Th. W. *Dialectic of Enlightenment*. Translated by J. Cumming. New York: Seabury Press, 1972.

Hübner, A., and Wuchterl, K. *Wittgenstein*. Reinbeck bei Hamburg: Rowohlt, 1979.

Humboldt, W. Von. *Schriften zur Sprachphilosophie*. Darmstadt: Wissenschaftliche Buchgesellschaft, 1963.

Husserl, Edmund. *Cartesian Meditations: An Introduction to Phenomenology*. Translated by D. Cairns. The Hague: Martinus Nijhof, 1969.

————. *The Crisis of European Sciences and Transcendental Phenomenology*. Translated by D. Carr. Evanston: Northwestern University Press, 1970.

————. *Ideas: General Introduction to Pure Phenomenology*. Translated by W. R. Boyce-Gibson. New York: Humanities Press, 1969.

————. *Logical Investigations*. 2 Vols. Translated by J. N. Findlay. New York: Humanities Press, 1970.

Ibish, Yusuf, and Marculescu, Ileana, eds. *Contemplation and Action in World Religions*. Seattle: University of Washington Press, 1978.

Janik, Allen, and Toulmin, Stephen. *Wittgenstein's Vienna*. New York: Simon and Schuster, 1973.

Kant, Immanuel. *Werkausgabe*. 12 Vols. Edited by W. Weischedel. Frankfurt a.M.: Suhrkamp, 1977.

Kasper, Walter, ed. *Absolutheit des Christentums*. Freiburg: Herder, 1977.

Kern, Walter. *Ausserhalb der Kirche kein Heil?* Freiburg: Herder, 1979.

Kenny, Anthony. *Wittgenstein*. Cambridge, Mass.: Harvard University Press, 1973.

Kippenberg, H. G., and Luchesi, B., eds. *Magie: Die sozialwissenschaftliche Kontroverse über das Verstehen fremden Denkens*. Frankfurt a.M.: Suhrkamp, 1978.

Knitter, Paul. "European Protestant and Catholic Approaches to the World Religions: Complements and Contrasts." *Journal of Ecumenical Studies*, vol. 12, no. 1 (Winter 1975), pp. 13-28.

————. *No Other Name*. Maryknoll, N.Y.: Orbis 1985.

————. *Towards a Protestant Theology of Religions*. Marburg: N. G. Elwert, 1974.

Kondylis, Panajotis. *Die Aufklärung im Rahmen des neuzeitlichen Rationalismus*. Stuttgart: Klett-Cotta, 1981.

Kraemer, Hendrick. *Religion and the Christian Faith*. Philadelphia: Westminster, 1956.

Kripke, Saul A. *Wittgenstein on Rules and Private Language*. Cambridge, Massachusetts: Harvard University Press, 1982.

Kuhlmann, Wolfgang. *Reflexive Letztbegründung: Untersuchung zur Transzendentalpragmatik*. Freiburg/München: Karl Alber, 1985.

Kuhn, Thomas S. *The Structure of Scientific Revolutions*. Chicago: University of Chicago Press, 1962.

Kutschera, Franz von. *Philosophy of Language*. Translated by B. Terrel. Dordrecht; Boston: D. Reidel, 1975.

Lenk, Kurt, ed. *Ideologie: Ideologiekritik und Wissenssoziologie*. Frankfurt a.M.: Campus, 1984.

Lepenies, W., and Ritter, H. H., eds. *Orte des wilden Denkens*. Frankfurt a.M.: Suhrkamp, 1970.

Lessing, Gotthold Ephraim. *Werke*. 2 Vols. Berlin/Darmstadt: Tempel Verlag, 1965.

Leuze, Reinhard. *Die ausserchristlichen Religionen bei Hegel*. Göttingen: Vandenhöck & Ruprecht, 1975.

Luckmann, Thomas, and Schutz, Alfred. *Strukturen der Lebenswelt*. 2 Vols. Frankfurt a.m.: Suhrkamp, 1984.

Luhmann, Niklas. *Funktion der Religion*. Frankfurt a.M.: Suhrkamp, 1977.

———. *Zweckbegriff und Systemrationalität*. Frankfurt a.m.: Suhrkamp, 1968.

———. *Soziale Systeme: Grundriss einer allgemeinen Theorie*. Frankfurt a.M.: Suhrkamp, 1984.

Lukes, Steven., and Hollis, Martin, eds. *Rationality and Relativism*. Cambridge, Mass.: M.I.T. Press, 1982.

Lyotard, Jean-François. *The Postmodern Condition*. Minneapolis: University of Minnesota Press, 1984.

Mann, Ulrich. *Das Christentum als Absolute Religion*. Darmstadt: Wissenschaftliche Buchgesellschaft, 1970.

Mannheim, Karl. *Ideology and Utopia*. Translated by L. Wirth and E. Shils. New York: Harcourt, Brace & World, 1936.

Marx, Karl, and Engels, Friedrich. *On Religion*. New York: Schocken Books, 1964.

Meja, V., and Stehr, N., eds. *Der Streit um die Wissenssoziologie*. 2 Vols. Frankfurt a.m.: Suhrkamp, 1982.

Metz, J. B. *Theology of the World*. Translated by W. Glen-Döpel. New York: Seabury Press, 1973.

Morris, Charles. *Foundations of the Theory of Signs*. Chicago: University of Chicago Press, 1938.

Nietzsche, Friedrich. *The Will to Power*. Translated by W. Kaufmann and R. J. Hollingdale. New York: Vintage, 1967.

O'Flaherty, Wendy D. *Dreams, Illusions and other Realities*. Chicago: University of Chicago Press, 1984.

Palmer, Richard E. *Hermeneutics*. Evanston: Northwestern University Press, 1969.

Panikkar, Raimundo. "Action and Contemplation as Categories of Religious Understanding." *In Contemplation and Action in World Religions*. Edited by Y. Ibish, and I. Marculescu. Seattle: University of Washington Press, 1977, pp. 85-104.

———. *The Intra-religious Dialogue*. New York: Paulist Press, 1978.

———. *Kultmysterium in Hinduismus und Christentum*. Freiburg/München: Alber, 1964.

———. "Man and Religion: A Dialogue with Panikkar." *Jeevadhara*, 11, no. 61 (January–February), 1981: 5-32.

———. "Der Mensch—ein trinitarisches Mysterium." In *Die Verantwortung des Menschen für eine bewohnbare Welt im Christentum, Hinduismus und Buddhismus*. Edited by R. Panikkar and W. Strolz. Freiburg: Herder, 1985.

———. *Myth, Faith and Hermeneutics*. New York: Paulist Press, 1979.

———. "The Myth of Pluralism: The Tower of Babel—A Meditation on Non-Violence." *Cross-Currents*, 29, no. 2 (Summer 1979): 197-230.

———. "The New Innocence." *Cross Currents*, 27, no.1 (Spring 1977): 7-15.

———. *Offenbarung und Verkündigung: Indische Briefe*. Freiburg: Herder, 1967.

———. "Philosophy as Life-Style." In *Philosophers on Their Own Work*. Bern, Frankfurt, Los Angeles: Peter Lang, 1978, pp. 193-228.

———. *Religionen und die Religion*. Munich: Hüber, 1965.

———. "Rtatattva: A Preface to a Hindu-Christian Theology." *Jeevadhara*, 49 (January–February 1979): 6-63.

———. "Le Temps Circulaire." *Archivio di Filosofia*. Rome: Instituto di Studi Filosofici, 1975: 207-246.

———. *The Trinity and the Religious Experience of Man*. Maryknoll, N.Y.: Orbis Books, 1973.

———. *The Unknown Christ of Hinduism*. London: Darton, Longman & Todd, 1964. Revised and enlarged edition: London: Darton, Longman & Todd, and Maryknoll, N.Y.: Orbis Books, 1981.

———. *The Vedic Experience: Mantramanjari*. Berkeley: University of Calif. Press, 1977.

———. "Verstehen al Überzeugtsein." In *Neue Anthropologie*. Edited by H. G. Gadamer and P. Vogler. *Philosophische Anthropologie* VII. Stuttgart: Thieme, 1975, pp. 132-167.

———. *Die Vielen Götter und der Eine Herr*. Weilheim/Oberbayern: Otto Wilhelm Barth, 1963.

———. *Worship and Secular Man*. London: Darton, Longman & Todd, 1973.

———. "Die Zukunft kommt nicht später." In *Vom Sinn der Tradition*. Edited by Leonhard Reinisch. Munich: C. H. Beck, 1970, pp. 53-64.

Pannenberg, Wolfhart. *Basic Questions in Theology*. 2 Vols. Translated by G. H. Kehm. Philadelphia: The Westminster Press, 1970-71. German: *Grundfragen Systematischer Theologie*. 2 Vols. Göttingen: Vandenhöck & Ruprecht, 1967-1980.

———. *Theology and the Philosophy of Science*. Translated by F. McDonagh. Philadelphia: Westminster Press, 1976.

Pelikan, Jaroslav. *The Christian Tradition: A History of the Development of Doctrine*. 5 Vols. Chicago: University of Chicago Press, 1971ff.

Pitcher, George, ed. *Wittgenstein: The Philosophical Investigations*. New York: Anchor, 1966.

Popper, Karl R. *Die beiden Grundprobleme der Erkenntnistheorie*. Edited by T. E. Hansen. Tübingen: Mohr, 1979.

———. *Conjectures and Refutations*. London: Routledge and Kegan Paul, 1963.

———. *The Logic of Scientific Discovery*. New York: Harper & Row, 1965.

———. *Objective Knowledge: An Evolutionary Approach*. Oxford: Clarendon Press, 1979.

———. *The Open Society and its Enemies*. 2 Vols. London: Routledge and Kegan Paul, 1945.

———. *The Poverty of Historicism* New York: Harper & Row, 1964.

Puntel, L. B. *Analogie und Geschichtlichkeit*. Vol. I. Freiburg: Herder, 1969.

Radnitzky, G. *Contemporary Schools of Metascience*. Göteborg: Akademiförlaget, 1970.

Rahner, Karl. *Foundations of Christian Faith*. Translated by W. V. Dych. New York: Seabury Press, 1978.

———. *Theological Investigations*. Baltimore: Helicon, 1961ff.

———. *Hearers of the Word*. Translated by M. Richards. New York: Herder and Herder, 1969.

———. *Spirit in the World*. Translated by W. Dych. New York: Herder and Herder, 1968.

Randall, John H. *The Making of the Modern Mind*. Cambridge, Mass.: Houghton Mifflin, 1940.

Ratschow, Carl Heinz. *Die Religionen*. Gütersloh: Mohn, 1979.

Ratzinger, Joseph. "Der christliche Glaube und die Weltreligionen." In *Gott in*

Welt. Festgabe für Karl Rahner. Edited by H. Vorgrimler, 2 Vols. Freiburg: Herder, 1964, pp. 287-305.

Ricoeur, Paul. *The Conflict of Interpretations*. Edited by D. Ihde. Evanston, Ill.: Northwestern University Press, 1974.

————. *Freud and Philosophy: An Essay on Interpretation*. Translated by D. Savage. New Haven: Yale University Press, 1970.

————. *Hermeneutics and the Human Sciences*. Edited and translated by J. B. Thompson. Cambridge: Cambridge University Press, 1981.

————. *Interpretation Theory: Discourse and the Surplus of Meaning*. Fort Worth: Texas Christian University Press, 1976.

————. *The Rule of Metaphor*. Translated by R. Czerny. Toronto: University of Toronto Press, 1977.

————. *The Symbolism of Evil*. Translated by E. Buchanan. Boston: Beacon Press, 1967.

Rorty, Richard. *Philosophy and the Mirror of Nature*. Princeton: Princeton University Press, 1979.

————. *Consequences of Pragmatism*. Sussex: The Harvester Press, 1982.

Sapir, Edward. *Language*. New York: Harcourt, Brace and Co., 1949.

Schleiermacher, Friedrich. *The Christian Faith*. 2 Vols. Edited by H. R. Mackintosh and J. S. Stewart. New York: Harper & Row, 1963.

————. *Hermeneutics: The Handwritten Manuscripts*. Edited by H. Kimmerle, and translated by J. Duke and J. Forstman. Missoula, Montana: Scholars Press, 1977.

————. *Dialektik*. Edited by R. Odebrecht. Darmstadt: Wissenschaftliche Buchgesellschaft, 1976.

————. *On Religion: Speeches to its Cultured Despisers*. Translated by J. Oman. New York: Harper & Row, 1958.

Schlette, Heinz R. *Towards a Theology of Religions*. New York: Herder and Herder, 1966.

Schutz, Alfred. *The Phenomenology of the Social World*. Translated by G. Walsh and F. Lehnert. Evanston: Northwestern University Press, 1967.

————., and Luckmann, Th. *Strukturen der Lebenswelt*. 2 Vols. Frankfurt a.M.: Suhrkamp, 1984.

Smith, Wilfred, C. *The Meaning and End of Religion*. New York: New American Library, 1964.

————. *Religious Diversity*. Edited by W. G. Oxtoby. New York: Harper & Row, 1976.

————. *Towards a World Theology*. Philadelphia: Westminster Press, 1981.

Stenius, Erik. *Wittgenstein's Tractatus*. Oxford: Basil Blackwell, 1960.

Strolz, Walter, ed. *Sein und Nichts in der abendländischen Mystik*. Freiburg: Herder, 1984.

Suppe, Frederick., ed. *The Structure of Scientific Theories*. Urbana: University of Illinois Press, 1977.

Theunissen, Michael. *Der Andere: Studien zur Sozialontologie der Gegenwart*. Berlin: de Gruyter, 1977.

Tillich, Paul. *Christianity and the Encounter of the World Religions*. New York: Columbia University Press, 1963.

————. *The Construction of the History of Religion in Schelling's Positive Philosophy*. Translated by V. Nuovo. New Jersey: Associated University Press, 1974.

————. *Gesammelte Werke*. Vols. I, IV, V, VI. Edited by Renate Albrecht. Stuttgart: Evangelische Verlagswerk, 1959-61-64-63.

————. *A History of Christian Thought*. Edited by C. Braaten. New York: Harper & Row, 1968.

————. *Perspectives on 19th and 20th Century Protestant Theology*. Ed. by C. Braaten. London: SCM Press, 1967.

————. "The Significance of the History of Religions for the Systematic Theologian." In *The Future of Religions*. Edited by J. C. Braür. New York: Harper & Row, 1966, pp. 80-94.

————. *Systematic Theology*. 3 Vols. Chicago: The University of Chicago Press, 1951-1963.

————. *What is Religion?* Translated by J. L. Adams. New York: Harper & Row, 1973.

Topitsch, Erst, ed. *Logik der Sozialwissenschaften*. Köln und Berlin: Kiepenheuer + Witsch, 1965.

————. *Sozialphilosophie zwischen Ideologie und Wissenschaft*. Neuwied und Berlin: Luchterhand, 1966.

————, and Albert, Hans, eds. *Werturteilstreit*. Darmstadt: Wissenschaftliche Buchgesellschaft, 1971.

Tracy, David. *The Analogical Imagination: Christian Theology and the Culture of Pluralism*. New York: Crossroad, 1981.

————. *Blessed Rage for Order: The New Pluralism in Theology*. New York: Seabury Press, 1979.

Troeltsch, Ernst. *Die Absolutheit des Christentums und die Religionsgeschichte*. Munich: Siebenstern, 1929.

————. *Christian Thought: Its History and Application*. Edited by Baron F. von Hügel. London: University of London Press, 1923.

————. *Der Historismus und seine Probleme*. Tübingen: Mohr, 1922.

Truzzi, Marcello, ed. *Verstehen: Subjective Understanding in the Social Sciences*. Reading, Massachusetts: Addison-Wesley, 1974.

Urmson, J. O. *Philosophical Analysis: Its Development Between the Two World Wars*. Oxford: Oxford University Press, 1967.

Voegelin, Erich. *Order in History*. 5 Vols. Baton Rouge: Louisiana State University Press, 1956ff.

Wehr, Gerhard. *Paul Tillich*. Reinbeck bei Hamburg: Rowohlt, 1979.

Wellmer, Albrecht. *Critical Theory of Society*. Translated by J. Cumming. New York: Seabury Press, 1971.

Whorf, Benjamin Lee. *Language, Thought, and Reality*. Edited by J. B. Carroll. Cambridge, Mass.: M.I.T. Press, 1956.

Wiggershaus, G., ed. *Die sozialwissenschaftliche Relevanz von Wittgensteins Sprachphilosophie*. Frankfurt a.M.: Suhrkamp, 1975.

Wilson, Bryan. *Rationality*. Oxford: Blackwell, 1971.

Winch, Peter. *The Idea of a Social Science and its Relation to Philosophy*. London: Routledge & Kegan Paul, 1958.

————. "Understanding a Primitive Society." *American Philosophical Quarterly*, 1, no. 4 (October 1964): 307-324.

Winter, Gibson. *Liberating Creation*. New York: Crossroad, 1981.

Wittgenstein, Ludwig. *On Certainty*. Edited by Anscombe and von Wright. Translated by D. Paul and G. E. M. Anscombe. New York: Harper & Row, 1972.

———. *Philosophical Investigations*. Translated by G. E. M. Anscombe. New York: Macmillan, 1958.

———. *Tractatus Logico-Philosophicus*. Translated by D. Pears and P. McGuinness. London: Routledge & Kegan Paul, 1961.

———. *Werkausgabe*. 8 Vols. Frankfurt a.M.: Suhrkamp, 1984.

von Wright, Georg H. *Explanation and Understanding*. Ithaca, N.Y.: Cornell University Press, 1971.

Wuchterl, K., and Hubner, A. *Wittgenstein*. Reinbeck bei Hamburg: Rowohlt, 1979.

Zimmermann, J. *Wittgensteins sprachphilosophische Hermeneutik*. Frankfurt a.M.: Klostermann, 1975.

Index

acculturation, 33, 34, 37
ahimsa, 152-56
Alaskan-Canadian pipeline, 99, 100, 131
Analogy, existential-functional, 71
anthropology, social, 91-101
Apel, Karl-Otto, 7, 131, 135, 136, 139, 140, 148, 149, 161, 184 n.44; on conditions of communication, 194 n.11, 200 nn.44,45; on critical social science, 195 n.13; ethics of discourse in, 131, 135, 136; on Gadamer, 199 n.40; on Hegel, 192 n.77; on language-games, 190 n.72, 191 n.76; on levels of language, 184 n.44, 187 n.63; on objectivism, 188-89 n.66, 192 n.77; on universal pragmatics, 185 n.53, 187 n.61
apologetic universalism. *See* universalism, apologetic
apologetics: Christian, in Schleiermacher, 25, 26, 27; influence of Hegel on, 27; method defined, 19-23; secular, 4, 10, 27, 169 n.68; theological, 4, 10, 19
argumentation: community of, 130; consensus in, 134-38, 194 n.13; defined by Habermas, 132, 135; in diatopical model of communication, 6, 48, 125, 131; game of, 129-31; in Kuhlmann, 137-39; pragmatics of, 129-35, 137, 141, 142, 144-47, 201 n.63; situation of, 135-37; universality of, 132-40, 196 n.23; validity in, 129, 132-36, 142, 144-46
Aristotle, 11
authority, principle of, in Descartes, 11, 12
autonomy, 11, 12, 106; in Descartes,

11, 12, 164 n.14; in Kant, 12, 164 n.9
Augustine, 11, 110
Azande, 92-98
baptism, 55
Barth, Karl, 27, 28; orthodox-exclusivism in, 27, 28, 170 n.69
belief, 54-58, 61, 62, 68, 69, 72, 151; and faith, 54-58, 61, 62, 68, 69, 72, 151, 175 n.25, 176 nn.35,36
Bernstein, Richard J., 80, 81; objectivism in, 80, 81, 182 n.22
Bitterli, Urs, 30-37; cultural encounter in, 30-37, 131, 170 n.78
boundary discourse. *See* discourse, boundary
Burgos, Laws of, 32
Chalcedon, Council of. *See* Council of Chalcedon
Christian theology. *See* theology, Christian
christology, 22
church, early, 18-21; Hellenistic influences in, 19, 166-67 n.33; heresy in, 21; relations with Jewish community, 18, 19
Clement of Alexandria, 21, 23
colonialism, 4, 10, 28-37, 77, 147; Christianity's role in, 32; collapse of, 30; cultural encounters in, 30-37; effects of, 28-37; ethnocentrism in, 31-36; history of, 29-30
communication: global horizon for, 157; in Habermas, 133; intercultural, 126, 131; pragmatic conditions of, 128-30, 194 n.11, 200 nn.44,45; universal, 124-31, 134-39, 147. *See also* diatopical model of communication

communicative action, 6-8, 121, 125-31, 134, 138, 142, 146, 147, 201 n.63; in Apel, 194 n.11, 200 n.45; in Habermas, 132, 193 n.3; pragmatic conditions in, 128, 129
confession, community of, 146, 147
Contract of Tordesillas, 29
conversion: confessional, 68; in Gandhi, 159; methodological, 50-61, 64, 67, 68, 70, 76, 131, 145, 147; in Panikkar, 160, 175 n.22
convincement, 50, 129, 130, 147, 151, 194 n.4; pragmatics of, 129, 130, 151, 160
correlation, method of, in Tillich, 16, 17
cosmotheandric reality, 7, 66, 123, 131, 151, 152, 156-58, 161, 178 n.58, 180 n.74, 200 n.48, 201 n.63
Council of Chalcedon, 22
Council of Nicea, 22
cultural encounter: Bitterli on, 30-37, 170 n.78; intercultural encounter, 34, 35, 36, 91-102, 131
cultural identity, 62
cultural relativism, 4
cultural supremacy in Western thought, 124
Dasein. *See* Heidegger, *Dasein* in
Descartes, René: *Meditations*, 11, 164 n.14; truth in, 11
diachronic hermeneutics (second level discourse), 46-50, 58-63, 67, 74, 125; conversion in, 50
dialectics, 49, 50, 173-74 n.10, 176 n.36. *See also* boundary discourse
diatopical hermeneutics, 45-76, 79, 80, 123-25; boundary discourse in, 48, 49, 125; conversion in, 50-57, 79; diachronic hermeneutics, 48, 49; defined, 49; morphological hermeneutics in, 48; symbol in, 64, 65
diatopical model of communication, 5, 6, 47-49, 61, 62, 89, 122, 125, 128, 131, 201 n.67
diatopical space, 150
discourse, argumentative, 131-37, 140-42, 146, 51, 157; five pragmatic conditions in, 132-35; hermeneutics,

149. *See also* Apel, Karl-Otto
discourse, boundary, 48-50, 58-63, 84, 109, 125, 138, 142-51; defined, 145, 146; first level, 84, 138; second level, 131, 139, 145-47; pragmatics of, 144-47. *See also* diachronic hermeneutics
discourse, community of, 118, 138, 158, 159
discourse, difference of, 150, 151
discourse, ethics of, 7, 131, 135-39; in Apel, 136; in Kuhlmann, 137, 138, 139
discourse, levels of, 125, 128-32, 138; in global communication, 132; first level, 48, 84, 125, 131; second level (boundary), 48-50, 58-64, 139, 146, 147; third level (disclosive), 49, 57, 61-63, 89, 152, 201 n.67
discourse, mythic, 6, 64, 65, 129, 130, 145-47, 150
discourse of conversion, 131, 145, 147
discourse of difference, 150
discourse of disclosure, 6, 63-65, 80, 89, 91, 102, 122, 125, 131, 132, 140, 150, 151, 157, 161, 162, 179 n.67, 197 n.28; and convincement, 151. *See also* diatopical hermeneutics
discourse of social sciences, 93
discourse, proclamative (boundary), 131, 132, 145, 147, 150, 151, 201 n.63
discourse, symbolic, 65, 66, 79
discourse, universal, 6, 94, 122, 126, 127, 129, 131, 140
discourse, universal community of, 114, 155, 156, 159
dogma: Christian, 21, 22; christological, 22; Jewish, 22; trinitarian, 22
Eliade, Mircea, 37, 38, 42, 174 n.14, 199 n.37
empiricism, 85, 86, 115
Enlightenment, 10, 22, 23, 82, 85, 148; critical rationalism in, 85; Kant's definition of, 12; in Panajotis Kodylis, 23
epistemology, 80, 142, 181 n.4
ethnocentrism, 31, 34-36
ethnology, 92-101, 108, 123, 130

evangelical, 12, 35
evangelical movement, 35
Evans-Pritchard, E. E., 91-97, 108, 123, 130, 184 n.52; Winch on, 91-97, 184 n.52; *Witchcraft, Oracles and Magic among the Azande*, 91
exclusivism. *See* Panikkar, exclusivism in
exegesis, biblical, 27
existentialism, 107, 188-89 n.66
faith, 1, 12, 13, 14, 175 n.25; horizon of, 61; ontological link, 55; in Panikkar, 54-58, 61, 62, 68, 69, 72, 151, 175 n.25, 176 nn.35,36
formal-logical criteria of meaning, 95-97, 100, 101, 105, 106, 184 n.44, 187 n.61
Frankfurt School, 85, 86, 172 n.102
Freud, Sigmund, 139, 140, 148, 164 n.9, 196 n.23; repression of the "self" in, 139, 140
fundamentalism, 12, 35, 36
Gadamer, Hans-Georg, 7, 131, 140-50, 161, 180 nn.79,88, 197 n.26; crisis of meaning in, 142-44, 148, 149; criticism of Apel and Habermas, 149; (debt to) Heidegger in, 142, 143; hermeneutical circle in, 140, 141, 147-50, 197 n.27; historical consciousness in, 143, 144, 147-50, 197-98 n.32, 198 nn.33,34; horizons, fusion of, 144, 199 n.40; "other rationality" in, 141, 197 n.26; philosophical hermeneutics in, 7, 140, 141, 143, 144; *Truth and Method*, 142, 143, 198-99 nn.33-36; universality of hermeneutics in, 140-44, 198-99 n.36
Gandhi, 150-59, 161, 162, 200 n.50; credo of nonviolence, 153-55; before Hunter Committee, 153; rejection of passive resistance, 158, 159; rejection of violent revolution, 200 n.58
global community, 28
global form of life, 7, 8
Gregory of Nyssa, 22
Habermas, Jürgen, 7, 131-36, 139, 140, 146, 148, 149, 156, 161, 184 n.42; argumentation defined in, 132; com-municative action, theory of, 131, 180 n.88, 187 n.60, 192 n.77, 193 n.3, 194 n.9, 194-95 n.13, 195 n.14; communication defined in, 133-35; criticism of relativism 184 n.42
Harnack, Adolf von, 27, 42, 166 n.33
Hegel, Georg Wilhelm Friedrich, 22-25, 27, 39, 164 n.9, 169 n.56, 180 n.88, 192 n.77; *Aufhebung* in, 22; Spirit in, 24
Heidegger, Martin, 4, 107, 142, 143, 146, 147, 180 n.79, 193 n.2, 197 n.28, 199 n.41; *Dasein* in, 142, 143, 147; hermeneutical phenomenology in, 142, 146, 147
Hellenism, influence on Christianity, 18-21, 166-67 n.33
hermeneutical circle, 140, 141, 147-50, 197 n.27
hermeneutics, 3, 74, 75, 140-50, 157, 197 n.28; and argumentative dis-course, 149; and ideology, 149, 150; universality, claim of, 140-44
hermeneutics, historical, 49, 143, 144, 147-50, 197-98 n.32
hermeneutics, intercultural, 81, 102, 108, 114, 162, 179 n.67; in Wittgen-stein, 102, 108, 114
hermeneutics, philosophical, 7, 131, 139-50, 160, 161; as fundamental ontology, 142-44
Hinduism: dialogue with Christianity, 46, 53, 59, 71-73, 177 n.43, 178 n.59
historicism, 165 n.18
homology, 70, 71
horizon of encounter: in nonviolence, 150, 151; in Panikkar, 37, 49, 50, 57, 61, 67, 68, 75, 150, 151
horizon, universal, in Wittgenstein, 114, 123
horizons: fusion of, 144; global, 4, 6, 77; in Panikkar, 46; in Tillich, 37-44
ideology, 5, 79-89, 91, 120, 121, 124, 148-50, 158, 181 n.5, 194 n.13; cri-tique of, 85-87, 124, 155, 161; defined, 82, 181 n.6; and hermeneu-tics, 149, 150; Marxist influence in, 82, 85; problem of, 80-89; (critique in) psychoanalysis, 181 n.7

inclusivism. *See* Panikkar, inclusivism in

indifferentism. *See* Panikkar, indifferentism in

initiation, 64

intercultural encounter, 34-36, 68, 98-100, 131; formal-logical criteria in, 95-97, 100-102, 105, 106, 101 n.51; psychological effects, 35, 36, 171 nn.83,84

intercultural understanding, 5-7, 90, 91, 121, 135, 140; in Winch, 91-102; in Wittgenstein, 108, 121

interreligious dialogue, 5, 19, 46-62, 67, 68, 70, 73, 74, 126, 131, 135, 163-64 n.1, 176 n.37, 179 nn.63,67, 180 n.80; limitations of phenomenology in, 174 n.12

interreligious encounter, 5, 6, 9, 50, 51, 61, 162; communication in interreligious understanding, 5, 6, 9, 50-52, 57, 58, 64, 68, 78, 124, 180 n.74; praxis in, 50

intrareligious dialogue, in Panikkar, 5, 68-76

intuition, in Schleiermacher, 25, 26

irrationality, 120-23, 193 n.80

Jesus Christ, 18-23, 26; as *logos*, 20-22; proclamation of salvation in, 18; universal claim of, 18

Judaism, in relation to Christianity, 18-21

Justin Martyr, 19-21, 23; *Dialogue with Trypho*, 19

Kant, Immanuel, 12, 25, 103; autonomy in, 164 nn.9,14, 185 n.53; definition of enlightenment in, 12

knowledge: sociology of, 82-86; theory of, 80, 83. *See also* epistemology

Kondylis, Panajotis, 23, 167 nn.53,54

Kuhlmann, Wolfgang, 137, 138, 195 n.18, 196 nn.19-21

language: Augustinian picture of, 110, 119, 120; ontological priority of, 144; philosophy of, in Winch, 91, 93, 94; philosophy of, in Wittgenstein, 102-26; as a picture of reality, 102-10; universal, 5, 70, 79, 109, 118, 140, 161, 162

language argument, private, 115-18, 125, 127, 190 nn.74,75, 192 n.77

language-games: argument in, 129-34; similarities with hermeneutical circle, 140-42, 197 n.27; structure of, 141; in Wittgenstein. *See also* Wittgenstein, language-games

Lenin, Vladimir Ilyitch, 85

Lessing, Gotthold, 23, 24, 169 n.55

liberalism, 15

lifeworld boundaries, 50, 142

lifeworld horizon, 6, 48, 58, 61, 64, 84, 89, 125, 127, 128, 133, 139-42, 160, 175 n.22

logic, 133, 194 n.9

logos, 20-22, 62-68, 72, 201 n.67; myth of, 151

Mannheim, Karl, 82-84

Marx, Karl, 43, 82, 85, 100, 139, 140, 148, 164 n.9; alienation of self in, 139, 140; critical theory in, 85, 172 n.102

meaning: crisis of, 84-86, 142-44; criteria of, 16, 93-95, 100, 102, 149, 161; criteria of, in Wittgenstein, 102-6, 108, 114, 115, 121, 128; horizon of, 84; theory of, 126

metanoia, 53, 145, 175 n.23. *See also* conversion

mission, 30-33, 36, 59, 64, 145, 147; under colonialism, 31-33, 36, 59, 170 n.78; Jesuit, 31, 32

misunderstanding, in hermeneutics, 148-50

morphological hermeneutics (first level discourse), 46, 48, 62, 67, 74, 84

myth, 62-69, 134, 145-47, 150, 157, 201 n.67

myth of *logos*, in Panikkar, 151

mythic-religious experience, 146, 199 n.37

mythologoumenon, 63, 64

mythos, 62, 65

neoconfessional, 12, 35, 36

Nietzsche, Friedrich (Wilhelm), 88, 100, 108, 110, 148, 164 n.9, 182 n.23, 196 nn.23,24

nonviolence, 151-59, 162; Gandhi's credo of, 153, 154; hermeneutics of,

178 n.58; passive resistance in, 158, 159; pragmatics of, 7, 151, 152, 160-62. *See also ahimsa*

objectivism, 5, 7, 79-81, 87, 134, 135; defined, 80; vs. relativism, 89-102, 126; in Wittgenstein, 102

ontology, 54, 55, 142

ontotheology, 151

Origen, 21, 23

ostensive definition, 110-14

other, the, 90, 91, 139, 140, 162, 183 n.26, 192 n.77

other-rationality, 120-23, 125-27, 137, 139, 141, 147, 192-93 n.79, 196-97 n.24, 197 n.26

Panikkar, Raimundo, 5, 43, 45-76, 79, 125, 129, 150, 160, 161, 173-74 n.10, 176 n.40, 194 n.4; dialogical dialogue in, 67; diatopical hermeneutics in, 47-76, 125; *epoché* in, 174 n.12; exclusivism in, 58-61, 66, 70, 124; fanaticism in, 59; faith and belief in, 54-58, 61, 62, 68, 69, 72, 176 nn.26,35,36, 178 n.56; free will in, 55; homology in, 70, 71; inclusivism in, 58-61, 66, 70, 124; indifferentism in, 58-61, 66, 70, 124, 161, 176-77 n.42; interreligious dialogue in, 45-53, 57, 68, 73-76, 124, 171 n.83; intrareligious dialogue in, 5, 68-76; method for theology of religions in, 74-76, 160; methodology in, 46, 47; on myth, logos, and symbol, 62-70; theological models for interreligious dialogue in, 58-62 (*see also* exclusivism; inclusivism; indifferentism); (fulfillment of) Tillich's five presuppositions in, 75, 79; truth in, 50-52, 57, 59, 60, 64; *The Unknown Christ of Hinduism*, 71

parallelism, 176-77 n.42

passive resistance. *See satyagraha*

Pelikan, Jaroslav, 18-21, 166 nn.31,33, 167 nn.34,40, 168 n.48

philosophy, as universal discourse of disclosure, 118-20, 191-92 n.76

Plato, 21, 80

pluralism, 4, 5, 10, 15-17, 28, 90, 159; cultural, 58; genealogy of, 17-37;

satyagraha and, 159; sociological concept of, 16

pluralism, radical, 3, 5, 10, 15-17, 27, 51, 77-79, 124; defined, 15, 16

Popper, Karl, 188 nn.64,65

positivism, 188-89, n.66

postmodernism, 90, 91, 138

praeparatio evangelica, 19, 23, 24

pragmatics, 17, 18; defined, 166 n.30, 194 n.9

pragmatism, 87, 88

proclamation in diatopical model of communication, 6, 64, 129, 131, 145-47

Rahner, Karl, 172-73 n.4

rationalism: critical, 85-87; scientific, 134; secular, 23

rationality, 120-23, 184 n.51, 193 n.80; criteria of, 92, 96-102, 121

realistic theory of meaning. *See* Wittgenstein, *Tractatus Logico-Philosophicus*

reality, 81, 83, 88; criteria of, 161; Western scientific view of, 92-98, 102, 105-8, 124; in Wittgenstein, 121

reason, 13, 16; autonomy of, 164 n.14; critique of, 187 n.60

relativism, 5, 6, 7, 79-89, 109, 110, 114, 120, 135, 161, 184 n.51; defined, 81; in Nietzsche, 88; vs. objectivism, 89-102, 126; postmodern, 89

religion: history of, 37-42; philosophy of, 13-15, 23, 24, 37, 50, 174 n.13; science of, 27, 49, 57, 66

religions: the Buddha on, 1; comparison of, 66, 67, 71, 72; critique of, 39-44; encounter in, 46, 47, 64; relationship with other religions, 1, 2

revelation, 14-16, 38-40, 42, 78, 168 n.48, 179 n.68; denial of, in secularism, 9; symbols in, 62, 63

ritual enactment, 146, 147

Rorty, Richard, 87, 88, 113, 119, 182 nn.22,23

salvation, 164 n.7; in Judaism and Hellenism, 22

satya, 152, 153, 157, 200 n.50; defined, 152

satyagraha, 150-62; *ahimsa* in, 152-56;

as alternative to theory of conflict resolution, 152, 158-62; and conversion, 159, 160; passive resistance, 158, 159; *satya* in, 152, 153, 157; *tapas* in, 154, 155, 157

Schleiermacher, Friedrich, 25-27, 42, 169 nn.58,61,65; Christian apologetics in, 25; intuition in, 25; Troeltsch on, 170 n.70

sciences of the social, 123; morphological and diachronical hermeneutics in, 49, 50; objectivism vs. relativism in, 91-102

sciences of the social, critical, 85, 86, 140, 148, 149; Apel on, 195 n.13; methodology of, 79, 80

scientific method, 48, 52, 57, 92, 105-8, 121, 134

secular humanism, 4, 8, 9, 12-17, 22-25, 28; autonomy in, 12; vs. Christian theology, 9-13, 37-44, 77, 78, 165 n.18; as religion, 38, 77, 79, 147; secular-rejectionism, 10, 38, 39, 44, 57, 70, 78, 147

secular universalism, 16, 22, 25, 28, 39, 40; autonomous rationality in, 25-27

secularism, 3, 27, 37-44

self-suffering, 154, 155, 157. *See also* *tapas*

semantics: pragmatic, 102, 110-123, 125, 126, 185 n.53, 187-88 n.63, 198-99, n.36; realistic, 102-11, 121, 185 n.53

Shankara, 66, 67

skepticism, 84

socialization, 64

solipsism, 107, 115-18, 135, 160, 183 n.27, 187 n.62, 190 n.75

speech act, 125, 128, 129, 132-35, 140, 145, 146

Spirit, in Hegel, 24

symbols, 58, 62-68, 70-73, 78; in comparative religions, 65; cultural identity in, 62; as ontomythical reality, 66, 67

synthesis: in early church, 21, 22; in Tillich, 16, 78

systems, 71, 72

tapas, 154, 155, 157

theology, Christian, 12-18, 147; apologetic universalism in, development of, 19; apologeticism in, 19, 25, 26; authority in, 12; claim to scripture, 19, 20, 21; historical criticism in, 27; orthodox-exclusivism in, 9, 10, 27, 38-41, 44, 57, 70, 78; vs. secular humanism, 9-17, 37-44, 77, 78, 147

theology, global. *See* theology of religions

theology of religions: horizon in, 3, 11; methodological foundation, 2, 3, 38, 80, 81; methodological presuppositions in, 38-44, 78, 79; in Panikkar, method for, 75, 76; in Tillich, 3, 9-11, 28, 37-44, 70, 78, 79, 162, 171 nn.85,86

Theophilus of Antioch, 21

theory, critical, 85, 86, 87

Tillich, Paul, 3, 9-20, 26-28, 37-44, 45, 57, 70, 75, 78, 79, 124, 162, 163 n.1, 165 nn.24,25, 166 n.29, 172 n.97; *Christianity and the Encounter of the World Religions*, 28; Christianity vs. secular humanism in, 9-17, 37-44, 78, 147; critical process in, 39-41; *A History of Christian Thought*, 19, 167 n.38; Japan, visit to, 28; orthodox-exclusivism vs. secular rejectionism in, 70, 170 n.69; "The Philosophy of Religion," 13-16; (five) presuppositions for any theology of religions, 38-44, 78, 79, 162; on Schleiermacher, 26, 27, 42; *The Significance of the History of Religions . . .*, 9, 10, 37-44; synthesis in, 16; *Systematic Theology*, 17, 37, 38, 42, 165 n.25

trilemma, 100, 101, 121

trinitarian mystery: *Filioque*, 24; Trinity, 22, 24

Troeltsch, Ernst, 27, 28, 42, 170 n.70, 172-73 n.4; mediating liberalism in, 28

truth: criteria of, 93, 100, 133, 135, 136, 145, 161; in diatopical model, 89; in ideology, 80, 81, 84, 87, 88; in Nietzsche, 88; in Tillich, 14-16; in Wittgenstein, 102. *See also satya*

universal communication. *See* communication, universal
universalism: defined, 4
universalism, apologetic, 4, 10, 11, 12,
17, 50, 80, 81, 121, 124, 147; crisis
of, 81, 124; defined, 4, 10, 17, 80; vs.
global culture, 57, 58, 162; and ideology, 80, 81; and the other, 183
n.26; pragmatic structure of, 22,
149, 150, 151, 166 n.30
universalism, Christian, 3, 19, 22, 25
universalism, new, 4, 7, 81, 124-62
Unknown Christ of Hinduism, The (Raimundo Panikkar), 71, 173 n.5
Upanishads, 54, 63
validity: criteria of, in argumentation,
83, 95, 129, 132-36, 142, 144-46;
pragmatic conditions for, 121
violence, 139, 140, 149, 150, 161; to
language, 149, 150
Weber, Max, 16, 86
Winch, Peter, 6, 91-102, 108, 120-23,
126, 131, 135, 160, 183 n.27, 184
nn.44,52, 193 n.3; on conflict
between religion and science, 97,
98; critique of methods of social sciences in, 91-102, 121-23, 160; on
philosophy of language, 91-95
Wittgenstein, Ludwig: *On Certainty*,
108, 109; critique in, of meaning,
91, 93, 95, 98, 102-8, 121, 125, 185
n.53; critique in, of modern epistemology, 115; intercultural hermeneutics in, 98, 114; language-games
in, 6, 102, 110-18, 191-92 n.76; linguistic philosophy in, 165 n.18, 187
n.62; ostensive definition, 110-14,
189-90 n.71; *Philosophical Investigations*, 110-20, 127, 185-86 n.55; picture of reality in, 102-10; pragmatic
semanticism in, 102, 114, 115, 125-
27, 131, 160, 185 n.53; radical relativism in, 109; rationality, irrationality of other rationality, 6, 7, 120,
121-26; realistic semantics in (*see*
Wittgenstein, *Tractatus Logico-Philosophicus*); realistic theory of
meaning in (*see* Wittgenstein, *Tractatus Logico-Philosophicus*); *Tractatus Logico-Philosophicus*, realistic
theory of meaning in, 102-10, 116,
118, 119, 186-87 n.59, 187 n.62; in
Winch, 9, 93, 95, 98